SILENT

Praise for Silent

"*Silent* speaks volumes. Profound and simple, *Silent* is golden."
Augusta Miller

"At some point, the beautiful lotus flower will spring out of the mud of human suffering and misery. This book helps to remind us that we are all human lotuses. Given the right conditions and spiritual awareness, it is possible to reach great personal fulfillment."
Dr. Sian Ong,
psychiatrist

"*Silent* is a revelation."
Clive Marshall,
company director

"Amazing. Malouf's courageous outpouring of thoughts, fears, and feelings is an inspiration."
Stewart Boag

"I loved *Silent*. Once I started reading, I could not stop."
Matthew Callahan,
music writer/producer

"A great book that really makes you sit back and reassess your life."
Jason Scott

"Someone once said: 'In silence, the darkness fell, and the stars began to come out.' *Silent* is one of those stars. Reading it has enlightened my path and brightened my vision."
Aurelie Nussbaumer,
accountant

"This book fell into my hands at the exact right moment in my life. It has helped me to live a more conscious and grateful life, to find my courage, and to develop the strength and insights to continue the journey."
Jessica Schebesta,
entrepreneur

"*Silent* shares the most precious message of life."
Cathy Wood,
real estate developer

"Raw, honest, and inspiring. *Silent* is a book that puts life into perspective."
Pascal Skelin,
director

"Ultimately *Silent* is a book about living life in a positive mindset. It will help you understand how to reach your potential and lead a fulfilling and positive life."
Melissa Smith

"A book with a tremendous message of hope and positivity. An uplifting read."
Kara Markovics

"Read *Silent*. It could be the best gift you ever give yourself."
Kellie Callahan

"The honesty and rawness of *Silent* put my life into perspective."
Jason Morris

"*Silent* helps us feel as if we are not alone when it comes to abuse. Abuse is more common than you would think and we need to learn to forgive it and to let go of the shame, and to seek help when we cannot accomplish these things on our own. At the end, healing is the key."
Guiddalia Emilien,
real estate agent

"A fascinating read! This is a book about the great journey of connecting with one's Self and the amazing growth and life-changing thinking that can be achieved from that."
Anne Alexander,
recruitment consultant

"Knowing Greg for more than forty years, I have witnessed most of his achievements, but I believe his greatest achievements will be attained in his sincere, heartfelt passion to help and inspire others. His writing is truly inspirational."
Robert Casarotto,
managing director

"Malouf's insight into relationships lifted a veil for me, and I no longer live in darkness."
Michelle Purves

"*Silent* is a powerful book that speaks for itself. You will be surprised!"
Levita Lau

"An honest account of how anxiety can cause loss and heartache and how to overcome it through silence."
Bianca Kunstle

"Informative and enlightening."
Cindy Tizard,
property manager

"Few people are brave enough to share the story of their journey to freedom. Greg Malouf's honesty and insight as he releases his past to claim the life he was meant to live is a gift. Accept it and be inspired to do the same for yourself."
Deb Orme

"A truly powerful read. Silent has made me realize just how my actions affect my children and put me in a better position to be able to help them in their development.
David Solomon,
director

"I recommend *Silent* to those who no longer want to be held prisoner by their own fears and dysfunctional behavior, and who crave a joyful existence full of possibilities."
Suzanne Stretton-Brown,
marketing director

"*Silent* will help you through the tough moments in your life. Read it and discover how to find peace and love, mentally, physically, and spiritually.
Erik Suryadi,
barista

"*Silent* has made my life a lot healthier, happier, and stronger."
Mahmoud Aljada,
sports physiologist

"*Silent* is a true masterpiece, a gospel for our times. It touched my soul. Bravo!"
Theo Vourakis,
company director

"*Silent* has had a great impact on my life. It guides us to confront the past in a very gentle, but incredibly honest way. Without lecturing, it advises us how to change our lives using a unique, natural approach to create a happier and more meaningful future."
Magda Danysz,
business proprietor

"Not only insightful, but a real key to life. Finally a book that puts it all together."
David Hammer,
property developer

"*Silent* was a brilliant read! It helped me overcome my worries and anxieties."
Douglas Griffiths

"*Silent* shed a lot of light on the events I experienced as a younger person, and it allowed me to connect spiritually with my inner Self. I particularly liked the way the author provides clear and succinct lessons on how to deal with issues as they arise."

Joe Necco,
licensing officer

"Life changing to how I see and overcome obstacles."
Andrew Panay,
portfolio manager

"*Silent* provides a way to overcome obstacles and difficulties, and find a new you!"
George Papadeas,
company director

"Every page of *Silent* has meaning and impact. It's empowering. Loved it."
Fiona Durazza

SILENT

THE POWER OF SILENCE

GREGORY NICHOLAS MALOUF

NEW YORK

SILENT
THE POWER OF SILENCE

ISBN 978-1-61448-321-2 paperback
ISBN 978-1-61448-322-9 eBook
Library of Congress Control Number: 2012940919

Morgan James Publishing
The Entrepreneurial Publisher
5 Penn Plaza, 23rd Floor,
New York City, New York 10001
(212) 655-5470 office • (516) 908-4496 fax
www.MorganJamesPublishing.com

Cover Design by:
Rachel Lopez
www.r2cdesign.com

Interior Design by:
Bonnie Bushman
bonnie@caboodlegraphics.com

In an effort to support local communities, raise awareness and funds, Morgan James Publishing donates a percentage of all book sales for the life of each book to Habitat for Humanity Peninsula and Greater Williamsburg.

Get involved today, visit
www.MorganJamesBuilds.com.

Habitat
for Humanity®
Peninsula and
Greater Williamsburg
Building Partner

Dedication

Douglas Joseph Malouf,
author and public speaker:
Thank you for all your love and support, Uncle.

Epsilon Healing Academy,
a place to share and unite, to help people with their unease, anxiety, and fear,
and to learn from each other in support and love.

www.epsilonhealingacademy.com

Contents

Foreword

Through the opening and reclamation of his true self, Greg Malouf became aware of the devastating effects contemporary society can have on relationships as the unhealed wounds of childhood surface.

In *Silent,* Greg has provided a passionate account of aspects of his life story. He draws attention to how powerless and bewildered we can become in life when we are overwhelmed by our experiences—how the impact of abandonment, abuse, and manipulation take us away from unity with ourselves. His awareness comes from his capacity to identify the factors that contributed to his separation from the Self, which are often classified as predetermined in our contemporary society. These include rapid social changes, family problems, and substantial pressure on family supports, major losses, addictions, abandonment, anxiety, fear, anger, and abuse. These aberrations led Greg to seek and lead an independent lifestyle, which led to drug experimentation and sexual relationships long before he was psychologically and emotionally mature.

Greg identifies how he pushed himself beyond his maturity from a young age, having been told repeatedly he was not good enough. This propelled him into an adult life where this continual push became an unbridled pressure to succeed no matter what. By nineteen, Greg had replaced all other addictions with work. Work provided him money to escape a horrible past of abuse and neglect. Money became the driver. He was in the driver's seat. He started to give himself away to others in his attempt to create a world of material wealth to be admired, believing it would save those he loved from the life he had led. Greg has led a life of entrepreneurial zeal. He employed numerous people in his business of real estate and property development over the past thirty years. With his insight into business, he has mentored staff and colleagues to achieve more than they could have imagined. He created an empire to be envied. As he inspired others, he also enmeshed himself into their lives—all this while attempting to manage a relationship with his wife and three children. The pressure of this lifestyle finally took a toll, with his marriage dissolving.

By this stage in Greg's life, he had lost three families: the family of his birth, destroyed at a young age through abuse; his first marriage; and now, his second marriage. Greg felt enormous guilt regarding the loss of his relationships. The breakdown of his second marriage broke him down to the truth. He had realized a dream through a lie—the lie being the facade he had maintained of keeping his feelings intact, managing to keep it all looking good at the cost of his own truth. His ego failed to see the success he held in his hands. A striving, successful business and a family meant success. He failed to see he had this and failed to hold it together.

The impact of being enmeshed with so many people took a toll. He wound down many areas of business to provide himself the time and space to create the opportunity for self-discovery and healing. Greg became an insatiable reader. He challenged himself to identify concepts and issues relating to his life. He then studied the cause and effect of these with gusto.

At the time of this loss, Greg started to seek support from a number of professionals. He resumed his meditation practice, which he had begun some fifteen years earlier. He sought therapy and spiritual guidance, which brought him to a new level of understanding. He started to understand how his world was destroyed by resentment and his unloved self achieved everything material while what he yearned for was Self-love, family, and a healthy life balance. Greg attended a live-in rehab program at South Pacific Private in Sydney's Curl Curl Beach to help him deal with his addictions, which he believes started as early as eleven years of age. These addictions include workaholism, relationships, and sex.

Greg has gone beyond the temptation to blame family dysfunction as a solitary factor underlying the conditions of his life. He has emerged from his path of living his life as a lie with his passion to help others intact. Greg has started a healing academy dedicated to helping people. Greg has been inspired to write about his life and his healing, in a wish to share the possibilities available to us all as we allow the healing process to commence.

In writing *Silent,* Greg has exposed the truth, which will shock you, the truth that is explicitly shared in detail within the early chapters. The truth will set you free. Greg's truth is in his stories as well as in the pages of discovery you will read.

He has delivered a thought-provoking and life-changing opportunity to challenge you to unbind the impact of your life experiences, to reconnect with yourself, and to heal the toxic wounds of childhood with ease and grace.

You are invited to find the courage to face your truth by reading and identifying with Greg in *Silent*.

—Leone Ziade,
Associate Diploma Psychotherapy, R.M.C.A.P.A., P.A.C.F.A.

Preface

It is in your silence that all your words are spoken.
It is in your silence that your conversation is understood.
It is in your silence that you hear the voice of God speaking to you.
So be silent to hear and be heard.

I have been very fortunate in my life.

I formerly employed hundreds of people, and I didn't find myself managing just one person an hour, it was probably five or six people every hour of every working day of my business life, and sometimes my working day was up to sixteen hours long.

I made fortunes and spent fortunes on life's pleasures, but I rarely gave myself the chance to enjoy them because they were all superficial attempts to fill a void.

The more I had, the more I was dissatisfied. I expended enormous amounts of energy to keep the wheels spinning, but no one in my life benefitted. Indeed, we were all left depleted—particularly those closest to me.

This book will intermittently change pace and throw you, the reader, back into a trying or difficult episode from the past that I had to face. I found myself driven to escape my past and connect to love, wherever it could be found.

This book will provide guidance and awareness to help you identify the potholes that keep conscious creation from your door. It is time to look within and to know why, to date, you have chosen not to truly look within. With this knowledge, you can let go of the past lessons and conditioning that limit you and cause you to regress, time and time again, to the old patterns of behavior that have kept you from finding complete peace, joy, and abundance in your life.

We all need to ask ourselves the hard questions and accurately determine where we are in our lives. We also need to face the truth of our lives, and in so doing, to start the process of healing, creation, and enrichment.

This is a journey that starts in pain, which had been felt very early in life, yet had been denied for many years until the realization that my life—as successful as it was in business and making money—was in fact the result of attachments and addictions created for the purpose of avoiding the painful truth. The truth will always rise to the surface and into our reality, which may be painful for us to face. I felt compelled to identify with the truth of my life, and through my experiences, be guided to my healing, fulfillment, and true Self-awareness.

Throughout this book, the term "self" is given two meanings. The all-loving inner Self is marked with a capital S, while the ego self, or adapted other self, is shown with a lower case s.

It was not until my world imploded that I faced my truth, looked within, and thought to myself, *There must be a better way.*

So often, we deny our realities and avoid our feelings—more from ignorance and our teachings of fear. These teachings have held us confined within the prison of our minds for eons. The uneasiness we feel and constantly live with is such a common occurrence—we could say an epidemic—that we no longer recognize the pain and unease. They have become part of society, who we are, and what we teach. We excuse these feelings through our own sense of rightness, and we normalize them. All problems are but one. They all stem from separation from Self, and thereafter from everything and everyone else. Without love of Self we cannot possibly hope to express and receive love from another. This book is a response to this problem. It will take you on an inward journey to find the all-loving place and connection to all that is—the silent connection to Self. In this connection, you will reclaim your inherent power, change your reality, clear your vision, and open the floodgates of abundance.

The people and things in your life will start to have meaning. The gratitude you will feel will bring more of life's joys to you—much more. Fear will be recognized for what it is, and in this awareness, by asking yourself difficult questions, you will start the process of removing fear from your life, as well as the associated feelings that restrict and deplete your energy or limit your imagination and creativity. This, you will come to realize, is to experience every facet of life for your greater purpose: your soul evolution.

Too easily, we ignore our truth. We are afraid to face our fears for fear of rejection, not being good enough, or not being accepted. I hope my truth gives you the courage to face your own truth, for it is in facing our truths that first stage of healing begins.

We need to reconnect to Self, life, and each other, to realize the power of knowing that unity is our ultimate path, and thus to realize that we are ultimately powerless without each other. We are made powerless by our separation, the separation we have all come to accept as a normal part of life. We are all made of the same stuff, so to disconnect from each other creates fear and anxiety, to the point where our lives truly become unmanageable.

We will talk about our children—the ones we love very much—and show why it is important to change what we are teaching them and how we treat them. We will learn to love and appreciate them more, and to accept them for who they truly are. They are beautiful, little, intelligent, creative souls, who, if given the chance, can and will change the misguided and distorted decisions we have made in this world—those that have led us into a world in crisis. We need to instill confidence in them. They have the power to change the direction of this world from crisis to peace, but the change, the healing, must start with us. In our healing, the world we see will no longer be a world in crisis.

We need to end past conditioning, trust, and go within to the place of our inner knowing: our core beliefs and values. Each of us possesses and unequivocally knows these intrinsic values at the core of our being, and we must be guided from there.

As I did after the failure of my second marriage, which imploded my reality, we must look at the impact of all the relationships in our lives and see how they have incredible meaning and purpose. In doing so, we can help stop our poor communication patterns and become aware of simplistic realizations and other things that stump our relationships.

We live in time, yet it is the timeless that we must face if we are to liberate ourselves from the physical handicaps that hold us back. We will brush the spiritual and link it with the physical so we can truly understand unity and our life purpose. We need to recognize the meaning of life and then remember who we are. The conduit of remembering will be felt first in the body as bliss and joy, permanent states of love within.

Perhaps for the first time in your life, you will see meaning to life—real, sustainable, everlasting meaning—and be shown reasoning with logic as to why our physical realities have incredible purpose and that we are not limited in any way other than by our reactions to life. We are creative beings who are failing to create the way we would like. We will bring back the power of creativity through connecting to the inner Self using techniques such as daydreaming. We will dream as our powerful, creative souls desire, and not judge our dreams as powerless or demean them any longer.

We will learn to value creation, to know why it exists, and to understand why we must create to fulfill our roles. We will recognize what our roles are in physical form and why they serve the greater purpose of our forever-expanding lives. Each of us is the center of our universe and is as important to it as any other part of it in existence.

We will look at the means of connection to Self, a connection that will become our sanctuary. We will learn the value in the power of silence. We will learn to go within and find solitude and rest.

By accessing creative thought, we will learn the answers that matter. We will be able to trust in Self, realize our feelings through going within, recognize them, and adequately deal with those feelings rather than finding alternative methods for coping, such as medication, disease, or anxiety, all of which are coping addictions.

The journey is to the Holy Grail, the part of each of us that is powerful, loving, creative, forgiving, and accepting. This is the part of you that can consciously create whatever your heart desires. The secret is in facing your truth, letting go, connecting, and then trusting in your Self and your greater power as part of the whole. It is about recognizing the importance of forgiveness and accepting life in its entirety. You will be given gifts which will strengthen in you on this journey, reshape your life, and create miracles within it.

This is our mutual journey, and it is one I sincerely hope and pray connects us all to each other and the greater picture of all life.

It is with much love and appreciation for all those who have influenced my life that I write this book, *Silent.*

It is time to reclaim your inner power.

Acknowledgments

I would like to thank all the people who have contributed to setting me on the path to healing. Whether through pain or joy, each played an important role in my healing, and subsequently helping heal those I love. You have reignited the passion in me to help others.

The opportunity exists in each moment of time to see a different reality. Our relationships are the greatest catalyst for learning and evolving. Thank you to all who have played a part and been instrumental in this journey.

To my second wife, for having the strength to find your own path and having the courage to leave, which was ultimately the action that set me on my path. Thank you.

To my father: Through your poor understanding of reality and love, you were led to do the things you did. Your lessons, I'm sure, will help many. On a car journey about three years ago, you told me you were sorry for the things that occurred. Please know you were forgiven long before that day. Now let's hope that our courage to speak and accept the truth gives others courage to face and speak their truths, and in so doing, liberate them and start them on their paths to healing, joy, and complete peace and abundance in their lives.

To my long-term friend, Theo Vourakis, who unrelentingly and unquestioningly supported my children and me during the worst period of our lives: You are a true friend who never let me deviate from every effort to reconcile my marriage, and who has only ever had loving words to speak of my former wife. Thank you for the incredible insights you shared with my children and me, valuable insights that I believe you must share and use to help many, just as you shared them with me.

To your beautiful wife, Anna, and your children, who welcomed my children with open arms and much love during this time.

To my three beautiful children, who endured much pain, found the path to healing in themselves, and allowed me the openness and love to do so as well. In particular, to my eldest daughter, Brooke, who was old enough to experience the pain in her father: Thank you. I love you all very much. Thank you for your patience when I was not able to be there to support you because my energy was consumed or depleted.

To my mother, sister, and brother, for your ongoing love and support.

To my beautiful lifelong friend, Robert Casarotto: Your support for my family has never stopped.

To Leone Ziade, counselor, spiritual teacher, and a wonderfully insightful person: You worked with me on this book and continue to help many people in life with your knowledge and wisdom.

To Maryrose Heffernan: Thank you for your contribution to finalizing this book.

To my dearest friend, Mick, the inspiration behind my writing and Epsilon Healing Academy, for your patience, love, understanding, and wisdom. You have reignited my passion in life. As Oprah Winfrey says, "Passion is energy. Feel the power that comes from something that excites you." Thank you.

A special thank you to the authors who have inspired me so much: I would sincerely like to thank the very special people who have contributed much to the healing and consciousness that many of us have now been exposed to. In their teachings are our seeds for knowing; in that knowing, we have the opportunity to heal and change the world.

• Steve Biddulph	*Manhood*
• Gregg Braden	*The Divine Matrix*
• Deepak Chopra	Through your literature you are one of the world's greatest spiritual teachers.
• Wayne Dyer	Thank you for years of wonderful literature and insights.
• Stephen C. George and Ken Winston Caine	*A Lifetime of Sex*
• Louise Hay	You are an inspiration to many of us. Your wonderful literature has graced my bookshelves for years.
• Deborah King	*Truth Heals*
• Herman Hesse	*Siddhartha*

- Pia Mellody — *Facing Love Addiction* and *Facing Codependence*
- Michael Newton — *Destiny of Souls*
- Karen Sawyer — *Soul Companion*
- Helen Schucman — *A Course in Miracles*
  And William Thetford
- Doreen Virtue — *Angel Medicine*
- Eckhart Tolle — *The Power of Now*
- Neale Donald Walsch — *Conversations with God, The Little Soul and the Earth,* and *The Little Soul and the Sun*
- Marianne Williamson — *A Return to Love*

A special thank you on behalf of my children to Disney Productions and Universal, who bring to the screen inspiration and creativity that open the imaginations of our young and teach them vital lessons and trust in their own imaginations.

Over the years, these inspiring people have influenced many of us and taught wonderful lessons of Self, love, and life. They are trusted teachers, spiritual masters, and special messengers who through their conscious awareness and knowing, have opened the floodgates to unity consciousness, our own healing, love, and acceptance. I thank you, and my children thank you, as I am sure millions around the world thank you.

A special thanks to the owners and staff of South Pacific Private and the owners of The Meadows Clinic, who brought their wisdom and understanding to many.

To Epsilon Healing Academy: May it be a light unto the world, a place to welcome all, and a place for all to share in love and peace together.

And last, but certainly not least, to Douglas Joseph Malouf, author and public speaker, to whom this book is dedicated: Thank you for being my mentor through life, your love, and your unceasing commitment to my family, mother, brother, sister, and children during their often painful experiences in life. You were always there in every way possible, as you have been for many people throughout your life. You are a guardian in life. I love you and hold you in the highest regard. Thank you, Uncle, for everything.

CHAPTER ONE

What a Journey . . .
Thank God It Is Over!

"Not until we are lost do we begin to understand ourselves."
—Henry David Thoreau

I was about three years old, and I was lying in my bed with the sheets pulled up just below my eyes, staring at the ceiling. The streetlight shone through the curtain and revealed a triangular pattern of light and shadows across the ceiling.

I lay there, hour after hour, staring blankly and waiting for the world to erupt, the violence to start, the deafening noise to rock my world. Sometimes I would be lucky and drift off to sleep well into the early hours of the morning. I escaped the physical torment, but often had nightmares.

We are conditioned to believe things aren't that loving. We call for love through our pain, and hear the pain of others screaming for help in healing from their childhood circumstances in reply. How do we free ourselves of these childhood afflictions? We have no idea for many years to come what normal is.

It is as if we walk around for most of our lives with a film of tinted glass covering our very being. It softens the impact of the world around us. We live within this flimsy covering, which offers us the illusion that we are okay.

Our experiences shape our thoughts, words, actions, and reactions. Yet we live almost blind to them, excusing ourselves daily for the subliminal discomfort in which we live. We need time to be—just be, nothing more—and a little silence to help us feel the pains we have grown accustomed to not feeling, feelings we have buried deep within.

When do we stop and take a good look at ourselves? Unfortunately, it is sometimes a little too late. Why do we wait for the dark night of the soul—extreme discomfort in our lives—before we look within (if indeed we look at all)? What is it about pain that makes us so comfortable? Is it the fact that it occurred when we were most vulnerable? Did it form such a part of our makeup that we now use it as the excuse for who we are and what we have become?

Is pain an excuse either for not doing much or for doing too much, thereby exerting the pressure of unrealistic expectations on ourselves and those around us? The pressure of our expectations can leave us grossly disappointed, more often than not, because those expectations are not met.

Do we identify with the drama in our lives and consider it as normal? The drama played out repeatedly in our daily lives gives us a sense of who we are. Although it is not real, we believe it is all we have. It has become who we are—an illusionary state of being, our reality, our lives—played out by drama and our reactions to our past, not inner peace felt in the present moment. Drama has become what we say and do, shaping our reactions to and interactions with others—often inappropriately.

Without drama, what do we have? Our fear is that we would have nothing in the absence of drama. What could we possibly talk about that would ensure people would listen? *Definitely not a good-news event or happening, as no one would be interested in that,* we think!

It is amazing how much comfort we find in the drama of life and how much comfort it provides our self-proclaimed "sorrowful" souls. If we hear the drama from another, our lives are made easier because we know our lives aren't that bad. If we speak and act out our drama, we do so to control or seek the attention and comfort of others, merely creating an illusion of our need for the love and attention we so desperately seek.

Stopping this pattern of behavior takes real courage. It requires us to stand for ourselves and not separate from others, but unite with them. It requires the courage to say, "I no longer dwell in a place that criticizes and condemns. I will only dwell in a place where I seek the experiences that speak of joy and happiness—the same places that will bring me peace of mind."

We criticize and condemn because we hold our past fears within, repressing those fears in order to forget them—yet we cannot forget them.

> *The violence and abuse became so muted in my psyche that every day I lived a lie, which was observable by the compassionate or enlightened souls, pitied by others, and condemned as bad by many. The lie continued. For as long as I can remember, I needed to prove myself to others. I sought approval from anyone, as I rarely (if ever) felt it while growing up.*
>
> *When I was eight years old and in fourth grade, my father asked me for my exam results. As my grades had fallen, I told him the results would be available the next day. I had tucked them away in the bottom drawer of my wardrobe, and I hoped he would not remember to ask me again.*
>
> *I was particularly nervous the next day, and when I arrived home from school, my father was sitting in his favorite lounge chair. I said hello and went straight to my room. My heart sank when I heard him ask, "Have you got your results, son?"*
>
> *My heart pounding, I nervously replied, "Yes, I will get them." I retrieved the results and took them to him.*
>
> *Silence fell over the room; even the cleaner stopped all activity around the home. A tirade of verbal and physical abuse began. His voice was thunderous as he unrelentingly bellowed his condemnation. Within minutes, the belt from around his waist was lashing across my back and legs. The leather belt burned into my skin thirty times, if not more. The next day, no part of my back and legs was visible other than the welts and severe bruising. This was a bad episode.*
>
> *Abuse often followed financial loss. There must have been serious losses at the horses that particular week.*

Continually seeking to fulfill the parts of ourselves that are devoid of love, we track through life in all manner of ways. Our exteriors portray only a glimmer of who we truly are. We are afraid to show the vulnerable side of our Self that could not possibly be loved. Wasn't it in this state of being our love of Self was lost? Believing any occurrence—bad or indifferent—is personally directed at us, we develop an ego, which is the survival mechanism designed to protect and ultimately destroy everything it experiences.

We begin searching for instant gratification, which eventually drives us. This searching and gratification becomes our escape valve. "What can I acquire next?" Material gain, self-pity, friendship, or a relationship—any gratification will do! We push forward relentlessly, seeking joy where it cannot possibly be found, but seeking it nonetheless.

We carry on through our lives with smiles and laughter, which seem real enough at the time. As our lives continue to improve with material things and things outside us, we believe we are genuinely happy. Regardless of the bumpy roads and potholes we cross each day, we drive on, our smiles and laughter convincing us—and others—that everything is just rosy. Inside, however, we are lost and starved of authentic connection to our Self and those others.

Our conversations become engrossed in judgments, petty jealousies, and criticisms. What matters is that the world we see runs how we see it. Any deviation from that world must be brought into line or eliminated. Our disconnection to Self makes us fear not being in control. This need to control everything as we want it and how we believe we want it leaves us forever wanting and never satisfied. This drives our seeking behaviors and creates our cycle of pain.

Our camouflage is so complete that we can only attract likeminded others to share in our glorious path to material gain or validation. It drives our constant need to be right, our need to be accepted for what we do, and reinforces and validates our behavior. Because we know no better, we choose the path of most resistance, believing it is the least resistance. This path, which we are conditioned to take early in our lives, feeds our anxiety. Each of us seeks something from another in the race to win all—all but nothing and all for nothing. When all is said and done, we are left with nothing. And when we are left with nothing, our greatest opportunity is presented to us.

Do we need to wait until nearer our final hours or that dark moment from the unseen when our dependency on other things collapses to see the truth in this? Or will we act now and open our eyes to know there may be another way? Maybe we can have everything we desire and feel total joy with what we have in our lives and those we hold close and dear.

We hide from the truth, repressing it—as we did when we were children—because it was too painful. When our anger is repressed from an early age, it turns to rage, and our love turns to fear. Still, we magnificently battle to disguise our torment and our grief with outer expressions of determination, confidence, and self-righteousness. We want to be Mr. or Mrs. Happy-Go-lucky! *Nothing is a problem, so don't make anything a problem—or else!* We are untouchable, ready for anything, and constantly willing to please until and unless things just don't go our way again.

> *I woke exhausted one night from a deep sleep. Screams and obscenities shattered the night silence. My senses were on high alert within seconds. In my haste, I crashed into a half-open door, which knocked me backward to the ground. But I jumped to my feet to protect the one I loved without knowing exactly how that was going to happen.*
>
> *There was no time to think. As I ran into the room, my father was sitting on top of my mother. Her clothes had been ripped from her body and her airline tickets removed. She'd purchased them because she wanted to go somewhere—anywhere—to get away from him. He threw her from the bed to the wardrobe. His hands were around her throat, strangling her. My mother was fighting, kicking, and cursing; and I, helplessly watching, was begging them both to stop.*
>
> *He relented for a moment, and she ran from the room to another and slammed the door. He followed, and the abuse from both sides continued. She tried to open the door, and he pulled it closed. She opened it again, gripping the door by its side and pulling hard. His hand was on the door lever, pulling it closed, with her fingers wedged between the door and the frame. All I could see were her fingers and the red nail polish she wore. I visualized her fingers being broken as he pulled even harder.*
>
> *Fear for her consumed me. I wondered what to do. Without a thought, I jumped on his back and whispered in his ear, "If you don't stop, I will kill you in your sleep; I will put a knife through your heart."*
>
> *The abuse ended immediately. I did not know it then, but I had just lost my childhood.*

It is no wonder that we cannot speak of love, joy, peace, and happiness or rejoice in it when we get it!

Why is it people are afraid to speak of happiness, peace, joy and love? Do we fear being ridiculed, perhaps? After all, look what we have put up with in our lives: survival of the fittest, innocence lost, a separation from true Self, and a "you against the world" mentality. It is no wonder many fear retribution for the joy of being.

Wasn't it stripped in one way or another from you in your youth?

How sad is it that the scenes play out on the larger scale of life and affect so many of us in unimaginable ways—war, famine, and hardship for so many. We are all connected. Each of us plays our bit in the fear-based reality we have come to believe is real. Our unity unconsciousness is a group manifestation, through our powerful creating energy, of our individual unloving, fear-based thoughts, words, and actions.

You are a beautiful soul temporarily lost from your inner, all-knowing Self, searching and yet not knowing what you are searching for. We keep up appearances to protect our identities: the *who* and *what* we have made of ourselves. Our ego self was self-made to protect us by the torment of our life experiences. The *who* and *what* are ready to ridicule anything or anyone that doesn't fit into the mold you created to protect your Self. It was a tough mold, impenetrable by anyone other than a mirror of your self—the victim mold that is always at the behest of others. Each person is looking for what can be gained from the other, until that, too, becomes resented and untrusted. Yet we continue to create drama to resolve issues, playing the hero or the poor victim, depending on our circumstances. What it is we seek, and from whom?

We are all motivated to discover who and what we are. That is our purpose in life. Our experiences shape our decisions. Yet what are the experiences on which we rely? To look closely at this very question is a start. All that is required is for us to stop, rest, and think quietly for a moment to offer us a glimpse of doubt that perhaps our reality is not as solid as we thought.

When we watch television news, listen to a radio to hear the news, or read a daily paper, it must confirm at some level that all is not well. Our world is a world in crisis and denial; some of us live beyond our means, and others are greatly deprived.

Our reality requires that to fill the void we feel within, we need to consume, on an ever-increasing scale, things outside us. We consume in such quantity, believing there is not enough to go around, and any threat to that belief is venomously defended. Nations are destroyed, and cultures are wiped out without any respect to their ancient teachings. Children are killed or maimed and left to survive without family or loved ones.

When do we stop the fear of realizing what is important and turn around to say, "Enough is enough"? When do we stand united in our love for each other across nations, races, and all boundaries?

A Moment in Silence

Rest the mind, and feel what it is you feel. Feeling is the key to living, to understanding more about the Self than anything before it. It is what a physical being is here for: to feel the experience of life and unite it with your true Self. Let yourself take time to rest the mind and feel what it is you truly feel.

- Just for a moment, stop and listen to the silence.
- Feel your body, your breath, your heartbeat.
- Do it for you. Be Self-(ish). This is not for anyone else. You do not need to please anyone else.
- Feel the life in your silence, and rest.
- Breathe slowly.

Put this book down just for a moment. Try. You deserve the rest.

(If you'd like to receive a free audio of a guided version of this meditation, go to my website: www.epsilonhealingacademy.com)

From a very early age, I acted out my unloved self.

When I was eleven, I fancied an older girl—she was twelve! Really, I fancied her eighteen-year old sister. Life wasn't working for me on that occasion. "Jackie" and I ended up at a drive-in movie car park. It was as if we were both searching for the same thing—love. You see, Jackie's sister, Nola, looked after her, because they didn't have a dad, and their mum was never around. It was my first sexual experience at the ripe young age of eleven. Jackie and I were in the front seat, with another mate and his girl in the back. Both were scrambling at each other's clothes! My heart was pounding. Although I cannot remember it as clearly as other events, I am sure it would have been a messy affair.

Telling my mates about it later was just as much fun as the act itself. I was the hero—the boy of the moment—and I was on top of the world.

The next day, Nola, who was babysitting, became the quest! She let me take her top off and play with her breasts. I felt the love, all right. Nola taught me how to slow down, and among other things, to kiss. Feeling the love became an obsession. Now I was on a roll. I'd succeeded with conquest number two! My mates thought this was magic. I was not a poor little helpless boy—no, not me. I was king for an hour—a minute, it didn't matter—as long I could distance myself from the helpless little boy I once felt I was.

The conquests never stopped thereafter, and the lack of love was playing itself out. For the next twenty years, it didn't matter whom I hurt or how much I got hurt. My life simply revolved as it began—loveless. I desperately searched for something outside myself. Women were the grand mummy of all prizes—and the older they were, the better! Did I know any better? How should another soul be treated, especially the opposite sex? I didn't know. I learned that was all it was to have sex—provide for them, protect them, and be in control—but I did what I wanted.

The cry for love has not stopped. More and more people are crying out for love—and even worse, they are afraid to admit it. They sit in silence—all for the wrong reasons. The silence is not from within, but from without, and it becomes the silence of incessant thinking.

There is screaming in our heads for escape—but from what? We don't know. We haven't a clue, because we live in fear of people knowing about us or our vulnerable past—the tormented past buried deep within, where people cannot see, that keeps us entrapped in a world of make-believe and illusion. This past consumes us with fear, so we portray ourselves as people who have it all, are unafraid, are victims, are disadvantaged, and who need to be rescued by a handsome prince or perhaps the person prepared to take on the world, believing we are right and everything else is wrong.

Do you just give up, believing you are wrong and everything else is right? Have you ever wondered why you cannot sit still, brushing it off as a mere excuse for the way you are? Or does your leg, arm, or finger twitch when sitting at work or in church, or at a restaurant or at home with the family? I heard once that this type of activity burns up to 1,200 calories per day. It seems to me like a good excuse not to think about such nervous disorders any longer.

We cannot sit still because we are unfulfilled, needing more to satisfy our insatiable thirst for outer experiences. All this is done at the expense of our health and that of our loved ones. "I haven't enough" is the mantra. We need to stop—just for a little while—and turn our thinking inwards. We don't need to do this for long, just for long enough to feel what it is that we so love, yet so hate, and to ask why this contradiction exists.

Confrontational as it must be for all of us, our truth needs to be told, the truth about our lives that has distorted our views and created our alter egos. The complete truth. Be unafraid to face your truth, because fear is what has kept you in the prison of your mind. Fear has kept us from standing and being heard. It isn't good enough for us anymore. Dare to ask why you don't feel good about your unease. You must ask yourself this question with courage and in the face of all past beliefs. Why? To free your Self from the many restrictions you live your life by and to find the peace and love within. The love that resides in each and every one of us is hidden by the shame and guilt we carry through our lives. Truth is the only remedy for this shame. It is in the awareness of past events that resolution of those events can eliminate all carried and toxic shame that created the other you, the ego self, or adapted other self, that was self-created to protect you. Challenge yourself, and ask the hard questions!

You hear the voices of many who are amazed that you dare ask about your life experiences, which are all too often too shameful for anyone to admit to, or the voices in your subconscious repressed by your experiences, forbidding you to search for the answer that you need. It's all too easy to forget—to repress your feelings and instead live your life in anxiety and concern for the future. You miss the moment when life means something: this very moment!

Know this: *Only the truth will set you free*. Find the courage, ask the questions, and challenge the status quo. Enough is enough. Do you feel sometimes as helpless as a little boy or girl standing in a room, watching someone you love get beaten, powerless to do anything about it? What story made you feel helpless, worthless, or powerless?

Another Moment in Silence

Sit for a moment in silence and breathe slowly. Focus on your breath. Slow your world down for just a few moments and feel how it feels.

In an instant, a small window of pure rest will be felt. It is in that instant that you are no longer helpless.

Eleven was a big year for me. It was the first time that the world I knew was to completely shatter. It was the first time my family and I were exposed to public ridicule. The police arrested my father for suspicion of murder and prostitution racketeering. My father ran illegal casinos. I used to frequent them often—either in the back seat of Mum's car at an ungodly hour, dragging him out of the place, or as a guest, sitting and watching my father play cards with the petty criminals and the desperate. It was lucrative for me when I went with him. I would sit at the casino tables with a world of saddened lives around me, listen to their laughter and down-on-their-luck snipes at life, and collect tips from almost every winning hand, obviously given me to impress the club owner: a tip for the son.

It felt good, all that attention and making a profit. Who could ask for more?

The body of man had been stored under the roof of my father's coffee house. The smell got to be too much, the body was moved, and when an investigation for the missing man ensued, the bloated body was discovered. The police took Dad into custody, and he was released on bail.

Over the course of the next three years, before my father's acquittal, our family went through a living hell. Mum was a strong woman, and I'm sure for our sake she hung in with him for this period, attending every court hearing and legal challenge. It was a difficult time for everyone. We were taught to keep our heads up, shut up, and power on, regardless.

I recall attending school just after the complete front page of the local newspaper read: "Local businessman charged with murder." I had no idea what to expect; however, what occurred probably scarred me more than any other event for the next forty years. I was in year eight, my second year of high school. A young mate whom I considered a great friend at the time—we had sleepovers, and often ate at one another's homes—walked straight up to me and said, "I can't talk to you anymore. My parents don't want me to be your friend any longer because your dad's a murderer." His parent's judgment of the situation before my father was acquitted scarred me for years.

The sickness I felt in the pit of my stomach I can still feel today as I reflect on those feelings. I was dazed by these comments, and nothing became relevant for at least a month or two thereafter. For the rest of my life, I would feel the need to continually prove myself. My confidence was gone, and my ego was about to rule everything I did from then on.

Is it the judgments of others that make us conform to a set of rules that we dare not break, even at our own expense? We have created this world in which we exist—where we are the beginning and the end. If we are not, then aren't we doomed at the hands of so many who would take everything from us and leave us destitute and abandoned? Isn't this the belief we have been conditioned by?

Have we all been so wronged that we cast our judgments freely, believing we are right and that we cannot possibly be wrong? Our experiences tell us we must be right. We all think the same way: *I need my mates/my relationship, because they validate my life journey, don't they?*

But what do these judgments say of us? We don't dare admit that our lives have lacked compassion and love to sustain us. We think, *Look at me; there is nothing wrong with me. I am at the pinnacle of success, my home life is great, and my mates support me,* until, of course, something goes drastically wrong.

Any feeling of lacking is a fear-based association with a belief that there is not enough to go around. This fear influences our actions and reactions. We demand something from someone for our gain until that illusion no longer exists and a new illusion replaces it. Each of us who believes that we exist as a separate entity to others will always be out to gain in any relationship. "What can I get out of this?" The more we can see ourselves getting, the more we adapt to another's beliefs, and we don't even recognize our motives until much later in life, if we are lucky.

When we no longer feel there is any more to gain, then the relationship turns sour. Our own judgments and criticisms side with another to form a new set of circumstances and beliefs, which are often made up, fictitious by the nature, and ignorant by design. These new beliefs enable us to project that which we feel is lacking in ourselves. What can we gain from this new set of circumstances, regardless of whom (even including our loved ones) we unknowingly hurt or affect?

How can we know any better when the world we have created cannot exist where we are not its center? We are the beginning and the end of all we are. How can we see what deepened hurts we feel? To show any weakness shows our vulnerability, and that means an end to the world as we know it. To many of us, this will be a fate worse than death.

Why can't we look at the world and know things don't feel right? And further, we ignore all the tell-tale signs, which appear as if in neon lights above our heads, yet we still refuse to look within. The answer to this question is too easily ignored by most of us on our quest to find the Holy Grail. Our inner sanctuary of knowledge, wisdom, and above all, peace, is the defining moment when changes occur so simply that our own lives and those of our loved ones can change forever. Is this not the belief we have been conditioned to?

Our judgments have been passed on from previous experiences and our thoughts in relation to those experiences. As we understand it, those thoughts and beliefs are then projected forward to shape our future. Past thoughts precede other past thoughts, and so on, and the cycle doesn't end. The past blends into past, experiences blend into more experiences, all reflecting the same outcomes and reaffirming our misguided beliefs. We continually try to change events, doing more of the same thing, but all the while expecting a different result. It is no wonder the world appears mad—mad by design—or that our design does not allow us to create anew.

Who is to blame for this state of our internal affairs? There must be someone—anyone but ourselves—because the world we know exists as separate from us and thereby deserves condemnation, doesn't it?

We are truly all responsible for each other, and surely any attack on another is an attack on the very Self. To know this is the first part of freedom. To know this is to stop the cycle of fear based on our past beliefs. Why is it that if our lives are so good we feel so ordinary—and when do we realize that our lives are not as good as they could be? Often we are alone when we have those moments. Does this give us a feeling of insecurity? Does it stir up the emotions and insatiable appetite for doing something to avoid feeling concerned and to disguise the fact that we are hurting?

Knowing this unease is awareness of self. It is the start of the healing process or the knowledge that you are not responsible for the way you were conditioned to live. By owning this—taking responsibility for your life—you can transform it to such a degree that life puts before you all the things you've ever wanted, desired, or dreamed possible. Your world will then be full of love, peace, and abundance.

Is it not worth the look? Did we act out when we were young and continue to do so as we shut our eyes, ever hopeful for the best?

It was a cold winter night. We had waited three days to fill our lives with meaning and were bored from doing a million things that amounted to nothing. Those things of little meaning were full of drama and were done to sustain our insatiable appetite for the lack that was felt within. We were doing anything but feel. We were taught feelings could not be trusted; thus, our feelings were discarded. We learned not to express our needs and wants very early in life. We replaced them with anything to avoid the pain of feeling those scars left from our early years.

It was a typical Friday night, and the local community hall was going off—girls, boys, and youth bands! Yep! It was all too exciting—girls and more girls! Love was on tap, if you were really lucky. All of us were competing for the affection of the opposite sex. You had to be in top gear for this event, but who could love me? Where was the courage to talk? Was talk all we were after? Who could possibly have told us, taught us, or even guided us? After a drop of courage, all would be well; the ego would do the rest—anything, everything in an attempt to medicate. It was a great veil to disguise the pain of the past. In effect, we were each saying, "I love my ego. Thank you, self, for inventing it; you truly are a master creator." We would meet in the thick scrub outside the hall with a bottle of Johnny Walker—always Johnny Walker! The sweetness of scotch whiskey often made us sick, but down it went, a bottle at a time shared between two, and that was just the beginning. Within ten minutes, the effects were felt, the courage shining forth like a peacock with feathers spread. The laughing and fun began.

Oh, yeah, it was good to be twelve!

Cannot the greatest euphoria of all—the silence within—replace the need for substance abuse? Why do so many of us seek the need to abuse ourselves and excuse ourselves for denying who we are and who we have become? We are, perhaps, afraid of our own shadows; we have no trust in the inner Self and no Self-love. Each of us is an all-loving Self; that is how we were created: We were born as an innocent (child), angelic, loving Self. Our life experiences conceal that pure Self. To be in tune with that Self is to enjoy—truly enjoy—the company and love of our family and our children, and better still, the company of our inner Self and the place from where all love flows. When connected to our inner Self, it is the greatest euphoria ever felt.

We cower in our secret lives, often living two lives, and maybe more. The world is made up of secrets—each with an identity and company to match. Yet can we still not see the pain that is hidden beneath the clothes we wear? Oh yes, it takes courage to take on these personalities—these ways of life that give us false meaning, however distorted. The more we rely on them, the more protective we become of them, and the grander our stature needs to be compensated.

Our images of the perfect family, perfect life, and perfect mates have been created individually by us. We have become so disjointed that the world we see is played as if on a projector screen. The movie we play is drama, and from that drama we create more drama. It is our life—it is what we are and what we have lived with, according to our view and perceived reality—but it manifests havoc across all aspects of life. We see, live, hear, and believe in drama, and we choose to do nothing about it until we have no choice and our lives become unmanageable. Don't keep ignoring it!

Encourage yourself to look within—to embrace the silence that exists within us and all things around us for just a moment. Just for a moment, rest your mind. Love awaits you—it is your love of Self. It resides in the only place it can be heard in the stillness and silence of Self. It is your core energy source. Your brothers and sisters need you, your neighbors need you, and your loved ones need you. Where are you? Come home (the home of Self-love) for just a moment, so that you might see clearly!

Your life can be anything you choose—anything! There is no limit or limitation other than the limit you apply to it. The ego cannot achieve what you seek, because it is made out of an illusion of self. It is a base of separateness from all people and all things that separates from the world around you. It takes without giving. It cannot love, because it is born from fear. It is a survival tool to disguise your many pains. You have been abandoned for long enough. Surely, it is time to come home.

What level of uneasiness do we need to feel before we relent or search for another way? Do our actions set alarm bells ringing, or do we simply turn the bell off, making excuses so that the path we follow and the consequences we will face seem to be of no concern? You cannot escape the reality of the consequences, and those consequences, at some point, are going to hurt. You feel it in the pit of your stomach at the first sign of being exposed to the fact that all is not right; still, you ignore the signs.

From a very young age, I preferred to medicate and to bury my feelings.

It was a regular school day, and I was hiding the pains of my private life, listening to no one except maybe the compassionate geography teacher, who was not like the rest. He was a priest, and he seemed to care about me. He could smile and be proud that I was in his class. It was an odd feeling to have someone care. I thought I might even listen back!

Then there was news that the cool kid in the class was supplying marijuana for five bucks a filled matchbox. My friends and I asked him to give us a box. Never had we laughed so much as we did after getting stoned! The more we laughed, the more pimples we got, because our laughter was rewarded with an attack of the munchies! The rest of the time, life was sheer bloody painful.

The old man was still fighting court battles. The town had all but turned its back on us—once the wealthiest family in town. The brothers of the murdered man visited with guns to ask my father questions. We were herded into our room for fear of trouble at the O.K. Corral. The gambling and legal bills were consuming all of his wealth, and the only part of our lifestyle that gave us some level of dignity—my father's money—was going down the drain. The abuse on the family was still as much a part of our lives. We wanted to deaden the pain.

At twelve, I used marijuana; at thirteen, I used LSD; at fourteen, I used cocaine; and at fifteen, I was needling coke straight into my veins. At sixteen, I did anything I could. At eighteen, I was snorting heroin; at nineteen, I came to a dead stop. I did not use another drug. It was time to go to work; my family was broke. That meant I was going to work!

My obsession with money became my freedom. I would never let my past experiences happen to me again. I would be in control of my destiny. I always thought that money was the answer.

I remember my mother dropping my father off at the Mandarin Club in the city. I was only seven. We were from a town a hundred kilometers south of the city. I was excited when I saw the high rise buildings. I remember saying to my mother and brother, who were in the car, "One day, I am going to build a building like that." Thirty years later, I did.

The thing I can remember well about my father was his ability in business. It never ceased to amaze me. He taught me well, although his methods of holding the money weren't so good.

I never stopped burying my feelings.

How do we know what our loved ones, friends, or neighbors are feeling? We are quick to judge them. Is their pain different from ours? Are not all pains the separation we feel from everything around us, including our own Self? Aren't judgments our own past fears made manifest into reality? How can we escape our condemnation of another? It is not possible, for what we dislike in another is something we fear in ourselves.

Think for a moment about stopping the chatter and criticisms that we all hook into based on previous thoughts and experiences in our lives. What would we have to talk about? God forbid if we looked like we did not conform, or if we did not see the wrong in others when it is so blatantly obvious that they are wrong.

We judge people because they are new on the block, they challenge our way of thinking, or they are quite obviously out to conspire against us. *They are different. They complain too much. They don't have money, so they cannot be successful. They are dark-skinned, they are light-skinned, or they are not from here. They don't listen, they don't understand us, or they try too hard. She's always smiling; what does she want from us? She's too nice for this job. She's too skinny* (or *too fat*). *My wife doesn't understand me. He expects too much from me.* On and on we go.

Each time we speak, how many judgments do we make? Indeed, what else would we talk about? We must project to control, feel good about ourselves, fit in, separate, or dare anyone to disagree with our reasoning. We might as well be saying, *My reasoning is sound, because I lived a hard time and survived. I made myself against all odds, and no one is going to be able to touch me again. Just ask my ego. It's easy to find—but be careful how you ask.*

To live in a present moment environment is to say, *I trust in my Self. I no longer rely on past experiences and thoughts that did not serve me well, as this is what has kept me from knowing who I am or from being who I wish to be: happy, joyful, and complete as part of the all that is, a part of everything and everyone. Now I will let down my guard and release the chains that have imprisoned me for so long. Now I will rest, and the joy of living in every moment is mine.*

I needed to surrender and live freely in the present moment. The hardest challenge to surrendering was to unconditionally forgive all those in my past whom I believed had played a part in the trauma of my life experiences. I needed a new framework! I needed not to blame, but instead to thank those I felt had wronged me for helping me get to the point in my life where I could actually feel liberated and at peace. These people had been instrumental in my lessons, and I love them for it.

> For several years, I toyed around with different businesses, and at age twenty-seven I entered into the property game. The first sale was made within a week, and six weeks later, I received my first commission check. It was only the smell of money, and I was off on the greatest hunt of them all: freedom! I could feel it, and I thought money was the answer.
>
> Not surprisingly, I was fixated on the chase for money. I was always exceptionally giving of it, as if it was a toy, a plaything. The hunt was relentless, and everything I desired materialistically was going to be mine. There was no second-guessing—I was going to own anything I wanted. I was going to have security for my family and take them around the world

to every continent, if that was what they desired. Wasn't that showing love? I knew no better. It was the best of me. It was what I had learned. However, they were my desires, and in my obsession I couldn't see or realize theirs.

Work was never nine to five. I recall my first business required sixteen hours of work a day, and I didn't even know the suburb where I opened my first real estate agency. All I knew was that it was an excellent suburb after I overheard a boardroom meeting of directors speak of it, and that they were looking for the right applicant to set up a real estate franchise in one of the largest areas of the city. Of course, I put my hand up for the role, and I was met with limited resistance before the owner of the franchise company, a friend of mine, awarded it to me.

Within six weeks, I was open. My first wife, who was inexperienced in administration, sat at the front of the office; I sat at the rear. The rental was $2,000 dollars per week—a lot of money at that time. Such was my desire that I worked the first year, sixteen hours a day, and I popped pills to keep me awake and antibiotics to keep colds and flu under control. I was completely driven with desperate yearning to succeed, and failure wasn't an option. I demanded freedom and an escape from my past. All things outside me became an obsession. In the first year of my agency opening, we were within the top ten franchises within the country.

I was divorced five years later. I had a beautiful daughter with my first wife, and the guilt I felt for many years after made sure of my commitment to her. I had an additional drive to work, and the only time I would leave work behind was to make sure I attended every available time allowed for my daughter. At twelve, she came to live with my second wife and me—one of the greatest days of my life.

We attract into our lives the circumstances that give us the greatest opportunity for growth at the very times we need them. My first marriage was riddled with difficulties. Communication was poor, there seemed to be a lot of competition for time together as opposed to work or attention sought, and the fighting was constant. History was repeating itself, and there was no escaping it. Learning and inner knowledge was needed, and I knew neither. I thought more work was the answer. It wasn't.

I kept acquiring all things materialistic, and work continued to be the be-all and end-all of my life. I fixated on outside material gain to fill the even larger hole I felt. In hindsight, I realize that the guilt I felt from my childhood had not been dealt with, and the guilt from feelings of abandoning my firstborn made the guilt worse. Guilt acquired guilt. Negative energy attracted more negative energy.

It was twenty-three years before I looked up. Another marriage had broken, and the only woman I truly loved—the woman of my second marriage—was gone. I had two more children and more guilt than I can ever recall feeling. My marriage to my second wife and the birth of my three children were the greatest moments of my life. Now my life was in tatters—all were gone. I was undergoing counseling or regressing in anger and self-pity.

God had not had meaning in my life since I was a young child. I believed in nothing other than self-survival. I was a fighter and thought I had to take on the world—and I did, quite successfully. But when my second wife left me, it was over. Without her, the desire was gone. It was a long way from being three years of age, waiting for the violence in my parents' household to start, before I looked up and wondered, *Could there be more? Dare I ask?*

I did ask, and to all those who played a large part in my experiences, I love you and thank you for helping me find my path back to a loving Self.

Forty-seven years on, my healing began. What a journey. Thank God, it was over.

CHAPTER TWO

Whispering Images
that Never Fade

"Awareness is the greatest agent for change."
—Eckhart Tolle

This chapter relates to two types of life: one that is over nurtured and another that is under nurtured. The question is, are the outcomes any different?

Too often we create images of our self, our ego self, by what we hear others say to us or from those who took care of us or were responsible for us when we were children. Thereafter, we go through life judging others by the same whispered images.

"You are not good enough!"

"You can't do that!"

"Who do you think you are?"

"Don't do that!"

"How does someone like you think you can have that?"

"Look at you! Get yourself together! You're hopeless!"

"You're an idiot!"

"You're too fat!"

"You're too skinny!"

"You don't look after yourself!"

At the end of a session with a group of work colleagues in which I talked about the importance of the inner, loving Self, and related some aspects of my past and the absence of it in my life, a young man came up and asked to speak with me. He told me that when he was growing up, his life was one of sheer bliss. His mother and father, who are still together and inseparable, nurtured him and provided for all of his needs. They loved him unconditionally, but at age twenty-two, he was finding it difficult to live within his own skin. He felt constantly stressed.

He described his life as "horrible, living with himself." Every night, he would go out with his friends and speak about all things in his life he could only dream of—money and living the life. He went on to explain how he was constantly stressed about money and referred to the two bills he currently had which were causing him enormous anxiety. He said that his dad, who hated seeing him stressed, had agreed to pay for one of them.

Here were two diametrically opposed lives—his and mine—resulting in the same set of feelings from completely different circumstances. I thought, *How is this possible?*

If it is love that we seek—and he was given unconditional love, and I was given love only sparingly—then why did the feeling of not living comfortably within our own skin affect each of us the same?

Over my lifetime, it was money that I sought. The purpose of my drive for money and material gain, I believed, was to achieve my freedom. It was through this belief that I felt I would be untouchable—and here resided my freedom. Without material gain, I could not live in my own skin. I thought it was the means by which I could create a world where no one but me could ever control me again and my self-image could be achieved. It was the means by which I could escape the horrible past. I found myself seeking it out and was driven to achieve one achievement after the other, then yet another.

We were two people with completely different beginnings, yet both in the same place.

The images we create in our children can be flawed, regardless of the circumstances of love or the lack of love. The lessons we provide our children create the images with which they will see themselves—within or without—which seem to either under prepare or over prepare them for the world in which they live. Ours is a world of make-believe and myth. It is a belief in all things outside us. We see ourselves as indestructible, invulnerable, and worthy on the inside as long as we have all the things on the outside.

Let us take one of the simplest "don'ts" and convert it to a whispering image. To our children, we say, "Don't climb that tree." What we create is fear in our children. Now while there is ground for this belief and our role as caregiver and parent is to ensure the child's safety, the reality is somewhat different. What we are teaching our children is fear, of course. The children will climb that tree in our absence. They will play and explore. The difference is that our children will climb the tree with an element of fear attached to the experience. Instead of confidence and knowledge of how to play safely, the children will be left with an element of fear. We create fear and want in many areas of our children's lives from our own fear. We pass on our fears in nearly all areas of our lives.

Perhaps we need to look at that part of us and our teachings. What is it we are teaching, and how did those teachings come about? How many "don'ts" does it take to create the whispering images that create fear—and then want—within us? Perhaps we have to adopt new strategies to prepare our young ones for what lies ahead. We should take the time to supervise, explain, and allow them—in the safety of that supervision—to experience life with confidence and trust. Does a "don't" suffice?

> In my life, I had been under nurtured and abused, whereas my colleague had been over nurtured. Let us look at these two lives and try to understand these realities, both for ourselves, as parents or teachers, and for our children, for whom we are responsible. Simultaneously we should try to adjust our thinking to our life purpose, which is to live as a fearless Self. We all have the same purpose we must align with if we are to truly experience peace and prosperity.

By the time I went into my working life with my toughened shield of survival and mental fixations, I was filled with images of my ego self, subliminal images of lack of self-worth, self-confidence, and self-love. If a compliment was paid me, I would question and distrust the giver of the message. *How could you like me? How could you compliment me? Are you just saying that to make me feel better?* My mind could picture these subliminal messages. Words, for me, became images in my head. Yet it was those images that ultimately further glorified my self-grandeur. I needed more success to distance myself even further from my past. *I'm succeeding, so keep pushing harder!* I kept going so as never to return to the place that represented the past. I wanted to bury it deep within, and never allow being judged again.

Here is the funny part. I didn't even know that this was my state of being. I had no idea. A driven soul normally doesn't have any idea, because it simply doesn't look at the signs. There are plenty of signs, yet the driven mind sees no barriers, and if there was one, it would be dismissed.

Negative words that were spoken would be met with immediate resentment and retribution. When called upon to defend my position, it was all too easy to attack. If a relationship suited me, the attack would turn to forgiveness, and then later open to attack again. No basis of stability can possibly exist in an unhealed mind. The notions of trust or lack of trust—being the persecutor or victim—play over and over to maintain an image and a sense of belonging.

Feeling deprived of something will create an attack in us. Our experiences have taught us of lacking. Through lacking, we attach to things. We label these attachments as things that are necessary. These things could be people, material possessions, or love. This is how we are taught. Love becomes an attachment. Things become an attachment. When we feel deprived, we project our lacking of this attachment onto another and attack them. You feel, in this sense of lacking, that something is being taken from you; hence you project, then attack.

The images in my head could never fade, because there was no place of healing or true expression of feelings. Feelings were dead; the images had replaced them. The images I created were so devoid of love that I only expressed images of love out loud. I was eccentric by conditioning, expressing laughter and love loudly, because I yearned for love and humor. By choice, friendships were minimal; after all, could I trust likeminded individuals sticking together in fear? We don't let too many people into our lives, because someone might see a flaw or have a different opinion—one that we don't like. Acquaintances were all too easy. There was much to be gained: among them, a sense of self-worth, validation, and acceptance.

Rebellion and fearlessness are born from fear. *Never say die, fight for everything, and create everything you dreamed possible. Keep going. Keep acquiring, for you are untouchable now.* And those images are still there, whispering sweet nothings in your ear. "You are not good enough." The voice would whisper back, "Prove me wrong."

A beautiful word is said, and attachment results, leaving you looking for more beautiful words, yet believing none, because the images were real to you. After all, you were conditioned from a young age.

When I met my second wife, she often spoke loving words and was supportive in many ways. I felt a real loving connection, yet due to my past experiences, I feared intimacy. While I loved hearing her loving words, I could not trust them completely. We often broke up and then would make up so that I could hear more loving words.

I would affirm her by what I perceived as loving action and words to show my loving intention; however, like me, she could not hear them much past the moment those words were spoken. She chose instead to continuously act out her jealous behavior from her own fear of abandonment.

You are conditioned early to stop believing in your inner Self and only to believe in your outer you, the separate you, the survivor. A picture of fear comes to replace any picture of inner trust and confidence. Outer pain suppresses inner love.

The exchange begins. "You give me this and I will give you that." But the people involved are rarely content! Yet the young boy or girl within constantly calls out, *These images I see are not me. Look, I will prove you wrong. Look what I can do.* You do, however, believe in the images, and they never fade—no matter how much you acquire. Love and trust doesn't exist here.

You are told, "You cannot do this," and you respond, "Yes, I can" to prove the images wrong—resisting, taunting, and controlling whichever way. Anxiety and concern are constant companions, which you actually make your friends. You hear the advice from someone less healed than you: "Leave the chip on your shoulder." This now drives you and guides you.

The time of the breakdown of my first marriage was the time I first started making serious money. I could not understand my unease or the guilt I felt for the breakdown of the marriage, or the feeling that I was abandoning my little girl. I asked my father, "Why do I feel so uneasy, and why can't I stop doing? I have no rest in me."

My father replied on the rare occasion we spoke, "Son, don't worry about it! Leave the chip on your shoulder—it will drive you."

The images are now your servants. You use them, for they are creating your world. Your perception of your freedom lies within them. How clever we are to create a world in which we are free from fear and pain. No wonder we are given the title of creators, creating in the image and likeness of God.

Yet what are we creating? We create distortion and illusion in place of joy and bliss.

Yes, we will prepare ourselves for the challenges and negativity we will surely face in this world. We will similarly prepare or under prepare our loved ones for what we believe exists in our reality—often in defense of what we see to be real, based on what we have or have not achieved, or based on what we have been taught. Our words and actions will be passed on. As a result of our teachings, we will pass on those whispering images of who we are and what we have made of our adapted self. If the images made us who we are—regardless of how distorted— then we believe in the images. They are us and are bred in us, and therefore we believe they must be right. *Look what I have created,* we say, believing in the images of who we have made of our self.

Do we pass them on? Of course we do—just like our parents, and their parents before them, did. It is generational.

"You did a good job." You ask within, nervous of the retribution for failure, *Did I?* We are comforted by the fact that we have been given a reprieve from the retribution that will follow for failure, but we ask ourselves, *When will they change their minds and realize I did not do a good job? When will I stop doing a good job?* The driven mind continues on its path.

Do we ever escape the images? No, not without awareness! Why do we wait for crisis in our lives before we look within to heal that unhealed part of us? The healing must come, as it is our physicality that creates the opportunity for remembering the true inner Self, the healed Self, complete, all-loving Self. We must return to it, for it is how we were created. It is inherent to us; hence we feel anxiety when we are separated from it. Why would we feel anxiety if being separated from the all-loving Self did not affect our value system? That instinctive aspect of Self that goes beyond physicality.

We look at a person who has been nurtured and ask, *Why? What basis has he or she for discomfort? What images he or she subjected to?* And it is here that the other half of the puzzle is answered. Are we overprotected and under prepared for the world at large? Have we nurtured our children to the point of inability? "Don't do that! I will do that for you! Let me do it! When are you going to learn?" What responsibility do we give our young? Cannot a six-year-old pick up his or her clothing and put it in the laundry bin? A seventeen-year-old can babysit a sibling. A child can help with the housework.

All of us need to experience life to know who we are. Without the experience, what would be the purpose of us being here? Life must surely have a purpose.

We have a purpose here on earth, which is to experience everything we are. In that experience, we grow and become more conscious. Teaching a loved one to believe in the inner Self and trust in that Self is the greatest gift we can give.

Consciousness is our connectedness with love, allowing us to be conscious of all the beautiful things within and around us. We cannot see the beautiful things outside of us, no matter how hard we try, unless we see the beautiful things within us. Without love of Self, felt deep within, the images of what you see are devoid of love. Therefore, everything we see is questioned, mistrusted, or distorted, because it cannot come from a loved-based place and thereby sustain trust and bliss within it. What we see, in effect, is not real; ours is a world of illusion. As we continue our discussion, you will soon come to understand in a healed Self the world's illusion is self-manifested for a purpose.

Life has a meaning and an intentional purpose.

Now the experience and purpose come into question. How do we know love without its opposite, fear? Yet love has no opposite, as it is the conscious energy of creation. It is the essence of all life. We would not understand the perfection and wholeness of that love unless we experienced its opposite: the self-manifested (ego) opposite of fear. Love, being the construct of all creation, knows no fear; therefore, it has no opposite. Love is real; ego manifestation is a distortion of true reality.

To explain further, how would you know what the idea of "left" is if you did not know what "right" is, what "fat" is if you did not know "skinniness," or what "tall" is if you did not know "shortness"?

> If we are born into a loving environment, that does not mean we are exempt from fear or pain, which were self-created for a reason. Our loved ones protect us and look after us so well that we no longer feel capable to look after ourselves. Two bills are in the mail, and we fall apart. Stress over the slightest thing becomes all too much to bear, and we project our concerns onto others, manifesting more of the same. Sadly, we wonder how kids from good homes and apparently wonderful lives commit suicide. Perhaps they were over nurtured and thus were under prepared for the world they would be exposed to.

Our purpose is not to abuse, enmesh, or abandon our children, nor is it to nurture our children to the point where they are incapable. We over nurture children only to satisfy a deep yearning or fulfill a deep-seated need of our own as parents, teachers, or caregivers. If we express love and it comes from a sense of lacking within us we can, in a sense, restrict our children from expressing their own creativity and pure potentiality. We must encourage them to use their creative and imaginative aspects to solve their problems and the many questions that life poses. We must teach them to trust themselves and trust in their inner Self without fear and thereby stop the cycle of whispering images. They must learn to solve issues for their healthy development, which will allow them to grow into functioning adults.

The answers are found in the silence of the inner Self, the silence that will be their home when faced with life's challenges. This silent place is the only place of knowing! By connecting to the inner Self, we restore our trust and love in our Self.

The outside world projects lifestyles of the rich and famous, and so we yearn for that which someone else has. We feel unworthy of the images we have created of ourselves. We say, "I can't do that," yet in an equally loud voice say, "I can do anything," feeling it deep within the recesses of our minds, but not believing it. We do not believe it because we have grown to rely on our teachings. Perhaps we have had everything done for us or have not been able to express a point of view. Perhaps we have had someone always there to over protect us and solve our problems, defend our cause, over esteem us, and make us feel nothing is good enough for us. Worthlessness sets its mark. Anxiety forms as much a part of our lives as it does the lives of the abused and abandoned child.

The time to prove those whispering images wrong begins as we fight to gain the upper hand. There is no escape from this. This is the very reason we are here. We need to know who and what we are—and who and what we wish to become.

For most of us, to do nothing is to deny our very existence. In the effort to prove images wrong, the doing becomes misguided, poorly perceived, and poorly directed. People or things outside us become our quests and our trophies. We say, "Look who I am or what I have!" The images are a constant reminder of why we are doing or not doing things, regardless of the relationships or the material gain we have or don't have. Things outside of you can never fulfill you and can only satisfy the images that you see of yourself. But they won't fade until you choose to recognize that they are a part of an unhealed past. In the inner silence of Self we can start to identify with this truth. It is in the silent place of knowing that our answers to our discomfort can be recognized.

It is in the awareness of this—and of those false images—that true healing can begin.

Fulfillment can only be felt in the body. Do you feel at peace, or are you constantly feeling a sense of lack, always thinking of the future, and delving constantly into the past? Are the images that whisper sweet nothings forever keeping you in a place of wanting? Do these images make you feel you are never achieving enough, nor appreciating or accepting what you have accomplished or what you have in your life in the present?

It's time to look for a new path. Can you see the signs of disillusionment in neon lights before you? Are you happy? Is the happiness short lived? Does it vary between highs and lows, love and hate? Do you truly know what joy is? Have you felt it for more than a day or a week without reacting to or creating drama? When was the last time you stopped for a moment and were grateful for everything in your life? Do you genuinely feel loved and secure? Do you know what love and security really are? Do you genuinely feel love in your life?

Our thinking never ceases its identification with our mind long enough to align with our inner Self. We are literally trapped within our minds and are constantly acting out those images that never fade.

The images are working overtime, keeping us from this place of knowing. To recognize such peace and joy would completely deny what we have created: the end to all we have grown to rely on and believe so well. *Do not say I am wrong,* we are saying. *Do not attack my sense of self, my sense of worth. It is all there is, and it is all I have.*

How wrong we are!

CHAPTER THREE

Dancing with Your Shadow

The shadow holds our deepest secrets. It is the choreographer
of our dance of life; it constructs our performance.

There are two of you: your inner Self, all-loving soul and your ego self, or shadow. The shadow is who you have created, and it takes over the body. To not create your shadow is to believe you are doomed to a life of toil or torment.

> *While we all understand ego and the many interpretations given to it, some will argue it is good and some that it is bad.*
>
> *I describe it as a negative, dark force that was self-created by an unloved self that lives in fear. It is the self that needs to impress, be continually validated, and control or manipulate for its false needs and wants. We think the ego guides us well because it was self-created in order that we can survive and provide for our false needs and wants that become our selfish attachments. Such is the fear that we live by and with.*
>
> *Your shadow is who you have become. You dance to its song, for the song is your survival. It is your other self that is nothing more than an illusion of the real you. The ego or adapted other was created for your benefit or detriment by you—the master creator. The ego's benefit is to experience all there is to experience, and the detriment is that the end can*

only be death. The cycle of life continues, for even in death is a benefit: the death of an old way or misguided teaching.

It is our shadow that will lead us to this path—a new beginning with new fulfillment and loving meaning.

It is our purpose and innermost desire to experience life to the fullest; yet we are not conscious of this purpose, believing instead that we are at the whim of life, not the creator of it.

Your shadow is created after birth by the physical nature of the form you are. Its appearance will take on, and reflect the essence of who you will become by your conditioning and learning. You create your shadow, but everything within it is the illusion you are taught to see. The image is the shape and form of your physical being. It is an energy of physical form that is similar, but directly opposed to, its host, your soul. It will follow its creator and act as you command. It believes it will protect you from harm; yet harm is all it knows.

If you are attacked, it will attack. If you jump, it will jump. If you sit, it will sit. Stand, and it will follow. Walk, and it will do the same. Sit in silence, and it will sit with you—reluctantly. It is your constant companion and a mere reflection of the false you.

The Shadow Effect

Sit in grief and draw a picture of what your shadow will look like.

- Will it slump and be still as it ponders the many thoughts of its creator?
- Will it move slowly, lost for fear of the unknown?

It will create thought, and then use the body to create pain to feed the thought. It will resist everything, for it trusts nothing, and resistance creates negativity. A cycle of more negativity continues.

Letting go is the mantra of the soul. Holding on is the mantra of the shadow.

My world was one of make-believe, yet I thought it was one of success and gain—even happiness, due to outward things; hence the need for more of them. I did not even know at the time the definition of joy, because I had so little of it to cross reference. Everything I did was from the point of escapism, yet I did not know it. I created a world with tenacity and doing. My incessant thinking was relentless, and so was my relentless doing. In that relentless place of doing, great energy was exerted. My shadow vibrated for all to see, and it was an attraction for many—many who gave up rather than fight. They hung on, and I hung on to them.

What, however, did I attract but more of the fear I had grown to know so well? My shadow danced for the world to see. More wasn't enough to allow me to escape the past—the place I knew well and could not escape, no matter how hard I tried. I needed to dance. My life was a dance show, and nothing more.

I had a passion for doing, and doing was the engine of the vehicle I drove. Attracting others was easy. Others wanted to jump on board, not knowing how to get to that place called success. The passion was so intense that it inspired others to action. I became the center of other people's dreams and the escape from their reality. We were the same, yet different; we had the same goals and dreams, but with different physical expression. Mine was driven. Relationships danced a while or faded away. Relationships came and went. The toll was too much for some; in fact, most of my relationships—if not all of them—ultimately failed.

I found I was particularly good at what I did—surprisingly so! I searched relentlessly for the vehicle that would lead me out of the dark, forbidding place I had lived in for so long—my childhood drama—and onto the path to somewhere—anywhere but where I was. I found a path, and it all appeared good. Yet what was I creating around me? I was creating a world of people, events, and material gain to fill the void of the discomfort and hate I felt inside myself. I was inspired for my own gain, and such was my obsessive control that I believed I could help them by my desires. My ego self, or dancing shadow, had no realization of another's desires.

I liked myself when I was successful, and my shadow danced for all the wrong reasons. Surrounded by love—but not knowing what real love was—I could not see it. All I could see was the need to control, protect, and acquire more and more so that I could feel good. I owned a business that employed twenty people—then thirty, then forty, and on we went.

I needed to build a high-rise building, then a shopping center, and then more, because it was there to do. My shadow danced with happiness for the world to see. I felt sporadic happiness until the goal was complete— but then what?

"Just one more thing and I will finish" was something I had said to my loved ones for a decade. I needed that shopping center, as it would underpin the financial position I created. It needed to expand to underpin its value—and so the task of doing continued. Each event took energy for itself, leaving little for its host to share with itself and give where giving would be well deserved and appreciated. I kept the energy up for everyone else of like kind so their performance underpinned my own. I needed it to survive. It was the law of return on investment, or give and take. Other than material possession through business, where were love and joy as true rewards for the effort and personal gain acquired over a decade or two?

The next real estate development needed to be built to acquire the cash flow to sustain the expansions elsewhere. One thing was underpinning another, and the shadow continued to dance to its own tune—leading, never following. Imagine all this vibrancy without clarity of vision: It was well-organized chaos, passion, and control, and obsession was its method of communication.

Our shadow dominates our life and separates us from our conscious, loving, inner Self. It is made apart from the Self, yet formed in the image and likeness of us. We become so enmeshed with it that we no longer feel the pain it creates. In my own case, my pain was expressed every day from people dancing to my needs, not their own, and resentment was the ultimate winner. We think, *Here is proof for all to see: a dancing shadow. We will follow what it says and see where it leads us. It seems strong, resilient, and invulnerable. We may get something from this; let's dance with it.*

We can become the glue for other people's lives. Have you ever felt that way or referred to yourself as "*the* glue"? Creating a world for yourself and others while the essence and energy of you is drained, you continue to hold on, fix, or resist, which sets you back on the path, looking for more to fill the void you feel inside. Nothing is fulfilling. If this is so, you need to just let go. Trust!

Who suffers the consequences of your actions? Who else but the ones you love or believe you love. Can a person who does not like his or her true Self truly like or love another?

We are not talking of the shadow self created out of the fear we were fed. That self lives on fear, creating drama to feel content and alive. Rather, we are talking about the true Self that was created at birth, the Self in perfect harmony with all that exists. It is all-loving and accepting of all that is.

I would come home to my beautiful wife and seek love in return. After all, didn't my efforts deserve that? What I received was the stark reality of what I was creating. High-intensity energy drained the essence of all I loved, leaving no room for my loved ones to be who they were. My world was based on expectation and result. Everyone had to fit within my world. I believed material things were a gift and an expression of my love, not realizing what the definition of a loving relationship was. I did not realize what a healthy relationship was or what love was in its true sense.

It was many years before I knew what love and being in a healthy relationship were. To love is to let those you love be as they wish to be, not expecting anything in return from them, having no expectation of them, and having time for them. To love is to listen unconditionally, to share, to be vulnerable and open, to be comfortable and accept the other for who he or she is and what he or she says, containing your reactions in a compassionate manner, expressing your needs, and being accepting of theirs.

Your shadow cannot accept love or a healthy relationship. It will sit in grief and despair because the other failed to meet something you expected and didn't receive. The shadow will be relentless at fulfilling your life, however amiss. It cares little about how another is fulfilling his or her life. It will control, judge, or play victim to meet its goal, and when that end is met it looks for more. We become so centered to the false self that we cannot see the needs of others, and we become disappointed when they no longer fit within our needs. Your shadow is nothing more than a shadow. It has no power other than the false sense of power you give to it.

You may say things like, "I'm doing it for them, how ungrateful they are." Slowly, the shadow absorbs the other's energy, and the craving intensifies the need to control and manipulate. The shadow needs to dance to its own tune, hoping all others will reinforce it. It continues to search for all things outside it to keep up the charade. We search in places we don't want and cannot refuse the journey, even though our inner Self demands we stop. What do we stop for— more of the same? Won't we lose everything? Have we got enough to protect ourselves? We keep dancing, forever in fear and never realizing it. How can you rest? The world you created is showing signs of wear and tear, but you must fight to restore and reinforce your creation. Resistance becomes torment. Relationships lose their gloss.

The more we fight, the more our lessons intensify, and the more we are drained of the vital energy of life. We search for it in others to prop us up. The false self needs to constantly be validated and seeks approval to medicate itself. It never stops dancing. It can't stop dancing, for it knows no other way other then death. We become fickle and attached to the highs, and suffer many lows in disappointment.

> When I arrived home from work each day, I was met with anxiety, resentful silence, and uneasy smiles. Misinterpretation was normal, for love was not adequately expressed by either side. The children—who could only love—were disappointed once again because of the negative energy felt within the home, and they would quietly suffer as a result. In the recesses of their minds, they would quietly wonder why, but they learned that this was normal.
>
> Gratitude no longer resided in this home, and our shadows would walk cautiously, fearing attack. The bodies were exhausted, but ready to attack. Both sides were locked in a duality of minds; both relied on their own self-opinions and beliefs. Disappointment wears its host down. The egos were playing their roles perfectly.

Our shadows are all we have to guide us on our paths. Many people find this a difficult concept to accept. Our egos contain our subliminal or hidden messages, and fuel our misguided beliefs and false perceptions. We have relied strongly on our adapted self to protect us throughout our lives. Any reaction we may have to this statement is given because our egos are not taking responsibility for our lives. Yes, the ego must control us, but it will take no responsibility, because that is its control mechanism and its belief in the distortion it creates.

We cannot follow the inherent values we failed to see or choose to look for. They have become clouded by a false reality that is self-created from the pain of our past. The ego is born from the pain of the past; that is why it is frail and ready to attack. The ego knows its foundation is weak and based on fear. It will always seek validation to feel the missing love, and when things do not work, it will blame.

The ego will be your constant reminder that you need to keep seeking acceptance from others. It will tell you to make a phone call, then another; to send text messages, looking for a reply and more validation; and to spend to make yourself feel better, then show off your wares to others, as if to say, "Look at me." Yet we fail to be able to 'not-do,' just to sit within, sit with Self and feel whatever it is that we feel. The path of doing is endless, because true feeling has been lost to fear.

We see a world full of everything we want, but we learn to keep wanting. We search out the means by which we can acquire this new reality or we become disheartened and give up on it completely and live with judgments and criticisms. The lives we were dealt were unkind and unjust—or overly kind, to the point of our loss of Self-worth.

We think, *What value will I follow but the value I place on survival, acquisition, control, opinion, or judgments? Surely I will follow no other. I can no longer believe in any inherent value I abandoned long ago or once believed to be right in the time when innocence knew itself within. This belief would mean I could no longer have what I have or the belief that those values abandoned me and left me forever wanting. It must mean I am wrong—and I cannot possibly be wrong, because that would make others right. If I am wrong, then I must be less than what I have made of myself—the person I made against all odds.*

When we reunite with love of Self, we start to feel the pain within and see the image we have created. The fickle, impermanent world we know deep within that we created is merely an illusion, a drama, an act; yet we have hung onto it tightly. The past and future became the intense focus; incessant thinking becomes a prison, and we believe that this is the normal process of life.

The only moment that will ever mean anything to us is now: this very moment with a loved one, this glass of wine and a good companion, the Self in silence and meditation, being aware of true Self, talking with our children and seeing the smiles on their faces, laughter overheard from another room, writing in a journal and realizing our blessings, acknowledging with gratitude the many wonderful things in our lives, taking the time to see and experience these things, or forgiving someone! These are the only moments that mean anything at all.

Life has blessed us with many wonderful sights and sounds, yet how often do we see or hear them? Rarely, if at all, for the world we see consumes our every thought. We become blind and deaf to the point of numbness.

You are numb, and it is no wonder you cannot feel anything, as a shadow can't feel. Who has shown you another path? And if they have, were you ready to perceive it, like you are now? Deep within, you know contentment is lacking; you feel separate from everything and everyone but still do not understand why.

Let Life Show You

Let a new song guide you.

Let it be the sounds of nature: the blowing of the wind through trees, the sound of birds singing first thing in the morning when you wake, the flow of a river, or some music heard in the background.

Hear the wonderful sounds you are blessed with each and every day and fail to acknowledge: the laughter of children playing, the happiness of your partner, or the sound of a friend's voice.

These are the only sounds that will ever mean anything.

We can choose today—right now—to connect with life in many ways. This is the beginning of present-moment awareness.

Observe all the things around you, and then feel what it is to feel in those moments of pleasure and silent rest.

We must learn to reconnect with our inner Self. In our inner Selves, our minds will connect with our spirits, and the peace that we have only ever desired will be found in abundance.

All our lives, we have either been over conditioned or under conditioned for the material world of which we are each a part. We judge abundance as if we are deserving of it. It is our inheritance and birthright to have all that we desire. We are here to create, yet we fail to create what we most desire. Now, while there is good reason in the creative plan of evolution for this, the moment we choose to heal and see past our belief in lack of what we think we don't have in our life, the quicker and more imminent abundance will be made real in our lives. While we believe there is scarcity in our lives, pleasures within it are substituted with judgments and criticism of those pleasurable things. We believe pleasurable things are beyond our reach. We might judge money and the people who have it, for example. We might judge sex as if it is a bad thing and should be limited or restrained, and we might judge anything else that gives us these pleasures and joy. These judgments then become our lessons and opinions, which we pass on or teach.

Let go of limited thoughts and attitudes. Just drop them. Accept people for what they have, and desire all you wish to desire without feeling any guilt or judgment. Whatever you desire, you can have. The secret to having is in the gratitude of receiving. The shadow lacks gratitude; it holds on to resentment and the past. Through fear, it believes nothing is forever and everything is susceptible to loss, so attachments become all too important. The shadow self believes what it has is never enough, and it is never satisfied. We create a world where limitation, and having without appreciation, or not having, becomes our reality. Attachments to people and things then become far too important.

Whether you are deprived of love and filled with lack, or overly loved and deprived of the tools to face the world we know, you are here to experience life to the fullest, and you will. It will also be your choice to feel the depth of pain in those experiences or celebrate in them. It is your choice alone. Your suffering will be directly linked to the length of time you allow your shadow to lead. The longer you fail to recognize or own the truth of your life, face the lessons you have been taught, and question their validity, the longer you will suffer.

To deny the very essence of us—the all-loving, resourceful, and complete Self—can only bring painful experiences which we must face. We cannot escape the reality of being all that we can be and therefore experience the multitude of possibilities awaiting us. How can we decide to deny ourselves the opportunity to be all we can be? We create the very things we need to evolve; it is our life purpose, who we are and, why we are here. It is through those experiences that we understand the relationship to the all-loving Self. We must all return to the loving, complete, and joyful Self that we are! In this state of being—referred to as our divine state of being—all that we seek is given, and all that we desire is made manifest.

The process of understanding this is made possible by, of course, the ego—our shadow. Yes, the thing that attempts to control you will ultimately destroy you. The ego is the very thing that will reunite you with your true Self. The constant fear that this aspect of your physicality will manifest in you assures your return to the peace that exists within Self. Be thankful, with no guilt of anything you have ever done. Recognize what it is you have done instead, and be grateful for this awareness. It is the experience of it that has brought you to this point in your life and to experience a new reality. It is your soul's purpose to experience love, peace, and joy in this physical form, with all life's ups and downs, and to live comfortably within it.

It is when we connect to our divine Self—our true inner Self—that all we have in our lives and all we have achieved or acquired can be fully appreciated. It is here that we do not depend on anything outside of Self. Thereby, what we have and who we have in our lives can be completely appreciated. There is no reason—through expectation, control, or feelings of never having enough—to cause anguish, because those behaviors will not exist in our lives. What we do thereafter become acts of love, and what we have will be totally appreciated, enjoyed, and accepted. Our lives take on a different meaning; we become grateful for the things in our lives. In gratitude, our lives will flower.

The shadow, by comparison, with all its suppressed secrets and hidden messages, needs to constantly seek out. Even when abundance is all around us, the shadow is never satisfied. Our failure to see that creates a hostile, unloving reality. When we are free of the affliction of an unloved self, the sight becomes all too clear. Life is instantly made easy. We no longer attach ourselves to people and things. Many of us create numerous attachments in our lives, although we do not even realize this until they are taken away from us.

A Simple Observed Attachment

A simple attachment to observe in this moment may be your mobile phone. Leave it for a day, and make no calls or text messages. Observe and feel your reaction. If this activity creates a body sensation or pain through anxiety, then you are attached to it. Your pain and anxiety means that you cannot be without your phone because you fear sitting with your Self. You fear being alone because you may have to face your feelings.

The need for contact and to feel loved, accepted, part of something, or validated becomes an attachment. A constant attachment to an outer form is such a common practice that very few of us even realize our attachments. It is only when they are taken away that the reality of these attachments is felt. Often, attachments are brought to the light of awareness through adversity, such as when a person or a material possession we are attached to is taken away from us.

Hence, there is a need to connect to the silence within to start the process of unraveling the truth of our lives that has limited our enjoyment of life. There is nothing lacking in our lives! Everything that happens to us happens for a reason.

When we grasp this concept, live it, know that nothing can harm us, and know that nothing is lacking in our lives because we feel complete wholeness in

Self, we release ourselves from attachments to outer form, which create resistance and anxiety within us, and thereby we stop the drama of life and the pain associated with it. Then, in the outer form, outer things will be enjoyed, accepted, and appreciated in gratitude, and more will be readily given. Without attachment, the people or objects that were once those attachments become the joys of life's abundance.

The transition of this, while difficult for most to understand, is in fact one of the greatest joys of life. The gifts of life are ours for the asking, while attachment will create resistance and anxiety and stop or limit more abundance. The limiting of abundance then fuels the need for more through feelings of scarcity, and the cycle of not receiving and forever wanting continues.

The shadow will unceasingly attach to an outer form, for it cannot accept non-resistance, letting go, and just believing in the process of life. The shadow was made by us to control, as we were controlled, and thus its dance must be distorted. By contrast, when we connect with our true Self, the joy in being who we are allows us the freedom to enjoy all the people and things around us. In this connection, all that we acquire or experience—money, a car, a house, sex, relationships, children, holidays, sitting in a park, going for a walk, or exercising—is made and appreciated in complete joy. Joy is felt when acceptance is the connecting point to life's blessings, and being aware of those blessings is the key.

A Boy Outside the Gate

When your soul has a blindfold on through its human life, it is virtually in an obsessed-like state; its outlook has been depressed, and its future—severed as the trap of your mind—is now in play. Look at your shadow, as it is leading the dance.

The reason? The blindfold , the ego, does not allow the light to come through, so it keeps your thoughts in darkness, enjoying the control it has over you.

Fear is now the ruler—uncontrollable jealousy, irrational behavior and swinging emotions that cannot be understood, less alone explained. These emotions are now running riot inside your head.

The pain you endure is self-inflicted; your wounds and scars are bleeding in the form of words, life's colorful theatre, now on stage.

And actually, these souls are very easy to identify.

Look at these souls; look closely. They seem to be stuck—caught in a deep place, going over and over the same thing, just rehashing it—and why? They cannot see their life's lesson they set out for; they believe they are lost. They have been abandoned; self-pity feels good and comforts their ego.

Will you allow the ego to suppress all that is good—to tell you that there is no spirituality? No enlightenment and no hope?

Let the ego go! To take off the blindfold is the highest level of detachment!

Meditate and breathe, and look inside you.

Connect to your inner Self.

Let the light of your inner Self enlighten you, allowing all to be, without judgment and only good intentions, as there is only good within us all.

And only good will stand to serve you.

Now your shadow no longer is.

It is your true Self that leads your dance.

CHAPTER FOUR

The Burning Log and the Stone

---

*"The more you lose yourself in something bigger
than yourself, the more energy you will have."*
—Norman Vincent Peale

When I was driving north along the highway on a beautiful sunny day, there was a chance to speak with Rhonda, a beautiful person and a colleague with whom I'd had the privilege of working for several months. She had spent the previous week crying off and on. As I no idea what was causing her anxiety, I asked if she wanted to talk about it. In response, Rhonda said, "Oh, it is just being at University; I've got too much work on, and with all your work, I'm feeling a bit pressured—that's all. I'll be okay."

Rhonda talked a little about her life. She told me that growing up in Hong Kong, she was a happy child. Both she and her parents lived in a very small apartment with a small kitchen and small oven, like all kitchens in Hong Kong, simply because space was an issue there. She remembered being happy. Later, however, her mum and dad grew apart, and her dad just gave up talking to her mum. She found herself trying to speak to her dad on behalf of her mother to resolve their differences—or at least get them to communicate with each other. She didn't have much luck, apparently. As she grew older, the apartment appeared to become smaller and smaller. She wanted to move away, but had no money. Proficient in playing piano, she started to teach children so she could earn enough money to study in Canada. She was successful and went on to study there.

During this time, she developed a romantic relationship with a man in Hong Kong, and they continued a long-distance relationship until she returned to him after her studies concluded. For six years, she was involved with Robert, who was totally absorbed in himself, had few friends—really none to speak of—worked continuously, and created his world with himself completely at its center. She described him as loving himself at the expense of every relationship he'd ever been in, including his relationship with her.

That relationship ended, and she moved to Australia to live. She was now going out with a person she described as loving, caring, and somewhat quiet. John was an engineer, calm by nature—someone she felt she was in love with.

She went on to explain how Robert had called her from Hong Kong only a few weeks earlier to tell her how he was sorry he had let her go, that he had another relationship with a woman who was always complaining about his work habits and therefore he ended it, and how he should never have let her go.

I asked how she felt about Robert calling, remembering how unstable she had been at work. She replied, "I'm okay. I like to stay in touch with him as a friend." Rhonda also said that she did love him, and it did play on her emotions. When I asked why she needed to be friends with someone who obviously cared only for himself, especially when she was in a loving relationship with a man who greatly cared for her, her reply was, "Because he is a friend."

Intriguingly, she had stayed in this relationship, despite realizing she got little out of it, for six years. In fact, she described the relationship as horrible and recalled the feeling of needing to get away from it. "He completely loved himself, and only himself," she said. I asked why she stayed, and she replied, "Because I thought I could fix him. I stayed with him because I thought love could fix everything."

I asked if she felt staying with Robert was a remedy for the relationship between her mum and dad that she couldn't fix—the relationship in which she had said she was always the intermediary between talking to Dad on behalf of Mum. Did she stay with him because she wanted to fix the relationship that she couldn't fix in her mum and dad?

It was apparent this girl was hurt that her mum and dad didn't talk to one another. She was a young child at the time who wanted her family members to love each other; she wanted to be in a place that she could feel safe and loved. In essence, she was the burning log that radiated love and heat into her mother and father until it exhausted her, as they were the stones.

I asked if perhaps Rhonda thought that her ex-boyfriend was her salvation and that this relationship with a selfish individual was an extension of her own family issues. After some moments, she agreed and felt that it was perhaps her reasoning.

Rhonda was the burning log, and all burning logs need other burning logs to spread the light and radiate energy together to feed the flame even brighter. However, Robert was a stone, and all Rhonda did was warm that stone. In that warmth, the stone felt something good, but could not do anything about it, because he was a stone, not a log. He wasn't ready to be a log. After a time, Rhonda's radiant energy—her flame—was spent. She was exhausted, for the stone absorbed all her warmth, and she left the relationship. She did well to do so.

I asked about Rhonda's current partner and how she felt a week or so earlier when she was feeling down on herself and overwhelmed. She replied, "John said I should just take things slowly, not put so much expectation on myself to achieve everything tomorrow—just let things unfold one day at a time." It appeared she found her burning log, and he was at home. There is nothing more important for a burning log than to be with another burning log. Be careful you don't become a stone and thus maintain, rather than deplete, radiant energy.

Have we healed those things in our past that we need look no further, or do we need to search for that which was lacking in our lives and try to make it right by attaching to expressions of false love—attachments to those we think we can perhaps fix, and in so doing, perhaps fix our past? Are we constantly attached to incessant thoughts over our true feelings? This self knows no peace. It continually challenges us to succeed, fix, make right, attach to things outside of us, and ignore the beauty of those deserving around us.

Rhonda obviously had deep feelings for John, and he was apparently aware that she had been communicating with the previous boyfriend. I asked how she would feel if John did that to her. Her reply was, "It would hurt. I wouldn't like it." It seemed a part of her still wanted to fix the ex-boyfriend a little—and in so doing, perhaps fix her past. What was needed was for her to forgive herself for all the wrong she perceived that was ever done to her and have the strength to say, "No, enough is enough!"

For Rhonda to accept Robert's phone calls and listen to him tell her she was the only one for him and the only one who could put up with his ways when she was in a loving relationship with a warm, caring soul was abuse. Robert was preying on her weakness—her past—and her shadow was dancing to its tune. Rhonda was accepting the possibility of being destabilized and her life being turned upside down, just like Robert's. As in all mind-identified states of unconsciousness behavior, Robert's goal was to control and ultimately take all he could to satisfy his own self-interest. Such people are stones, as their consciousness is weak and their love is clouded in fear.

After awhile Rhonda found the strength, courage, and inner wisdom not to take Robert's calls anymore and to tell John that she would not take these calls anymore because she cared for him too much. They became two burning logs energizing a truly loving relationship.

Unity Consciousness

Unity consciousness is when healed souls come together in the inner knowledge of the oneness of which we are all a part. It is immediately recognizable in Self-love. Unity consciousness is the individual, loving energy of two or more people manifesting loving connectedness. It is a powerful, loving creative manifestation of form from the formless.

Unity consciousness is very important for all of us. It is the light of wellness that manifests abundance, peace, and love in an instant. It is felt by many others within its radius. It is contagious, as all love is. It expands to families, communities, and globally, as people of high-loving vibrational energy come together to meet, talk, and share. Unity consciousness is the path to peace on earth.

We must choose the company we wish to keep. People in the process of healing will not heal while absorbing the energy of unhealed others. To associate with another whose flame radiates with the light of love can only increase your light and energy, like two logs burning—one perhaps greater than the other. However, when the logs come together, the intensity heightens and radiates even more love. Regardless, if one is removed from the fire, both will burn at a far greater intensity. The light radiated from unity consciousness can help many others reach higher levels of consciousness.

The world is in desperate need of people who represent burning logs. We must let go of our past and seek out our consciousness by forgiveness of self and forgiveness of all others, knowing that we are all inexplicably linked together to experience every aspect of life so that our consciousness grows stronger by each experience.

It is important to know that to forgive also means not accepting the projections of others that would deplete that light you radiate. A stone will deplete a burning log's intensity, for no matter how much you warm that stone, it will never burn.

You were born the light—the burning log—until you were made a stone. Through divine alchemy and the experiences of your life, you have the chance to be that burning log once again and radiate light to all those seeking this knowledge. Are you going to let the opportunity pass and deny the very thing you search for, yet can never seem to find? It is in front of you, reaching out. At what point are you going to embrace your destiny?

Love is all there is.

CHAPTER FIVE

Soundproofed Words

"Resentment is like drinking a cup of poison and expecting the other person to die."
—Carrie Fischer

Soundproofed words are words we do not wish to hear. They tell us one reality, but another reality is acted out. These words often come from our caregivers. They say they love us, they feed and clothe us, yet they all too easily express words of an unloved self. We pick up these lessons, and from then on, we act them out. Later, the words we have heard so often distort our reality. Any love expressed by another is no longer heard, because the words are soundproofed, having been suppressed within us. We cannot know love as, or give love from, an unloved self.

Too often, children are told they are not good enough or that they will not amount to anything. The actions of those we love cut to the core of our being and turn our reality on its head. Grave disappointment becomes all too commonplace, and we learn to live with it, feeling safe that we have a place to call home. What is our alternative? Eventually, we feel comfort in those words; they represent the only feelings of unity we felt—the unity of a family. At least someone apparently cared for us; they fed us and clothed us. This is certainly different from the separation we created—growing to maturity as we fought our many battles—as a consequence of our early experiences.

In the face of public perception, your world takes on completely different characteristics. From early in our lives, we are taught to hold our heads high, smile, and pretend everything is okay.

What lies beneath the surface of your skin has a completely different reality, and too often, we are taught to hide our truths, conceal our pain, deny any wrongdoing, and create a picture-perfect world. When we are not allowed to express our truths, they become suppressed. It is the smoke screen of our lives. This continues well into adulthood.

It is little different to the experience of children of addicts, who grow up feeling the comfort in physical pain as a consequence of another's addiction—a pain they are all too familiar with. What have we created in our young and those around us is more of the same. Unloving words affect our physical bodies and minds, creating physical anguish through our unforgiving thoughts of a past lived and our misperceptions created by them. Such words never cease to alarm us when spoken by another and create all sorts of reactions in us. Words can easily be taken out of context, misinterpreted, and then acted upon accordingly by the illusion we have created in our minds.

Our youth masks these types of words to allow us to hide our feelings deep within—feelings that lay dormant. These feelings are dormant until someone close to us, someone we trust, or think we do—the "other half" of us who, through our attachment, we value—triggers a reaction in us through words. These "soundproofed" words remind us of our past. We relive our past, but now with the luxury of age and a hardened shell, we attack, cover with humor, ignore, build resentment, indulge in all sorts of medication, or simply deny our reality.

Toward the end of my second marriage, the words "I'm leaving you" triggered abandonment issues I could not deal with. My reaction was to verbally attack, because I couldn't attack when I was vulnerable and young. Then after my wife left me, words as simple as "no more silly goodbyes" brought up feelings of worthlessness. The issues from actions of my childhood arose. I pretended I did not care, but I keenly felt a lack of importance. At that time, however, because my former wife had my children, even greater feelings of resentment resonated within. These feelings are easily triggered when we cannot identify the truth behind these soundproofed words.

Any word spoken by a loved one, someone with a vested interest in us, can trigger powerful emotional reactions. The shadow waits to defend its illusion of reality. The shadow leads the dance with its secrets hidden deep within, yet unresolved, because most often, we are not even aware. When we react by using any of our defensive behaviors, we add to the layers of resentment, and our unresolved anger builds. Anxiety becomes a way of life until our lives simply become unmanageable and we are forced to deal with our truth.

Simply put, we cannot deal with the same issues that trigger our deep-seated pain using the same mindsets we have always used. Rather, we need to find an alternative—and preferably before it's too late or we are too exhausted from the years of living with anxiety to adequately deal with it, thus suffering as a consequence for many years after.

Why can we not look at our lives and observe what we are doing and feeling?

The words and actions you were subjected to early in your life simply built up, layer by layer, until you create a new "me"—a me that was dependent on self-image. This image of your "me" is forever protecting and projecting; it is the same image that taught the rest of us, as it was taught to our teachers.

The words and actions to which we have been subjected while growing up—regardless of how lightly or humorously said or how they were interpreted by us at the time—built and reinforced those layers. We toughen our exteriors, and to harden our resolve, we create identities that are forever ready to defend a position in whatever way we think appropriate.

> Dad: "Son, can you get me that shirt for this gentleman?"
> Me: "Which one (among one hundred to choose)?"
> Dad: "There—top shelf—green." (Now there was a selection of ten.)
> Me: "This one?"
> Dad: "Not that one—next shelf up."
> Me: "This one?"
> Dad: "You bloody idiot—what did I raise? You and your brother are useless. You will never amount to anything."
> The customer laughed, and my father's ego was given a boost.

We may not realize that the time it took to build those layers was long compared to the length of an average life. The conditioning was slow and steady, cementing those teachings well within us. The process of undoing them must be a patient journey, allowing the integration of knowledge to work. Through awareness, we will realize when we regress to old ways, thus enabling us to try again. This is the path of healing. Yet the process of connecting to inner Self will be your refuge—your peaceful abode—and it is through reading about, and practicing the lessons in this book that you will be able to access this silent place of knowing.

Most of us suffered emotional or physical abuse or abandonment during childhood, as the words spoken to us were less than appropriate to develop and nurture our mature development. These words separated us from ourselves and those around us. We repressed our feelings of hurt for many years to come. Our caregivers felt the guilt of their neglect and all too readily dismissed it for the reason of self-protection. A whisper of discontent from their children, and those soundproofed words were heard within their own past that triggered reactions within them. The lessons are always passed down from one generation to the next.

Anger and rage are all too commonplace in the modern world. Almost everything, to the loveless mind, is taken as a threat. Those of us who live in constant stress and concern worry about what is said and done, thinking all is directed at its self. Their world is relentless, the thinking not ceasing for a moment. There is no rest and inner peace for these people. It is disguised with doing, humor, food, sex, money, and too often, substance abuse to soften the impact or to deaden the constant pain they feel. Yet these temporary solutions are mere substitutes, and when the deadening effect wears off, the pain becomes more intense.

Whether we were abused, abandoned, or enmeshed with parents who needed our energy and love to fill their lacking, the words used become soundproofed. What we hear is often contrary to what we experience. The words spoken later in life by others close to us are often misinterpreted from the intention used, and the images created in our past replace them with unloving reactions. We lose trust in words spoken; they are soundproofed. We no longer hear their meaning, nor see the call for love through those words in another. Within the relationship, two lives were acting out their pasts, each calling for love, but not knowing where to find it—not knowing how to communicate with the other.

From an early age, through our responsibility for or expectation placed on our young, we create feelings in them of not being good enough. Simple, everyday comments create these feelings, things like: "You're foolish!" "Don't let your sister do that!" "You are responsible—watch them!" "I will do that for you (as if you are incapable)!" "Don't do this; don't do that!" "I'll do it; at least that way, it'll get done!" It is no wonder we grow up not trusting love or hearing words of love and becoming attached to false hope, constantly wanting, never fulfilled. We lack trust in those who express and show us love, and our attachment to them is all too easy. We try to fix our past through these people. It is a past that we wanted very much, but rarely felt as a loving connectedness with self and family.

Words become soundproofed. We see words of love said to us, but do we really hear them and just cling to the dream of love becoming a reality? When words are expressed in private or public, we smile but feel muted by them. We almost believe in them, but we know these words are a beautiful dream only. They are said and received in fear, so they are not heard.

"You will never amount to anything!" The verbal abuse of our parents and their past lives are now in play. "How can you do that?" "Don't be an idiot!" "Stop that foolish behavior!" "You can't do that!" "I'll be back soon!" "I couldn't make the sport today; too busy!" Your subconscious is bombarded with these negative messages until they reside within every cell of your body. Your DNA becomes saturated with these viruses. Words like these condition us and manifest our reality—a reality that prepares us for the world we face—a world created in the same way. What hope is there, other than the hope of Self-realization and love?

You must heal your Self, and then the world you see will no longer be the same! Those around you will heal by your healing; there is no choice in this. Negative responses require other negative responses to survive. If you are aware of your reactions to unloving words, you will then have the choice to change those reactions or behaviors. Change, therapists have told me, is behavioral! You will start to see the meaning in the words spoken when you see your reactionary behavior to the uneasy feelings triggered in you. The past experiences in you react to the lack of ease. You can then consciously stop any reaction to them by getting to the thought that triggered this behavior, and thus choose to be unaffected, realizing the words are another's reality only, not your own.

Unloving words are often spoken from ignorance. Each person has his or her own set of soundproofed words which are repressed within and too easily trigger a reaction to the perception we may have of another's spoken word. Often, expressions of love are seen as expressions of anger, neediness, fear, or jealousy.

Do not whisper criticism or think false judgment of another. Have only loving thoughts for everyone and everything around you, no matter how difficult the forgiveness may be, for this is about you, not the other. Remember Carrie Fischer's comment: "Resentment is like drinking a cup of poison and expecting the other person to die."

Cure the Unease

Try an exercise for one day of your life—just one! Throughout the day, stop yourself—as best as you can—from criticizing, judging, attacking, or acting out behaviorally when an emotion or uneasiness is triggered within you. For just this one day of your life, make a conscious effort to forgive everyone whenever you feel uneasy. Forgive the bearer of your unease, and watch what happens.

Indulge only in loving thoughts and your day will be beautiful. Feelings that you have not felt in a long time will greet your day. Let's not expect that miracle until you are ready to create your life consciously. Here, however, is a chance to experience a mere glimpse of bliss, calm, and joy all around you. Are you afraid to give yourself a chance when the primary beneficiary is going to be you? In this one day, you may feel what it is to liberate the soul. Try this simple lesson of forgiveness!

Forgiving: A Simple Test

We can make the decision to consciously choose to forgive. For one day, when you feel resentment, anger, or grievances, replace these feelings with the thought, "I love you, (name), and I accept you as you are."

- Repeat this each time you feel a change of mental state or an uneasy feeling.
- Identify the thought and at whom this negative energy is projected.
- Forgive, using loving words and affirmations. Repeat the words above until you release yourself of any negative energy and unease!
- Do not whisper criticisms.

Why are you continuing to drink the cup of poison? Stop drinking it. Change your restless world to a loving world. Only you can do it, and you must take responsibility for it. We must see the words that create our unease as soundproofed.

These words block love from entering. They block love as sure as bullet-proof glass blocks bullets. The reality of their intention does not belong to us, and even though it may be directed at us, it is not about us. It is another's pain triggering our own.

Our reality is ours. Another's reality belongs to him or her. We must remember this when on the path to healing.

Take responsibility for your reality by owning the feelings that trigger any reaction within you. Own them! Accept them! Then you will have the power to change them.

What confidence do we take with us in the world we must face alone? What words do we hear to console us and tell us everything is okay? Our facades build slowly, and it is in this slowness that their foundations are strong. The ego is formidable, and we take with us the negativity and hidden, destructive subliminal messages that are so well ingrained within each of us to face the world alone and to survive with all we have learned. We keep drinking from the cup, for we think there is no other way. Do we let our resentment be felt by others so they conform? How is it we came to believe this actually works? We were conditioned, as our teachers were conditioned. Fear was the basis of learning, and our learning was the basis of separation. Words are the simplest and most effective form of communication—communication that is easily lost in translation.

We fear separation and react to it almost all our lives—until now, when we have become aware of it. What is it that we have created? A world of pleasure found in things outside ourselves, yet steeped in constant pain and unrest. We believe this is the place where we will find love and security—the basic desires which we were deprived of from an innocent age or when growing to adulthood. We desperately crave love, joy, and peace, yet they are inherent in our every cell.

The inner Self has what we seek! The inner Self holds those inherent values of love, joy, and peace within it and is the state of being from where we have originated and to where we will return. It is our birthright to seek them out for the soul's purpose of truly knowing this state of completeness and love.

In our experiences, we learn to be exceptionally aware of love, and therefore, peace and joy. The opposite of a thing must exist for us to be aware of its existence.

Words of love are spoken and felt at our deepest level. We initially accept them—smile nervously at first, perhaps—but do not really believe in them. Instead, we attach ourselves to them and the person expressing them—but do we trust them? Of course we do not!

We can't hear these words; they are soundproofed, muted by our past. We pretend to hear them, desire them, and dream of their reality. We try to return loving gestures, but we are too easily diverted as pain is triggered—the same pain felt by someone afraid of intimacy who abandoned us and drained us of energy early in life. We now stand in the public arena of life, proud of our achievements, our trophies on parade for all to see. Our lives are reliving themselves as we were taught, and we are passing our messages on to our loved ones, who are playing out their roles according to their acquired learning.

What becomes sustainable in a world of trophies, more trophies, and then more, to fill the void of lack we feel within? Will they replace the love we yearned for and still seek? No amount of external pleasure will fill that void—the hole has no bottom. We seek love—but for what purpose? Can we complete a picture of feeling whole within—completed by another or complete in the public arena of life? We just don't know how to love; we were given no base. Who were our mentors? How did they act?

Do we keep striving for more and more, disguising the hurt until it all comes crashing down around us? We have been wronged. How do we feel? In protecting the fragile world we have created, we reinforce the belief that it is worth fighting for, but when words of love are spoken, we cannot associate their meaning. We prefer instead to distance ourselves from anyone appearing to get too close. Didn't we try to get close and become bitterly disappointed?

Doing becomes our cover, and expectation becomes our demand. We expect a return for the effort we put into life—the effort we perceived necessary and then created for life to exist in perfect harmony. Yet perfect harmony requires no effort! Instead, we believe we are alone to fight battles—each on our own, separate from everyone and everything. Who else got you here against all odds? Not God, surely—didn't he abandon you long ago? *No, it was I who created me,* you may think, *and the world owes me. You owe me, so what can I take or gain from you?*

Despite our inability to perceive it, love is all around us. When the love we have felt from our genuinely beautiful life companions is discarded in the face of more doing and wanting our companions may call us with loving words, but again, they are muted. We try to return love from an unloving self—the self that is never content, always thinking and doing, wanting more and never satisfied. They stop calling with love in the way we have always dreamed of, for now their love is expressed as pain from feelings of abandonment. Their love is expressed through raw emotion and behaviors such as grief, pain, fear, anger, resentment, or blame. The words, feelings, and actions we know well are born from the addictive words and actions that create attachments in us. These actions remind us of our past with ones we loved. We hold on to a reality of miscommunication and poor perception. Surely this is love—this is what we learned. It has become our way of expressing it.

If a soul companion has similar yearnings of pleasure outside Self, the facade can be maintained only in the short term. Soon, cracks will appear, and that companion's own demands and expectations will surface. His or her own needs and wants that have been suppressed for a long time will surface and rear their ugly faces. Each person—with his or her own expectations and demands—will fight for control of his or her life and the control over another to have his or her own needs met.

What words can we express to have our needs met? We have not been taught. Our words become soundproofed, and their meaning is not adequately explained or heard for fear of seeming vulnerable, weak, helpless, and ultimately afraid to express our true Self.

I remember that this is how I felt growing up, didn't you? It drove my addictions and behaviors. *I can do anything,* I thought. *I know better.* To all appearances, I was invulnerable, strong, resilient, and fearless. To a conscious soul, my thoughts, words, and behaviors were nothing other than fear, but I couldn't see it, nor could I hear it. My words were soundproofed, and any expression of love had been lost.

Without love of Self, nothing real is sustainable long-term. Words will become soundproofed—muted by our past experiences. We will fail to recognize the meaning of words in others and equally fail to express words of our heartfelt Self. Everything else becomes far too important, life becomes a method of ownership, and we can't treat it like we own it. With ownership comes control, and control is resistance—forever fighting for survival. No one is immune.

It is only Self-love that is eternal and everlasting, for Self-love can see past words to their true meaning. After all, we are good at disguising the truth through our fear, but a healed mind can see through this fear. With it, joy and peace will reside. It is here that heaven on earth can be found. Nothing outside of you can give you lasting joy and peace.

> *As I flew over Dubai and saw the palaces with their magnificent gardens, I wondered how such beauty could exist in such a barren place. It was said to me that the gardens were fed mineral water, which was shipped from abroad, to survive.*
>
> *I had another realization when I was told that some of the happiest people on earth come from the poorest countries on earth, countries like Zimbabwe.*

Isn't the story of Dubai so much like life? Here we are, with our palaces and beautiful gardens full of fruit. We believe all that is. The ravages of the world are waiting to consume us, and we do all we can to survive. We ship in water in an effort to feed the garden that we believe will feed us.

Yet the home is filled with an urgency to survive over the need to look within and find true beauty and love. Expectation becomes a way of life, and the pressure of survival slowly claims its victims. First, pressure claims the young, who move to the city to seek new paths ingrained with self-creating lessons they have learned. Then the loved ones who cannot keep up with such demands and pressures are consumed with anger and resentment for the paths they selected and the guilt and disappointment they feel. Finally, the self-proclaimed master of the palace who worked all his life to acquire the things he thought would bring love and security—the only things that were ever desired—loses them to the elements.

The only palace that exists is within you. The treasures of the palace abound. It is within this palace that no outside element can affect its demise. The palace is indestructible and permanent. It offers complete joy and peace. Only love can live there!

We must go within. Find the silence and stillness of Self. Here, life is accepted and understood in kindness and love.

CHAPTER SIX

Forbidden Love

"The focus of your feelings becomes the reality of your world."
—Gregg Braden

In her poem "Solitude," Ella Wheeler Wilcox wrote, "Laugh, and the world laughs with you; weep, and you weep alone." Today, however, the opposite appears true: Cry, and the world cries with you; laugh, and you laugh alone.

It is increasingly difficult to live enmeshed in people's lives and see the reality of what lies beneath the surface of a happy façade. Rarely is the happiness we see in others anything more than a façade. It is often a fragile and impermanent illusion that everything is okay within their lives. The feeling that everything is okay is often played out against a backdrop of fear—and as a consequence, the reality we see and live with.

We fear not being liked by everyone else. Perhaps we feel the need to fit in and then have a problem doing so. We talk about our worries to make others feel good about themselves in the hope that we will receive some validation and acceptance. We talk too much as a consequence and idle chatter replaces the ability to speak in a loving way. We are afraid we just aren't good enough, smart enough, or worthy enough—the same way we have felt for a very long time. Too easily, we put on a happy façade.

Bliss and Happiness

Bliss and joy are states of being held within the contented, loving Self. They are permanent states of belief in love and unity, and are expressed through connectedness to our permanent and stable inner selves.

Happiness by contrast is a temporary lifting of ourselves above fear held within us. A picture-perfect reality or a happy moment, which is short-lived, occurs when an external goal or connection is made. Happiness is fickle and impermanent.

Most of us cannot show any internal bliss or joy, for our understanding of love is lost. Dare we express that which we have come to fear in case we may appear different to others, thereby leaving ourselves open to criticism and judgment, perhaps through jealousy or their resentment? Forbidden love is all too real. Instead of joy and bliss, we use a happy façade to conceal the truths hidden behind our fear of love.

If you are like most people, your relationships are attachments to likeminded people who understand your pain by their own, yet have regard only for their own pain. These people are often willing to offer opinions over your life and your pain as if they know the answers. You decide to accept your life, expressing it as "less than," lacking, unfulfilled, burdened, or whatever form of acceptance from another you seek in self-pity or attention.

We accept the judgments of others, as if they know all the answers, or we give our opinion to be accepted, further creating our false illusion with another. There is no love in this type of exchange, just a greater degree of another painful expression of dissatisfaction. We feel good in this company for a short while. For the moment, we feel validated.

This becomes our fix: Being with other likeminded individuals to whom we outwardly express our fear. The happy façade is lost for a moment, and we cry. We release our fear for a moment, attack in anger, or control or medicate our pain. Reinvigorated, we go back into our world and show that happy façade again.

In all my years of business and within the hundreds I employed, rarely did I witness a person with a sustainable, inner loving connection to his or her inner Self. The very few who seemed somewhat centered and Self-loving became the attachment of so many others within the business. These attachments of others literally drained them of all their energy. Authentically Self-loving people are rare.

Having lived my life with so many people, day in and day out, I could see the majority were driven or motivated by their own fears. Their own pasts were expressed all too frequently, and their attachments to outer forms were all too important. The quality of life was lost to their fears, yet many of us do not see it until much later in life.

People are all too willing to cry with us, for it seems their own tears are what they express. Too often, we do not laugh other than superficially and to cover our stresses and concerns or to avoid our true feelings.

Our lives are full of signs to see this reality; yet we dare not look at the signs, because many of us do not want to face our fears.

Why do we demand so much of our self? Is it to justify how we have become? Seeing is merely an illusion, and what you see is the same as what most of us see. The world where love is forbidden represents a threat to the core teaching we have all become reliant upon. We choose to forbid love, as love represents a truth against our very unconscious reality and the world we are currently living in. It is an unconscious reality that exists in the absence of inner spirit. We all are familiar with the reality we see. We live in a world of suffering and pain; it is all we know. Our lessons of forbidden love touch every facet of our lives.

We are told that life is hard, people are different, everyone is out to get what they can, and people are jealous of what we have. We criticize others for having more or less than us and judge anyone for fear of not being accepted or validated by them, making judgment a norm. Idle chatter becomes commonplace for the lack we feel inside ourselves.

Whom you choose to associate with will greatly impact your outlook on life and the evolution of your life purpose. A physical being ready to heal will see through this veil of expressed pain and live comfortably within it. If it is this path you desire, then you must be strong and climb the mountain alone. You must climb to the summit of this mountain before you can truly help others. We must dismiss unconscious minds, for now, as they will hold us back.

This is a frightening thought, and putting the thought into action is not easy to do. We have, for the most part, become attached to other unhealed minds. They are all that is left to validate us. We feel secure by likeminded individuals. We are attached to the idle talk, negativity, and need for acceptance of any kind. These attachments to others are what we believe is our reality, and without them, we believe we will be abandoned or left alone. The thought of this creates fear. It is this fear that restricts us, limits us, and holds us in an unloving place—the same place the world currently resides. We have no internal or external boundary to say no. We believe, *My life is better than that which I am expressing or others are expressing over.* Obviously, to date, our lives have become so unmanageable that we look for an alternative path.

We allow others to condition us with forbidden language for the purpose of fitting in. We would rather fit into the mold than create our own mold.

You cannot be in the company of unhealed people if you are starting your path to healing—not alone, anyway. Certainly, they are wonderful in a group, all expressing the same desire to release pain and heal. All your strength will be needed to climb the summit, and conscious minds working together will create and maintain the energy you need—the love and support you need to heal from an unloving state to a loving state. It is not easy to face the truth of our lives, which is that perhaps there is a better way, that we need to deal with our past, and that we need to find a path that leads to a healed Self. It is a stark reality for most to face this truth, but ultimately, all of us will face it.

There exists no sustainable peace and love in our lives, yet we fail to see the signs of our unease, because we do not express our needs and wants. We ignore them in favor of being accepted. None of us like to be disliked, so we constantly justify our positions in an attempt to appear right. After all, we have spent our lives being right and being justified for our cause. An exhausting effort is expended in merely living life in whatever manner or path we chose to follow.

In the many mind battles we have contended with, haven't we earned this right—the need to be right? Why would we look for another path?

It is the mind that feels separate from others. It is the mind that reasons without love—and continues to reason to justify its existence. It needs always to be right, so when challenged, it defends its position; it reasons everything out to anyone with a different view. Acceptance of another's opinion—particularly opinions of people who are close to us, such as loved ones—is often discounted. The fear in this stems from abandonment issues, past abuse, and living life disconnected and alone—fighting and resisting life rather than accepting it. It is how we have been taught. Control is the basis of our lives. We are too afraid to let go.

You know the reasoning—the same reasoning that destroys friendships and families. Relationships fail because a union lacking love cannot be sustainable in any healthy relationship. All must comply with a mind that only reasons for its survival. You see, reasoning is not feeling, and feeling is the natural process of the soul expressing itself—the loving Self into physical form. Through our souls, we instinctively know what is right and wrong according to our value systems, and our feelings take us to this knowing place. Without recognizing feelings, the mind is left to wreak havoc in order to protect us from the fear of the disconnection we feel. The disconnection from love is purely our perceived reality alone with the ego seeking its validation from a world existing as separate—a world to serve it and it alone.

Are you greeted with comments such as, "Who gave you a happy pill this morning?" "Why are you so happy today?" "Did you just win lotto?" It is as if being joyful is a form of insanity. To be joyful is not normal. Have we all become so discontent and bored with our lives, or do we carry the shame of our past that creates the lack we feel within and therefore refuse to accept contentment in another? Is it jealousy that causes this reaction? Is this reaction caused by a yearning to have what you fear you cannot—what is out of your reach because you have never been shown connectedness to Self, Self-love, or love for all and all things around us?

Are we so disgruntled by the substance of our own lives that we churn through life in a desperate search for the things which are going to raise us from our silent dread—things outside us—and belittle anyone who gets there before us? We feel discontent with the ones that mean the world to us—our loved ones—and attack them to maintain our sense of control, which we fear has been lost in many other areas of our lives, without realizing it. We fail to recognize their love for us. We do not accept our love for them. What is love, after all?

Of course, we will connect to joyful people if we come into contact with them, but the connection to a truly joyful person is often fleeting. We attach to them, and of course drain their energy by wanting what they have. It is an unsustainable union. Conscious souls attract other conscious souls, but we rarely see these people.

We need to find our conscious path now—find it so that we can authentically connect to Self and others. We need to share a laugh from a sustainable, loving base and offer our healing to those we hear crying.

In a healed state, we will choose to be kind over right. Kindness is about listening to another without opinion. It's about acceptance, about not always needing to be right, and instead allowing another his or her opinion (right or wrong) until he or she can come to the answer that suits his or her reality. It is from this place that you become unaffected by life's drama and those who create the drama. Healing is choosing Self-love and acceptance. In that way, we can love and accept all others. This is the place where love cannot be forbidden. We no longer cry with others, but lovingly laugh with them instead!

Lack of acceptance in ourselves, our reality, and the ones we truly love causes anxiety. There is no gratitude and appreciation left in us, because we have become so conditioned to life's so-called norms that gratitude seems to be taken as something people owe us, not what we owe anyone. What sense of permanence and tranquility are we going to get from this disconnection? The Self knows and waits patiently for us to remember permanence and tranquility. Yet we only understand the meaning of life to be impermanent, separated, or full of anxiety. We reflect this impermanence back to others through our counsel. Our relationships are built on fear—fear of the unknown—the place of impermanence and restlessness. We seek validation and justification of who we are and who we have made of our self.

The only permanence, tranquility, joy, and bliss that exist are in love! Yet we live anything but love.

Why do we attach to those who express positivity and joy regularly, make demands on them, and then condemn them? Is it because it is too hard for us to keep up with them, or is it not considered normal by society's standards? It threatens our perception and understanding of who we are: entities made by our own hands from lives of turmoil, the shadows of who we really are.

Many of us don't know the truth of a joyful existence. If we did, we would choose no other path. Yet it is through expressing pain and fear that we are led to remember joy, for it is the only true reality that completes our soul's purpose. Our soul's purpose is to evolve, and it is within the loveless self that love is understood. Joy, peace, and bliss exist in love, and our being—which is composed of the body, mind, and spirit—must connect at a point of love that allows complete acceptance and forgiveness in this life. Without the drama of life created from our conditioning pool, we would be aware of joy, but we would not experience the opposite of it, or truly know joy. Our experiences are born so we can experience the opposite of it and know it!

When everything else seems lost—when we feel confused, overtired, pressured, stressed from living day to day, bored, and unforgiving, and non-accepting of life, our partners, our relationships, or our children—that is the time that we must seek out a new path and realize there must be more! There is no escaping our return to love. The wonderful thing is that the harder we try to avoid Self-love and acceptance, the faster our lessons for remembering them will be, and the faster we meet our soul's purpose. We must experience all there is to experience to know who we truly are, as distinct from who we have become!

Our return to love is the only thing that is real in this world. All else is impermanent, an illusion we create to experience pain in order to evolve and learn. This is the gift of pain. Surely we cannot believe there is no purpose to pain when pain is unavoidable in physical form. Pain is a given in life! Givens in life are death, loss of jobs, relocation, divorce, money problems, abandonment, resentment, war, poverty . . . and the list goes on. The purpose of our creation is to experience the opposite of love so as to know love. Without the experience, we have only awareness that something exists.

Does the concept of Self-love trigger the subliminal sense of failure and separateness on which we have become dependent, or does Self-love trigger our criticism of self, thereby forbidding it? Preferring instead to keep separate, do we acquire more or just give up, believing it is all too hard? Fear of any loss of this perceived self will leave us totally without.

Your life must turn. It must, because there is no other option. The only option we are in control of is *when*. When do we face the truth of our present realities? Your life will turn. It's your choice as to when that will happen. It is love of Self that you will need in order to turn your life around. The love you seek is within you. The journey we are on is to merely remember this knowing Self, to know it completely and experience every facet of fear to truly know love. The journey is our destination. The destination is the cycle of universal consciousness—a consciousness that is forever expanding. We need to evolve individually, like all things universally. We are one and the same.

It doesn't matter what you acquire or what you achieve. The feelings of "never-enoughness," dread, and boredom are always there to drive you harder to acquire just one more thing. It is no wonder love is forbidden—it's a forbidden language, lost long ago. Love would mean letting go, trusting in others and the process of life. How can we be asked to derail all the things we have trucked around for years and learned to trust?

To be joyful and express love has become so foreign to many of us that we no longer understand its language. The more we search, the more it is lost. We believe the thing we are searching for is found in the things and places where it cannot exist. Love does not come from things outside us, and the more we strive for them, the more it will allude us. It must, as the lessons we seek are not yet obvious—our alienation from love felt within and the painful intensity we will ultimately face.

Love is held within; it is who we are. Yet we dare not look there for fear of annihilation or alienation. How odd that the one thing that can resolve everything is the one thing we fear most!

Why has love become so forbidden?

The world doesn't love itself. Our lives mirror the unity unconsciousness of all. Our individual lives are governed by the minority, which influences our global decisions and affect the lives of countless millions of people. Presently, those countless millions are experiencing expressions of love lost. The forbidden language is taught to us through our life lessons and handed down from one generation to the next. All is expressed to us to prepare us for tomorrow—the harsh reality we must face—a world without beauty. It is sad that our young must learn the lessons of an unforgiving past.

Would our world leaders rather us remain in a state of fear because it is easier to manage us? Why would they want many healed souls running around, questioning everything they did—actions and policies that separate us from everyone else? They couldn't face this reality. There would be too much to lose, so fear is bred and passed down the line. Each generation is doing its bit for the lesser good through lessons taught to our young and bred into society by the chain of events which make up our modern society—a community in fear.

Our world displays external happiness, which is often shortlived. We find ourselves forever chasing our dreams, the reflections of everything we wish our lives to be. We are never content and grateful for what we have, and we never have the courage to stand up and say, "Enough is enough." We will choose instead a world of beauty and ugliness, adrenaline and exhaustion, playing hard and fast or not playing at all. We will choose a world of happy moments and many more grave disappointments. We will live in complete denial of the illusion we create to feel good. We believe the world owes us a living and we owe it nothing. What can we take from it? We keep taking!

How dare we be happy, let alone allow another to be happy? Where is the joy felt in the joy for another? It is said, "What you give away is given you." With that, all you have will be appreciated; this is the law of attraction and the truth of love. Love is the matrix of all things in existence. All you desire will be brought to your reality. Simply give it away. Forbidden love forbids love. Love will breed love, and our teachings of love to the ones we love dearly—our children, spouses, family members, friends, and neighbors—will become a passion of love. The cycle of love replaces the cycle of fear; generational conditioning stops with you. Begin to change the world through loving eyes. It starts and ends with you.

A dear friend of mine reminded me of a television interview of the captain of one of our premier football, or soccer, teams. The interview was given straight after a quarter final victory against the team's arch rivals. After the match, the first comment by the captain was one of humility. He commented on the brilliance of the other side and continued this line throughout the interview.

A week later, the same team lost a very important game, one that was vital for the final matches. Once again, showing pure humility, the captain was gracious in defeat. His first comments were to give credit to the winning team.

The value of people like this is they show us that it is important to be gracious and humble, whether in victory or defeat. We should not ride the shirt tails of success and let it be an excuse to glorify ourselves, but sit quietly with success, within, to fully appreciate the moment. In so doing, you would gain a true sense of your Self, the place where all love originates from.

Metaphorically speaking, grandeur is the opposite of grandiosity. The captain's speech was a display of grandeur—the grand moment of doing one's best with expressions and appreciation of the love of doing, win or lose. It is felt in the silent expression of the love that can only come from Self-love. Openly expressed, it was not judged; the words were accepted and respected. Why could we not do the same, express the feelings of positivity, happiness, and joy, which are reflective of Self-love, without condemnation and judgment of others or the need to aggrandize ourselves as better than others? Are we unable to do this because sport carries the dreams of so many? The place where victory can overcome defeat is an escape from the realities of day-to-day life; we experience the turmoil and discontent, yet have become numb to the unease, not realizing why. Perhaps that is why sports people are the most highly paid on earth. They carry our dreams of victory. They give us the win factor. This is the factor we crave and search without doing—or perhaps doing too much.

It is through forbidden love that love is limited in its expression. Love is often misconstrued as anger, grief, sadness, self-pity, blame, attack, or resentment. If love was more readily accepted, not feared, these displays of emotions and behaviors would be less commonplace. Only someone who is very comfortable within his or her skin can freely express parts of himself or herself in comfort and ease without being affected by these feelings and behaviors on a day-to-day basis.

Wisdom sees forbidden love as a cry for love and has the strength to convert it through inaction. Just sit with Self, express no judgment, give no reaction to another's loveless self, and allow no personal judgment in another's unconscious reality. Look within; this is the place where very little negativity can affect you, regardless of what it is that is said or done. This is freedom—the path to enlightenment.

"Happiness is not found in perfection, it is found in the acceptance of imperfection."
—Therapist, South Pacific Private

The number of people looking for change in their lives is growing rapidly. They are seeking change from their grappling discontent and anxiety, and it's happening now. Do not be afraid to face the truth of your life; it is in this awareness that change can occur. Express love with graciousness and humility, search it out, and seek out conscious others—those who are willing to change and those who possess willingness for life. Be in the company of healed souls, and your life will turn. You'll reap immeasurable benefits.

Do not be afraid. Be strong. For it is Self-love that we have lost although it lies within us. It is close, and we must access this Self in the silence of our inner being. It is this love that will heal you. It is through this healed Self that your view of the world will change.

It is funny how we fear the thought of expressing love when it is all we seek and fail to see until our experiences make our life unmanageable, forcing us to look for an alternative. We get knots in our stomachs when we think people or our partners will think we are weak for expressing love. How sad is the conditioning-pool of your life? How ready are our defenses to show our feeble strength when we perceive attack? Look within fearlessly, and have faith in the power of your Self.

What words feel better to you, love, joy, happiness, peacefulness, gratitude, bliss, contentment, fun, and laughter or jealousy, resentment, unease, blame, anger, self-pity, anxiousness, worry, concern, stress, and grief? Say these different words out loud, and feel their sensations within your body.

What do you have in your life? Probably everything you need right now. But how do you feel? Are you worried and concerned about the next deal? Perhaps you are uptight and have a sense of uneasiness, jealousy, and resentment. Do you constantly blame others for your own perceived wrongdoing? Do you engage in gross amounts of thinking, planning, or controlling? Are you concerned about what others will think of you? Do you worry about not having enough money? Do you feel you are not doing enough?

Certainly we can't accept those who challenge us, for defense has become our reality. But our perception is misguided! The illusion we live within is an illusion designed to bring us all to a point where we can accept the truth of our current reality, learn from our experiences, and change the ways we live. To live in a place of tranquility and joy is to live today in acceptance of and appreciation for life and all those who participate in it.

We did not make ourselves; we just create our experiences. Those experiences shape our lives and our perceptions of ourselves. It is our choice, then, to live with the consequences of the experiences we create in whatever way our willingness to accept or deny permits.

Love must be forbidden for now and will remain that way until we accept ourselves as pure potentiality—as creative beings in a world of all possibilities. Our lives aren't based on love, but many perceptions of false love. It is taught in our schools; our history tells us so. Love cannot exist in this world of thinking, which separates us from everyone else, for it undermines everyone and everything we truly know deep within that we are! We know! It is our genetic makeup to know! Searching for it outside of our Self is a futile journey to nowhere. It creates unrest and anxiety within us, because we become separated from our value systems, as we do in life itself—all from our learning.

Separation-Belief-Realization

Do you think about how separation makes you feel?

Think of any problem you have ever had. Then look at the problem as a separation from something, someone, or your Self. See that separation. Sit quietly, close your eyes, and think for a moment on the separation from someone, something, or inner Self. Is it a feeling of abandonment or lacking, the need to prop up self-worth, or loss of control?

Once you identify with the separation, feel whatever it is you feel, such as, for instance, anger, hurt, fear, grief, or anxiety. That's all you need do: just feel how this separation makes you feel. Where does it attack the body?

Identify the pain, then sit silently and question your feelings in relation to it. Why do you feel this pain? It is in the awareness of your feeling that you can see beyond the pain you experience, which triggers your reaction to it.

If you can be aware at the point of these feelings, then you are aware at the moment the mind identifies the separation from its core value beliefs, the beliefs aligned to your true Self. The core value system (aka moral law) is born in you. It is directly linked to the soul. When the mind and body venture away from the soul (the core value system), they will experience all sorts of pain.

Now you are starting to identify with the experience through feeling, you are starting to catch the thought at the beginning stages of separation-belief. It is from this point that

you will develop the skill to cut the link to the resistance you
create or the negativity you materialize in your life.
(If you'd like to receive a free audio of a guided
version of this meditation, go to my website:
www.epsilonhealingacademy.com)

Start today, and don't ignore the signs. The body is designed to feel. The signs are evident in feeling; thus we must relearn to feel. Look within, for this is where feelings are found, in the inner silence of Self. It is an all-loving and all-knowing place. Accept love, and by giving it away to others, especially to our children, the love will strengthen within us and light our paths to know it and thereby acquire it in abundance. All problems can be seen as either a call for love or an opportunity to return to love. If you have enough problems, your experiences will either wear you down or make your life unmanageable. At this point, we are given a choice to face our truth and liberate our Self from our constant unease. We need to ask about the cause of our unease—what it is, how it came to be, and why it was there.

When we ask these questions, we are at the first stage of recovery. It is from here all possibilities for you exist. We will deal with them throughout this book. We must remember that any separation from love will create the opportunity to return to love. Fear will be felt in the body and used by the mind to distort our view of the world. In that distortion, more pain and negativity will be experienced until we become aware and desire change.

Love is all there is. It is the only true reality; all else is an illusion—life's illusion—a masterful plan to allow us to know through this illusion our inner spirit and who we are! This gives us the opportunity to go beyond and evolve to even higher levels of consciousness to who we wish to become—mirrors of universal intelligence that are forever consciously and lovingly expanding.

Love will no longer be forbidden when the Self returns to the radiance of its completeness. Body, mind, and spirit all aligned, and it is through the body that the alignment can be felt. Simply choose to no longer forbid it. It lays dormant within you; it will never leave you. It cannot leave. It is how you were created and exists within every cell of your body. Your life of experiencing forbidden love is for the soul's purpose of remembering pure love. Your courage will change it in an instant. The courage is to desire it; the desire will give your life meaning and purpose. The purpose is not subjected to the elements.

When I first found the courage to change, it was after I was stripped of all my defenses. A time that was perceived as the worst period of my life, yet wasn't. Even the statement, "This is the worst period of my life," was merely a reflection of my ego. How could I perceive this time as the worst time of my life when it was the only time in my life that I looked inward to Self? Forbidden love hangs on to statements of fear, not letting go and not accepting. I had to find the courage to change the statements I was using before I could change from an unloving self to a loving Self. Without changing the phrase the "worst period of my life," the ego, my separate self, used forbidden love and its attachments to all things external to control my false reality or belief. Yet this same ego manipulation, using fear, was imploding me and releasing me. I found the courage within this fear-based reality to let go, forgive, and no longer accept the fear.

Once I was totally aware of my perceived reality, I was no longer affected by feelings of the worst period of my life or times when I was unhappy with my life. The change was automatic, and the return to true Self was imminent. The worst period of my life became the greatest opportunity of my life. Healing began!

The secret to affecting change is in forgiveness and acceptance of all that happens. In the silence of my inner Self, the answers freely came; however, the awareness of knowing the secret was in the knowledge of Self-love through expressing forgiveness.

There were many people to forgive. First, I had to forgive myself; then I had to forgive all those in my past who contributed to what I perceived as my journey in pain. Then I had to forgive all those I perceived as being associated with the breakdown of a moment in time when love was abandoned. Forgiveness came, and release began. Forbidden love had no further hold on me. My children began to learn the secrets of love. The word *love* was lost to me at birth, and thereafter, I searched for love relentlessly—as most do—until the realization that a life spent hard, abandoned, and in self-pity, attack, and blame had broken it down into the simple reality of forgiveness and acceptance.

CHAPTER SEVEN

Hear with Your Eyes and See with Your Ears

"The most important thing in communication is hearing what isn't said."
—Peter F. Drucker

The pain someone experiences can be seen but not heard. The pain is expressed as a denial of that person's true feelings. This is how we communicate together. Our secrets create a false reality we are too willing to communicate to another in a number of ways—silence and resentment, anger and attack, drugs to medicate, alcohol to dull, humor to ease, denial, excessive work, judgment, and criticism. How can anyone be aware of his or her truth when he or she is in pain? The truth of a person's life has been concealed for so long that it cannot be seen, let alone felt. If the pain of our past was evident and brought into our awareness, would we truly choose pain and illusion as an option?

It is our awareness that transmutes our pain and creates the knowledge to express love and forgiveness. In that awareness of these attributes, we can choose not to participate in another's pain. This is a state of conscious forgiveness, and it is from here that all will be healed.

My second wife and I had not been able to communicate effectively from the time we met, although we thought we did. We were caught up in a great sex life, which was our perceived idea of intimacy.

Her fits of jealousy were always met with my love-avoiding responses. She needed to be loved, and I was always trying to please or rescue her. Our love and hate was extremely passionate. This is what we perceived as real; both of us were caught up in our past fears.

In hindsight, I only need to look at the wasted energy of having to respond. Here was a woman with whom I had a wonderful sexual connection and with whom I shared similar attributes of humor, compassion, and caring. She often screamed in anger at her perception of the attention I paid to others. She was calling for love—in particular, my love—but all my reality heard was her neediness.

All I had to do was put my arms around her and reassure her, but I couldn't, because love was absent in my unloved self. I was afraid of love, expecting it to drain me of energy. It is what I manifested, and over the next decade, our family imploded through our lack of awareness, knowledge, and Self-love.

Imagine your partner in despair and expressing himself or herself in anger, with grief, perhaps in a jealous fit, or with self-pity or sorrow. To hear only what you hear is to identify with the illusion that they are experiencing. In so doing, you respond in like manner of similar frequency as your own emotional pain is triggered. However, hearing with your eyes will create an entirely different reality.

All too often, we express the counterpart equal to what we are hearing. Our hearing, however, is poorly conceived if it reacts to another's pain with our own pain. To see the words spoken is far more powerful than hearing them. In other words, create a mental picture of what is being expressed by first observing without evaluating, and then by not taking personally what another says to you. Leave the other with his or her reality, and simply acknowledge it. In therapy, a response to another's reaction would often be met with a simple phrase, such as "I hear you, thank you."

That is why we spend countless millions on therapy. It is the principle of hearing from sight rather than through the words spoken that an objective and compassionate response can be made.

Love has no barrier; nor, in reality, does it have an opposite. To say we love is only true if we do not attack a situation, but rather show love in return, regardless of the pain expressed by the other. The highest form of human intelligence is to observe without evaluating. Confusing love with attack is a mind-identified state. The ego's need for completeness is based on its interpretation of love made real from this illusion. Love cannot be real if you identify with another's pain from your neediness, feelings of lack, or defense, thereby expressing your fears towards the person in reply. This then, becomes our ego in control of our thought process—not love, by any means.

Love is the basis of all life. If love had an opposite in reality, then life as we know it could not exist. Hate is not loves opposite, for hate is not real; rather it's an ego-based state of a self-created identity under threat. Hate and fear take from everything. They ultimately destroy their host and everything around it. Love is the cornerstone and the central pillar of all life that exists, both physically and non-physically. Once we separate from it, we develop scenarios of illusion from fear and escalate that illusion by the actions we take to justify our separation. The separation or lack we feel creates feelings and emotions, disease (or dis-ease), and anxiety, because we know instinctively that separation is not a part of our greater Self. It contracts the essence of who we are, as it contracts all energy associated to it.

Separation is the reasoning behind war, famine, hardships of any kind, and illness. We have created it for a purpose. It takes on the fear-based association of separation felt from ego identity—the separate self created by us to separate. It gives birth to fear, hate, grief, and despair. It is created by us alone.

Love has no opposite in reality; it cannot. Ego identity is mind identity about who we are in relation to everything else. It is about what we own and our social, religious, and political status. It attacks or defends to protect its identity or protect the adapted self we have created out of our past conditioning. It is based on a neediness or lack felt within the host body. When one individual expresses his or her fear to another, then the instinct takes over, and that pain is expressed quite violently, at times triggering the same pain in the other. The ego hears words of pain and immediately takes it personally, often describing the other as ungrateful, unappreciative, demanding, or controlling. Your own feelings of lack of Self-worth and failure reflect a past that is unresolved. Perhaps you felt unimportant, unappreciated, unloved, insignificant, or unsafe. You hear words spoken, immediately assume a position, and try to reason out, attack, or defend that position.

When you are aware of this reaction, then awareness—by its own definition—will dissipate the feelings of anger, blame, resentment, or self-loathing. Simply by being mindful of the illusion that an ego carries with it, you will realize what it is you or the other person is trying to express or communicate, regardless of how frustrating it may seem at the time. This can be very liberating for the soul, for little awareness exists. Yet awareness can free the mind and the body from the constant, relentless thoughts of having to defend or attack in reply to mind-identified conditions that practically run and ruin our lives. Let go. Accept others and their expressions of their realities as they see them, because these realities belong to them and them alone. We must understand the difference if we are to start the process of healing. We can only control our own feelings, thoughts, and behaviors.

You literally begin to see the call for love in each of us. You begin to have an intense desire to feel whole and complete in the oneness of Self—the place from where we came and where we will return. The place is so inherently strong that while separation is the journey of our lives, we do not feel complete. It is so inherently strong in us that we cannot ever be free of the call to return to it. Self is complete, whole, and at one with everything else in existence. This is the reasoning of our sense of separation and the instrument of our fears. It is through these feelings and the illusion of a fearful reality created from them that our lives will meet their crossroads, where we can turn in one direction for more pain and fear, or take an alternative path to discover their opposite: love. Remember, it is love that has no opposite. Fear does.

We have chosen to feel self-created from the misinterpretations of our life experiences. Our perception of those events and circumstances in our lives were outside our control. As life unfolds in your separate world, the perception of separation creates more separation and loneliness—regardless of what you think you can acquire, control, or take to satisfy your unease. The incompleteness within you will search for all things outside Self for the purpose of self-identity. This self-identity is forever searching, attacking a threat, or defending who it thinks it is, but never knowing true Self and its wholeness. Therefore, without knowing incompleteness exists within us, our wholeness can never be realized.

Why would we search for wholeness if we were not spiritually aware that we have created ourselves as less then whole? In our experiences, awareness is born.

If this is how the majority of people live and their quest is to find the path of love and feel safe and secure, then how can hearing the words they speak or seeing the expressions of pain they feel be taken by an enlightened soul as anything other than their call for love? Think of the worst thing that ever happened to you or the worst problem that you have experienced. If you think about it, you will see that it started from the feeling of separation.

Now we look at a colleague, friend, lover, or loved one; and see that person's pain; and hear his or her words. The closest person can experience his or her pain.

What do we do? We follow suit, in most cases, taking it all personally, registering our own pain, and attacking right back. Unless, of course, you have the power to stop it, attack begets attack, fear begets fear, and so on. Others cannot cause anger in you unless you feel anger already. They can, however, in the absence of knowledge, bring out of you what is already at home in you.

Defuse Your Fear

To stop another's pain and to keep your own from being triggered, try the reverse of what a normal, expected response may be. Sit back and watch—simply observe—and instead of hearing the words, see them. In an observing state, you are intentionally aware of a painful situation.

Another cannot bring out an inappropriate response in you if that response is no longer a part of you. It will not be a part of you if you filter the words through your eyes, for what you hear are lies. Hearing an expression of pain with awareness—regardless of the form it takes—is now correctly perceived by you as someone's call for love or help.

Observe without evaluating and now you are actually seeing a different reality. You hear the words spoken, but now, in the present moment of time, you see a different reality. Your seeing will change based on what you hear but will be unclouded by your previous thoughts or past judgments. Your pain body cannot manifest longevity once your present moment awareness is maintained. This will cut the link to your thoughts in relation to your past.

Hold your observation. Do not evaluate, just accept the person's reality as his or her reality. Give yourself permission to take time to assess what you see. Perhaps you can respond in a supportive, not attacking manner later.

We are conditioned to believe that what we see is real. What we see is exactly what we see. Yet what we see is anything other than real, because it is not seen from love! Therefore, it is a self-created illusion. We see the expression of abuse from a loved one and take it as an attack on our belief system. We protect that position in whatever manner we feel appropriate. We do not see it as another person's misguided belief or see the pain it creates in others we love. Our seeing is to believe in another's sense of separation. Who takes the effort to heal? Divorce is too easy—the path of least resistance. Yet our most trying relationships can be revived and be miraculous if, after living through such emotional intensity, the effort to heal them can be made. Can you imagine the depth of understanding that would result from another attempt to resolve a once passionate and loving relationship in whatever form that love was understood? With acceptance, a greater degree of appreciation, respect for Self, and Self-love how good would that revived relationship be?

There are many instances where a relationship cannot be revived and the love pertaining to the wholeness of one partner is in letting go of the other, particularly in association with abuse. The need to say enough is enough is a loving act in itself, even if love is not your initial intention. Saying no to abuse is as important to the abused as it is to the abuser. Do not give permission to abuse. It is very important to say no to abuse!

> *I grew up in a family where my mother said no to abuse. As children, we are too young to say anything. However, while my mother said no to abuse, it was her choice to stay within the relationship; this in itself was giving permission to the other to continue. Regardless of how sorry my father may have been each time, his acts of abuse and violence were perpetuated—they continued and continued. Life was unbearable!*

No one wants separation. A person creates toxic expression to punish another, to have the other conform or be controlled. This all stems from a feeling of lack, which is almost always regularly communicated through abuse, blame, guilt, shame, or self-pity. Separation begets more separation, and the cycle of negativity consumes both the giver and the receiver of the message. An unconscious person will react to another with the same sense of lack if the feeling of separation exists within them, and disagreement will ensue. It is important to note that all people only ever want acceptance and love.

You can choose to perceive correctly, not to respond, and simply to allow another person to be. Acceptance (non-emotional attachment) of a situation is releasing it or forgiving it. In forgiveness, the other person's pain cannot exist for you. If another's response continues and you have maintained awareness and been vigilant in observing without evaluating, then it will be your decision whether to continue communication or simply to remove yourself from it. This act alone denies permission for the other to continue. However, your own assessment is essential before making that decision.

With this knowledge, you are no longer caught in the energy field of others. You do not take their situations personally, nor are you subjected any longer to the whim of unconscious behavior. This is the start of enlightenment. This is the start of peace.

It is very important to gain the knowledge that love is all there is and all there can be. Love is the core essence of everything. It is the source of creation, the reason we exist. If we allow hate to continue, then it would be true that we would not survive as a human race. Fear and hate are manmade, and to identify with them is destructive. Nature will tell you bad weather cannot last indefinitely and the sun must shine. Hate also cannot survive indefinitely. It cannot, because it is the opposite of the sustainable energy of all life, including our own. Love is the source of all consciousness and all things in the universe. All matter is made up—to some degree—of consciousness. Consciousness is love.

The secret knowledge that we all possess is the knowledge of love and creation. That is why we are said to know the answers to life without ever having to ask. To remember the knowledge, we must start with our inner Self. In that inner silence, we have an awareness to hold steady when others choose not to. It is within our inner silence that we are given the power to forgive, accept, and surrender!

There is a chance in every relationship to acquire this knowledge, heal another, and heal ourselves. To hold steady and see the pain in another's words is virtually to see yourself as a director of your life—the relationship is the actor, and you are in charge. You can choose to act along in a mindset of fear and panic or sit back, watch, and walk away in grace, giving a thought to the performance.

While you may think this sounds odd, the only odd thing about it will be how good you feel after the event. This good feeling is something I'm sure many of us are not used to. To not be affected by others is to be on the path of enlightenment. To accept all that happens with an inquisitive mind—aware of the moment and seeing words instead of hearing them—is to be conscious of the present moment. It is in this present moment that nothing can affect you and you can reclaim your power. The power is in the all-loving Self in whom and by whom you were created.

To hear with your eyes is to hear your soul's calling for you to return to knowing, and in that knowing, to give your love to another. That love is then given a chance to prove it is the essence of you. Why allow another to keep their pain by adding your own? Give that love a chance to be. Realize if it is love or the attachment to love—a remedy for past lack of love. This is the secret to life. Forgiveness and healing begin here. We are surrounded by a world of ego.

Each ego is looking to saddle with another in the game of "take what you can, and look at me." We have come to believe protection of our identity is our entire existence, and after it, there is only death and finality.

The amazing illusion of this unreality is to believe that the purpose of life was meaningless and the grandeur of our universe exists without us. That we are merely specks on the radar of creation without purpose or thought is a weak conclusion at best! How could such a complex being—the human being—surrounded by a complex, never-ending phenomenon, be not even a bleep on the radar of life? This senseless thinking keeps us in the prison of our minds. We are all one being, and our purpose in life is to experience who we are and what we choose to be, evolving spiritually in each moment and experience. In each moment of our lives, we are given countless opportunities to experience exactly this through the relationships we engage in.

In each relationship, we are given the means to create a different reality than the one we have become dependent upon. Our distorted concepts see everyone and everything as separate. Now it is time to forgive and know that we are all made of the same stuff. We are all energy vibrating in the larger energy field of everything else. We are part of the oneness that is life—life that is not separate or affected by fear. It is the perfection of creation manifested in us. We are all one, and in relationships, we encounter the potential to remember that our divine purpose in life is to know our oneness with life and all other lives in a state of love and perfection. To acknowledge and live in this oneness with all life and others in physical form is to master your existence and your life. In this knowing state, all your experiences will be as heaven on earth with complete peace and joy.

Life in the physical form is about knowing the perfection of creation by experiencing the opposite of such perfection through our experiences. Human beings—through experience and their feelings—are a creation of the opposite of this perfection or the spirit; thereby, they create the experience of the opposite. Each small part of perfection or pure love is broken down into tiny bits and experienced over and over in many different ways through our experiences. All this is for the purpose of knowing pure love! We evolve endlessly and create abundantly. Hence, God's perfect creation is ourselves, or our Self, whereby the supreme energy of all truly knows itself and forever expands. The enlightened soul is the one who lives a life in a form with the knowledge of oneness in all forms. Your path to knowing and remembering is given at every opportunity in a relationship. Relationships are the greatest form of remembering, for in their pain, the treasures of knowing are realized.

*"Your most difficult relationships are normally associated
to a soul mate rather than a chance passing."*
—Wayne Dyer

Stand back and observe the constant uneasiness of people. The truth we speak of here is where love replaces fear and you create a reality of peace and joy from the countless opportunities given to you each day. Over and over, the universe gives us the opportunity for growth and the opportunity to remember the source of all: love. Start to express it with forgiveness. Forgiveness is easier when you have the understanding that separation from yourself and others is causing all the pain.

As you become aware of this knowledge, others will also. However, this will not happen initially, and you will be the director of your movie, as the events of your life unfold and clearly show you a mirror of what you once were. The feeling gained from this awareness is liberating. The Self soon needs more of its Self in truth, as love is contagious. It is in the consciousness of your responses that others will no longer have the power to attack or resent you. They will only hold their own resentment for a certain time until they start to question it. It is in the silence of your actions that the perpetrators see themselves. If not, then you have a responsibility to remove yourself from them. This will then allow them the chance to see themselves more objectively—and give yourself a safe environment to continue to grow and evolve spiritually, free of their obstructive actions.

Hear What You See

To see with your eyes is to see a world as we have always seen, subject to the whim of ego.

Hear what you see. If you hear what you hear, then you will see exactly that.

Instead, hear what you see, and the words are lost to illusion. Simply observe without judgment.

To be the witness of your world is to understand it. To understand it is to accept it. Your acceptance will transmute the drama that unfolds in front of you.

You will hear yourself answer the many puzzling questions you have long sought. Observe without judgment, and you will hear the truth in self where forgiveness and understanding will prevail. The world you see thereafter will take on a different reality than the one you have always known—a world without fear and only seen through loving eyes. This will be your new world!

Remember any angry moment in your life, and then describe to yourself the false sight you created with another (or several others). What you heard offended you, perhaps, and the unreality you saw may have been projected outward and intensified until you were in a complete state of anger—even rage. Each person was hearing what he or she heard and seeing what he or she wanted; no one forgave, and the cycle of abuse was relentless and spiraling outward. No one could persuade you or anyone involved differently, and the drama unfolded for all to see. Their reactions were similar; no boundaries existed for anyone. At times, you have caught yourself out in this charade—this illusion—and a new reality hit you. You laughed it off, feeling ridiculous at how far your reaction took you on that wild ride.

> *Several months after my second wife left me, I was feeling hopelessly abandoned. I was angry, and grief consumed me. Anyone who didn't stand in and defend our family was seen as against me. I had nothing but anger and rage within me, and those people who did not defend our relationship became the object of my anger.*
>
> *I excused my ex-wife as misguided and attacked those I perceived as being the cause of our separation. It was an illusion, totally false; my perceived love had blinded me to the truth of my unloved and abandoned childhood.*
>
> *I was simply unable to accept this reality at the age of fifty.*

How often do we create this type of drama—a false reality—for ourselves and others? It usually ends in apologies—and later, more apologies—as the drama replays over another scenario, like just another take in the director's film. The pain created from seeing what we see and hearing what we hear becomes a constant and never-ending cycle of drama. The drama becomes an addiction, as the mind easily identifies with it as a reason for its own identity. Without drama, the mind believes it is separate, so it becomes addicted to it. Yet it is what keeps us separate. We must change what we see as our reality, for nothing in this world is as we see it.

The world is full of beauty, and all we see is ugliness. Consumed by egos, we hear the words and trigger our own latent pain.

If you see all things as blessed, then what you hear will be the sounds of peace and joy; if you hear all things as another's call for love, then what you see will be forgiveness and acceptance.

CHAPTER EIGHT

As Pure as Snow— Connecting to Self

All problems are but one. They stem from our sense of separation. The disunity felt from Self or others creates the conflict in us and the world around us.

A dear friend of mine said to me during a gym workout, "Do you know what I hated when I broke up with Caroline? It was the loneliness I felt." If we reflect on our own lives, how many times can we say this of ourselves? How many times do we feel lonely? This is a feeling of being without or a feeling of lack. If we can be honest about this very question, then maybe we can find that moment necessary to reflect and perhaps discover how much we really do like or dislike ourselves.

The need to be with another to feel good is what loneliness is to everyone. Does it need to be ignored until the answer becomes obvious? We attach to other people rather than connect with ourselves. It seems we cannot be left to be with our Self for the unease we feel. To love our Self would eliminate this need or attachment to be with someone to fill the scarcity we feel within.

Instead the completeness of you would make any relationship worthwhile. Yet we all too easily ignore the very obvious signs that we are separate from our Self and other people, no matter how close they are. This separation creates the anxiety. No amount of seeking, wanting, or acquiring will sustain you in this stage of life.

We need to be able to sit with our unease, own it, and know we are powerless against it.

The challenge we all face at different times throughout our lives is to ask, "When do we let go to life? What the hell is all this about, and why do I not feel content most of the time?"

These questions were very confronting, but I confronted them in my fiftieth year. My life was, from my perspective, in ruins and unmanageable.

I started to wonder how I could break the cycle of attachments and addictions I had created in my life, which was born from a feeling of lack of love. I had a great business, a beautiful wife, kids, an open ticket to travel anywhere in the world, and the envy of many. I was on top of the world, in fact, and I wasn't happy within my own skin—I only thought I was.

I couldn't effectively communicate with my wife. No one had told me that validating my partner or understanding her wants and needs was important. In fact, it was only later that I was told that this was more important than buying her a car, which I've also learned is not as relevant as buying a rose and spending a little time together regularly. Some might laugh at my ignorance. I don't blame them, really. I couldn't believe it either. I do now!

I bought my wife everything she ever wanted. I could afford it, and that was love, wasn't it? The less time I spent with her, the more I seemed to pay for! Her feelings of worthlessness and loneliness escalated into resentment. We both suffered immense loneliness in the thirteen years we spent together.

My idea of love and her idea of love were on two different train tracks. Both trains were moving in different directions—away from each other.

Neither of us was able to express our true needs and wants; neither knew what they were. These are the effects of disconnection from one's Self.

When does money, the perfect exterior, or the happy façade connect anyone? These things cannot. It is all exterior to the Self.

Didn't young boys have to be brought up tough to face a tough world? Obviously not, but I was raising my son to be tough. My family had taught me that lesson, just as they were taught it. Children need to be treated as all young, beautiful souls deserve; that is how you give them the skills to handle life and be confident and fearless. It is called loving them and showing it. I simply didn't know that either. Tough is how I was conditioned, and that is what I was teaching. Lucky for me, I learned differently early in my son's beautiful young life.

From all outside appearances, my married family life was picture perfect. But from within, a whole new picture started to be created—a picture that involved expectation, demands, discontentment, neediness, lack of communication, and then a complete breakdown that painfully and slowly destroyed the marriage and everything I ever truly desired and loved. I came face to face with my past, which was the cause of my problems and the separation I experienced.

How could it have been any different? The collision course I had been on was set long before the illusion I lived imploded for the second time. The first implosion was after my first marriage ended fifteen years earlier. In the absence of loving yourself (which is the absence of knowing and accepting your Self) what is the meaning of love around you? No matter what the effort from another, the receiver cannot feel its depth. It is as lost as you are, and you don't even know it. Often by the time you realize, it is too late to change course. This is when great learning can apply. This is when you are given the greatest opportunity to learn to connect.

How good would it be to observe, as the participant—perhaps to see into a crystal ball—the lessons that lie ahead well before time and set a new course? The new course or path would give you everything your heart desires—love, joy, abundance, peace of mind, inner peace, a sense of belonging, and connectedness. It takes far less effort to achieve this reality than it did for most of us to live the way we did. In your knowing Self, this path is possible and readily obtainable.

Would you not agree that our lives were filled with noise, stuff, and incessant unsettling thoughts that lock our minds in the prison of a world we and most others have created for ourselves? This prison is a place where unrest is our reality. We have grown to depend upon this unrest to feel what we feel is not real. What we express is a reaction to the fear created by the illusion we believe exists for us. Where and how can you rest?

What tools do you have or have you learned to help you through life? Where are the freethinking, elderly, culturally minded, creative people who aren't trapped in the grip of life's controls, rules, or regulations? Where is the wisdom to teach us the love, connect us with our Self and thereafter, connect with life?

We eradicate cultures that can teach us, ignore the elderly, and deny those who have lived incredibly hard lives, who could teach us much, and who have now opted for a spiritual change. We condemn spirituality in favor of religious beliefs and deny a higher power to help us, guide us through life, and connect to our all-important Self that, when it is healed, can be and do anything we choose. This Self that can create total joy within everything it experiences. We must notice that things aren't right before we can change them.

What will it take to make us look within or seek the Holy Grail of teaching and the spiritual quest of the minority? What will it take to make more of us aware—starting with you, right here, right now—and to feel things just aren't right before it all comes crashing down around you, which it surely must? In the absence of Self-love, there is only fear; and in that fear, a world of illusion and wrongful perception exists.

Who has the right to ask someone to look within and feel his or her reality? That reality just may be wrongly perceived. You are being asked to truly feel and then look at your truth. What has brought you to this point in your life? You will require courage to face your truth because it is harder than you may think.

You hold the key to the Holy Grail, the key to the inner Self. It lives in your heart and radiates from there. It is pure love, and it emanates from within you. You have simply forgotten how to access its power. It starts with the truth of life. It is accessed through owning your feelings. We are so clouded by our distorted vision that we cannot access its power, meaning we cannot create the lives we desire.

The universe we all live within waits patiently for this knowing to return to you. Your experiences will lead you to the connecting valve.

> *A wonderful friend of mine was suffering severe depression. When I asked him to go out to get him out of the house, I would always be met with his somber reply: "No thanks." Prior to this, however, we often hung out and had many laughs and good conversations. In fact, he helped me through some difficult periods in my life. His world was catastrophic, his mood depressed, and his shadow lifeless by all description. He was sleeping sixteen hours a day to pass the time away.*
>
> *Who was I to ask him to change his reality, as if he didn't want to already? What right has anyone to ask someone to look within?*
>
> *My friend perceived his world as devastating. He saw himself as a failure. Financially speaking, he felt he let his family down. For thirty years, he worked hard, supported his family, and gave them a great life. He felt he had come to a point in his life in which he could no longer live the lie of doing something he really never enjoyed. His motive for*

doing all this was originally to please another. Thirty years later, he met his dark night of the soul. He wanted out, and when he finally had the courage to do it, his world collapsed.

Not realizing the financial consequences, he went from doing everything to doing nothing. It was his time to seek inner sanctuary and discard the old attachments to outer form. He was courageous just in making the decision, but it was one he felt necessary to make. He wasn't asked, because his reality bit hard, and he had little choice. He could have wallowed in suffering or found the courage, as he did, to look at the benefits in his journey to that time.

He was caught between a rock and a hard place. He was being squeezed. He had been the eternal optimist and intellect. He had been full of humor, but he had no real peace to speak of. He was ready and always armed to defend his position. He faced his demons for the first time in his life. All his life, he had been the financial supporter for his family and a wonderful father to his children. He had always been there to give his family members whatever they desired. He had money, status, and for the most part, financial freedom.

It was this attachment to what he'd created—the ego state of attachment to things outside Self—that was no longer there. His world—by his own perception—was not worth living. He wanted to die, but he knew better. He needed peace and Self-love. The abuse he'd endured at the hands of his mother when he was growing up ensured he'd never rest until he faced those demons.

How could anyone ask my friend to change his reality—his perception—until he alone was ready? In his moment of grief, he had to make his choice. It is easy for us to expect others to get a grip, face their demons, get over it, or get on with it. It's easy to make a number of judgments over another based on our limited understanding of facing our truth. I felt that I knew what he was experiencing from my own grief and anxiety over the previous two years. I felt tempted to take care of him—to fix him as I thought I could. The reality is that no one knows the reality or feelings of another, and each of us must come to the decision ourselves as to when and how we need to address our reality.

My friend was in a state of depression, and he saw no hope. No reality was possible other than the clouded, distorted, painful belief in the unworthiness, guilt, and shame from a past lived separate from his Self.

He was always doing things for others, and he falsely believed his needs were being met. He was totally disconnected from his true Self. Self-pity and resentment consumed his every thought.

I recall very well his support of me. He sat with me on many occasions, allowing me to vent my feelings regardless of how distorted they may have been. He allowed me the opportunity to express myself without offering his judgment or opinion. I was simply not willing to look within—not until I vented or until I was ready. It was this lesson that gave me the strength to stop fixing and validate him; our roles had become reversed.

Listen to the other within your relationship, guide him or her, and when he or she is ready, this person will make the decision to look within. Yet be there—be a friend to someone in need. Give your friend time, not things, which could potentially hurt him or her further. For example, giving someone more money will ultimately drive the person further into debt and guilt.

Do not discard other people's reality as unreal. Do not criticize their lack of effort to change from their negative state, for their reality is real to them. To discount their feelings is to say to them, *"You are less worthy than you currently feel."* Choose kindness over being right! We do not have to always be right just to be heard or feel worthy or validated. Be kind to other souls. Listen without evaluating until they are ready to connect to the truth of their Self.

The support we offer is the best way to help another look within—to connect to Self and the all-knowing state of acceptance and love. You cannot say to another person, *"You are not a failure"* when that is his or her reality. Nor can you tell people that they have been a marvel to their family and community or to be proud of what they've done, for they cannot hear in despair. The time to heal and grieve is needed. The courage is found to start the process; then the process needs to be accepted, allowed, and developed. This is an individual journey. Many of us, at different times in our lives, must face our own journeys. This is a given in life—a certainty that pain will come.

My friend's path was to find inner peace. The gift of grief is growth, so with many of life's givens, such is the opportunity for one's growth, both personally and spiritually.

The inner Self, which is felt within, is the only place in us that is permanent, full of love and hope, and can never be affected by outside things or subjected to the fickle elements of life's colorful bounty. Yet it is in this fickle reality that our greatest seeds of learning and growth are made possible.

The process of grief in physical form is to heal and grow. The stages of grief are first to deny it is happening, acting out as if the people around are mad or responsible. The second stage is anger vented to anyone within firing range—an incorrect perception that plays a very big role in the life of the person who is grieving. But this is okay; it is the process. Thirdly, the grieving person will not make sense of grief. He or she will question it and be victimized by it, asking, "God, why me?" Often, depression will follow as a normal part of the cycle. Then, finally, comes acceptance. Acceptance will vary in time, but ultimately, it must come. Acceptance cannot come without this cycle of growth. Quite literally, in all grief, there is hope and wisdom!

Now you are being asked to consider yourself. You are not being asked to change your reality, but to merely look at it. If you believe it is not worth it at this time, then so be it; you are supported in many ways. But if you feel the determination to find peace, desire, and permanency, then have the courage to ask questions and find support. It is all around you. Beautiful souls, group meetings, people who care and will love you for who you are—seek them out. It will take courage, but look at where you are. You are perhaps at the worst period of your life so far. Perhaps nothing appears good, beautiful, or hopeful, yet you are here, at a crossroads. This is your destiny, whether you believe it or not. You are ready for spiritual evolution. You put yourself here! You wanted this, because you are aware deep down that change is important. You just can't quite remember why it is so important. You are a master of creation. You are marvelous in every aspect, and you will endure and grow strong. This is your plan and your destiny. While you have a say in it, the conclusion is final, so accept it with an open heart and mind and realize you are steering your vessel.

It was your courage that got you to this junction point in your life, so don't give up now! It is time to excel—to go beyond, as you have already. That's right, you have already! Your constant fighting of an uphill battle, which has taken courage and strength, was intended to bring you to a point of choice. You have the choice to know who you truly are and what you wish to be.

No one is asking you to change. You are being asked to take a chance. Believe in the purpose of life and the greater evolution of your soul. Look within! Be fearless for your Self. Remember, it is the absence of the within that caused this fear and pain in the first place. It is now time to seek the path of permanency—the path to within.

The world my friend created, like the worlds that most of us create, was one of impermanency. His life hinged on the status and the financial position he created, like most of our lives do. When we are disconnected from Self, this is all we have or all we can rely on in times of need. In effect, this has replaced our higher power. If it is lost, then we are alone. This is not reality, but merely an illusion of reality. Reality can only exist in love. Love of Self will bring to you love of all others and life around you. This is the only permanence to life and to you. Love can never be at a whim or subject to an outer form. A loving reality is not a palace in the desert, but a palace in the rich, green, fertile grounds of universal love and support. It is untouchable.

Money is not real. This doesn't mean you cannot have it. You just should be mindful not to be attached to it, feel you need it, or want more of it to be happy. Just allow that which you desire to happen. Success is not real. Status is not real, because what is real cannot change. Like the love of creation from where we were born, only love is permanent and real. Money, success, status, and all things outside Self that make yourself grander are subjected to the elements, easily taken away, and will ultimately leave you feeling as you do now—or worse. See the signs, and act fearlessly. Having the courage to face the truth is what is needed. Look at the telltale signs in your life, and act accordingly. Do it for you.

Connecting to your Self is real. That's the only thing that is real. It is no different for any of us. When my second wife left me, I had thoughts that I did not want to live any more. I felt there was no reason for being here. I was self-absorbed. I felt my children would be okay. *I will leave them to her,* I thought, as if my final action would be an act of retribution—my final lesson to my ex-wife and my final possibility to manipulate or control her. I would make her realize how my pain felt in retribution to another and bring her under control. Could my reality have been any more distorted? The ego can only win by your death; that is how you feel and why you attach so strongly to it. This is another distortion.

The reality was that I would have never committed this act—yet my mind projected this action, venting hopelessness and worthlessness from feelings of abandonment. I was playing the victim. Yet it need not take the grief felt in this moment of my personal suffering to define a reality as distorted and derailing. We are often faced with life's givens—pain from death, abandonment, divorce, job loss, rejection, illness, separation from a higher power, abuse, or loss of assets—and we feel riddled with grief. The most severe grief seems to come from our relationships. We are, after all, relational beings, which is why relationships are our greatest challenges. Therefore, this is the area that we can truly look at to define our reality—to see where we are truly in connection to Self.

Our reality is based on how well or poorly we feel within ourselves. Often we will not know what we are looking for, simply because we have become so conditioned to life's pain. We can live in fear and anxiety and think it is normal, because the majority of people live with fear and anxiety. Our society values normalcy according to the majority, not the minority, thereby giving us the grace to dismiss our actions and behaviors—which are fundamentally flawed—as acceptable or even approving. You may start to see how we can condition our children by passing down the lessons we were taught—lessons that are fundamentality flawed. Our relationships will show us these flaws.

Are you sure it is not worth looking within? Could anyone win by any act of resentment or harm brought to self, believing these acts to be acts of retribution upon another—leaving my beautiful children behind in misery or guilt by a final act of retribution? Do you think that your courage to look within is possibly a better solution? This solution is not just for you, but perhaps a solution or salvation for your loved ones—in particular, your children, who are the beautiful little souls you bring into this world—your spouse, your friends, and even the world at large. You are magnificent, and your magnificence is what got you here. Be assured that your magnificence will take you home—the home of Self. It is within the stillness and silence of Self that your intended destiny will be made real and its completion manifested; here, it will know love.

You are at this point in your life for a reason. Your reason is your creation, your destiny. Take a chance for yourself, and believe in the greater power of you. All you are asked is to believe a new path is possible. Accept your past—it has gotten you to the point in your life where a door of opportunity has opened for you as a consequence. It is acknowledged, and you are supported unconditionally to accept where you are right now. You are on a new path, which you may choose to follow. In this acceptance, you are ready to change. Change to a new reality, and make behavioral changes necessary to realize there is an alternative—the only alternative that will lead to joy, bliss, and peace in your life. Look for yourself, look within yourself, and your world will never be the same again.

My friend took his chance, and his world changed rapidly. He had every reason in the world—the world of illusion we all know well—to remain depressed. He just decided to believe and have faith in the greater power of all things. He pulled himself out of bed—out of depression—and remained fixated on a positive and trusting state of being. It shocked me how strong he was. I took great strength from him. This was a time when he dismissed his outer form after a life of attachment to it, and he truly was grateful for the meaningful things that mattered. His family supported him. He was open and truthful about his current reality and optimistic about the future. He disassociated from anyone who was in a negative state, believing he needed all his strength to stay positive. He turned his life around within six months. He was offered a major franchise, and he created the opportunity to make far more money than he had ever dreamed possible. This time, however, he worked with complete gratitude and appreciation for what he had. He would never again forget his lesson. Gratitude was his greatest blessing. He was connecting to Self and loving it!

Do you know that you—and you alone—can change the world instantly? I had a hard time with this concept when I first heard it. "Me?" I would ask. "How can I change the world? Little me, change the world? Sounds crazy!" In fact, it was all too real. You see, the world of drama we create creates more drama, and the drama helps us feel alive, just like it did when we were kids. We heal, and we start to see a different reality. At a moment in time, the reality is clear; expressions of love replace expressions of fear. The world we see changes in a heartbeat. Life is not about a distorted view of what we can get out of it or what we can gain from another. Instead, it begins to work in unison with others. All benefit is for the greater good, abundance is rightly perceived, and more given as a consequence. Life is all about the power of love, and it will support loving acts completely. Give yourself the chance to experience miracles.

If you think a moment on this, you will see its reality. As you heal, your whole world heals with you, for the world you see is based on love. The world around you can no longer affect you, hurt you, or cause you pain, because you act rather than react. The love that will emanate from you will be perceived by others; it will then be ultimately adopted if they choose to stay in your energy field. Love of Self is vital to all loving acts. You will be able to meet your needs and wants, say no, not give in to another's demands or abuse, give your time to others who may need time, distinguish between takers and givers, be in the company of healed or healing souls, and add to the light of consciousness. Be grateful for what you have in your life, let go, and trust in Self and the connection we have to the greater power of all things. These are all loving acts that come from Self connection.

As you heal, the world around you heals. Look at the reverse—if you see the effects of your negative patterns of behavior or look closely at one person's negative actions in a family environment, you will understand how many people you will actually be healing by your own healing.

The world we see is based on fear, and fear has a tremendous negative impact on you and everyone around you. Criticizing, being discontent with everything and everyone, reliving the past through our judgments, living in denial of our feelings, and worrying or being concerned about every little thing becomes pretty tiring stuff—and we still don't stop.

We attack and defend; then we reverse roles, and eventually, it all simmers down to the ego's lust for conflict being temporarily satisfied before it all starts again, only to finally break down. This constant, mind-identified state of being is draining, and over time, it absorbs most of our energy and the energy of those around us. It comes from the place of lack—lack of love of self and forgiveness of our past.

Your life lessons are being played out on stage, and the ring leader is the dreadful ego. Some could argue that ego has a place; this is heard many times in counseling sessions. Quite frankly, what place has the ego after you successfully arrive at the point of readiness to change? This is a big statement—especially when your whole existence is wrapped up in this ego-driven mentality. Your ego is the adapted self you created in childhood to protect you and keep you safe, and it did a good job—until now. Now it is no longer useful.

You have the power to change the world, and that power comes from the strength within you. To change the world is to affect your new perception of a world that is love-based, not fear-based. This is how the world changes. What you see in a loving world derives seeing from Self-love. You notice the trees in the park, the view from your window, your neighbor's smile, and the pain of the cafe waitress, not the rudeness you once perceived. You see your children's laughter and your wife's call for love—even the way your new car drives. You will live in the now.

Change the world. It is no longer appropriate to live in a cruel, vengeful, unkind world—a world of hate, suppressed by fear, and separated from all things. You can and will change your world in an instant; it is your decision. Find people of like mind, turn off bad news, and stop negativity. Simply decide to evolve spiritually and live life. You will be very effective, as countless people will benefit by your action, and the universe will support your every action in return. What you give away, you will receive; you will strengthen your Self. Give love, and love is all you can strengthen within. This is connection with Self.

When you next walk into a coffee shop and feel that the waiter or waitress is rude, consider that perhaps understand it is his or her issue and not an attack on you. Forgive that person in the silence of your knowledge. Do not let it create a cycle of negativity in you. This cycle of negativity is the ego wrecking havoc at every chance it gets. It is you and your past creeping up and finding a position of worth against the backdrop of worthlessness that you and many others may be feeling. All self-importance and grandiosity are feelings of worthlessness. You are not that person, so stop the self-importance, because you are very important. You are important to the cycle of life and the creation of all that is. You are pure, creative energy expressing itself in the physical form; thus, you experience each aspect of all that is to truly know all that is. The purpose of the soul is the pure knowledge of perfection from where you were created made real by your imperfect experiences—true knowledge of who you are and who you wish to be.

You can create everything you desire, because it is your will and the will of creation that you do. The rewards you receive will be greater than anything you could ever imagine. It is your birthright by the power of your creation. You are a creating being, just like your creator. In order to know this, you need to not know this. In other words, to know something is to experience the opposite; otherwise the being part of it is just being: accepting, but not really knowing.

You can create anything. Often, you do so, and you don't realize it. Believe such is your power. You are unlimited in power, and how you choose to use it is entirely up to you. Here, we are satisfied with the mere crumbs of life we feed ourselves, or we humbly accept the crumbs fed to us by people who are top feeders, and we say thank you. It is contrary to everything we are and everything we stand for. Life's abundance is for our total enjoyment: to be shared and appreciated. It is there for the asking. Our experiences are purposeful for this reason. We will get this message.

The question is, when will you act? When you do, your life will change dramatically.

Connecting to Self is also about being able to identify the people and things in your life that are preventing you from having the experience of joy and peace. It is being able to say no. It is recognizing the signs, having the courage to change course midstream, and moving forward in life to a place of contentment.

For eighteen years, I was content to allow a business partner (actually, several business partners) to keep their hands outstretched and ask for more. Yet the devil I knew kept me in a place of comfort, particularly in light of the fact that we had expanded the business within the previous two years of that period. Whenever my partners needed six months off, needed pay raises, gave excuses for not performing for the remuneration paid to them, or a myriad of other reasons, they would simply take the opportunity to express or do something without consideration of others. They felt everyone was okay with that behavior, because I never set a boundary.

The more I gave, the more they demanded. My partners felt as though they could behave this way because I failed to say no or to set that boundary. Why did I allow this to go on? Don't think for a moment it was a one-sided taking. I didn't react, because regardless of their aggressiveness to clients, childlike behavior, constant demands, and greediness on a scale often unmatched, they made money, so I made money. The ego demanded that I maintain the façade, regardless of the pain it created. The ego demands all things superficial. The world it creates eats away at you, because its demands are relentless. Nothing is ever enough. Can you fill the void of lack within? You cannot, so it keeps seeking—and the cost is huge.

How many times will you say, "One more thing and I will be happy," until you acquire it? You cannot be happy unless you acquire one more thing after that, and then another. Constant acquisition takes away the very essence of you. The ego's demands burden your life and the lives of everyone party to it—your family and loved ones in particular. "Oh, yes, the loved ones," you say. "I'm doing it for them." Regardless of the constant reminding by them that you said you would take it easier, you are home less than you were prior to that promise.

The insatiable appetite to fill the void you feel within comes from the separateness that was created in you from childhood because love in your family was lacking, smothering, or over protective. Judgments and criticism are passed on to you by others who endured the same upbringing or worse; the circumstances are different, perhaps, but the effects are the same. We are made feel separate from everyone and everything. This is the reason we live in constant anxiety and are worried about the past or concerned about our futures. We seem never content, and our connection to Self is absent from our understanding of life's purpose.

We create lives that are in place where we do not exist, where our needs and wants are abandoned, or where we are the center of the world and everything must revolve around us. It is amazing to have lived the second part of my life in the latter and reflect on all the people who would allow me to live it, conforming to my ideas and ideals because I created this extraordinary world or perception.

You attract people of like energy—those who are similar to you in many ways—to tolerate the ego's demand to be right, loved (even if superficially), able to control and barter, involved in the drama, help you feel alive, or get something from you. When the getting is done, so are the relationships. This is cruel, but unfortunately, accurate. People stay around while the going's good. As soon as the situation turns, most of them turn too.

A life of overindulging in just about everything you do and have, or a life where you abandoned your ideals, values, and needs for another or for others provides lessons that lead to spiritual growth. Life under these conditions gives us the greatest seeds for opportunity. You are given the chance to connect to Self. It is through the pain of these experiences, which must come as a consequence of not recognizing the signs within these realities, that your connection to Self is felt. It is as pure as snow!

All outer forms are subject to change. Love of Self is not. The more fixated we become on outer form (often created by acquiring and never appreciating), the more unfulfilled we feel. Enough becomes never having enough. Material gain can only be beneficial if abundance in Self is felt. This is the sign we must observe. Ask yourself, "Do I have abundance in my life?"

Does a house, family, a partner, business, travel, or money sustain you in its own right? Those things cannot sustain you, because they are subject to change. Love of Self however, can completely sustain you. With this love, those things are made joyful and pleasant for you and for those you care about.

Material possessions and attachments in life are meaningless and stressful without Self-love and a connection to, and appreciation of your Self, and the abundance felt in life's blessings, appreciation of the elements, nature, and life. They are meaningless and stressful without spiritual balance, appreciation for others, the receiving and acceptance of love, the ability to express and give love, gratitude for what we have, acceptance of life, the ability to just let go, and the ability to live in the now. In fact, life is merely a smoke screen without this connection.

"Your vision will become clear only when you can look into your heart. Who looks outside dreams; who looks inside, awakes."
—Carl Jung

The physical and mental need for this connection to Self—the spirit within—is obvious when we take the time to analyze or reason where we are and why we are not content. Why can we not live in peace, without control, or just let go and trust? We must connect to the purest form of connection to all life. Connection is within the purity of Self. As pure as snow, the perfection of nature itself is parallel to the connection within Self. The purity found here is as wondrous, creative, and as awe inspiring as fresh snow on the tops of mountain ranges. It is your freedom to go within. It is an escape from the ravages of our incessant thoughts. It transforms our lives from fear to love, anxiety to peace, confusion to sure direction, uncertainty to confidence, and dark to light.

My second wife is a beautiful soul. She blessed me with two small children and cared for my eldest from a previous marriage. I had material possessions that people envied—not that I cared for their envy. I would go so far as to say that when the cracks appeared in my worldly domain, that envy turned to jealousy. The chance to break apart something that was founded on a perceived enviable, loving, abundant foundation was too much of a temptation to ignore. Comparing lives to feel better, judgment, and petty jealousy are all too easy. Very few thought of the kids and the family unit, and what surprised me was that people I had known for fifteen and twenty years were rarely seen.

It would have been wonderful if someone had the courage to offer positive words of support. Someone who knew us could have perhaps taken judgment out of it and thought of the children and our past as a family or as friends, but that rarely happened.

My wife and I would entertain a hundred people for lunch at a time and show them more hospitality than they had dreamed of. I did it from generosity, but even in that generosity—and perhaps without knowing it—my ego needed others' approval to fill the void in me once again. It was all fun: laughter, music, alcohol, and more food than anyone could eat. People were appreciative. Of the hundred, however, only a small handful would call after and say, "How wonderful. Thank you." Yet like the image maintained with the business partners, my wife and I kept up appearances and image in the social arena; we kept on giving and inviting the same people.

The invited guests turned up to the best barbecue in town. Missing it was not an option, everyone turned up. It was a big, happy event. They were appreciative when they were there, all smiles. You would rarely get an invitation back, however, other than from the handful that called each time to say thank you. Those who expressed thanks were normally the ones who were full of appreciation and love. They were people who seemed to like themselves; they appreciated and were grateful for most things in their lives.

When the cracks in our lives appeared, most people disappeared. What can we get from this? Nothing? My feelings of low self-worth did not help. Friends whom I had previously helped in their marital disputes were taking sides and judging accordingly. Their judgments and criticism caused more pain for our family. My children suffered, as did my wife and me. The egos were in full play, each ego taking what it could to satisfy its intrinsic need—taking what it could until there was nothing left to take.

There was no forgiveness or love, just separation. This mirrored life in general; individuals create more separation, for this is what our world knows to teach. My wife wasn't connected to her Self, and I wasn't connected to my Self. We were both connected to everyone else, and unfortunately, people got much satisfaction in this. It gave them a sense of worth and validation.

My quest to find the Holy Grail, the meaning of life, and connection to love of Self was born. It was to be a journey of love and completeness. It was based on forgiveness and gratitude. I wanted to have gratitude for all of that I did have in my life, not what I didn't have, and the knowledge that nothing outside me could satisfy or sustain me permanently. It became my blessing and my freedom. I incorrectly thought when I was a child that freedom was only in money and material things. With money, I would say, "I will control my destiny and never allow what had happened to me or my loved ones to happen ever again."

My perception was wrong. For my life and all the pain I experienced, however, I say thank you, for nothing would have gotten me to this point in my life other then the chain of experiences that led me here. I feel truly blessed.

When do we look for the signs in our own lives—the signs which are easily felt, yet dismissed to keep up the facade?

Who feels? We think and create, and it is this incessant thinking that creates our experiences, which, by their nature, are the essence of the decisions we make to better our lives. Yet we don't know what it means to better our lives. It is the soul, the inner Self, that guides you through those experiences. That is why in life, we attract what we think. As the Greek philosopher Plato once said, "Where I go, I am."

Perhaps now we can start to really identify with the law of attraction. What you think today, you become tomorrow. Create pain to receive more pain; live in fear to create more fear. Pain will ultimately lead you away from it to search for different answers. It is then that you will find a new path through knowledge of the feelings of an old path, and you will follow. You will not follow a new path unless you see, own, or identify with an old path—a path that does not work for you anymore.

Repeating an earlier question, who has the right to tell someone to change before they are ready? Obviously no one. The joy of part-time highs, quick fixes, or addictions may still be considered as life enhancing for you and something you have control over, even if you really don't. Until the pain of this reality is realized, no one is ready.

Now we can decide to look for the signs that all is not right. We should save what we have, appreciate and love what we have, and enjoy life to the fullest. It cannot be done unless we identify with our truth, observe clearly, feel this reality, and connect within.

Most of us are caught in the trap of our ego self. The state of our world tells us that.

How often do you feel anxious, worried, or concerned? Are you angry and upset with others? Do you have feelings of discontentment—feelings of being unfulfilled and unappreciated?

When does your mind stop for an instant in time to do nothing, think no thoughts, and truly rest in solitude and silence, so that your feelings can be felt, acknowledged, observed, understood, accepted, and then released?

Resting your mind in nothingness rests your body. A well-rested body finds its path to passion to live with energy and vitality. A mind of no thought is a mind living consciously in the present moment. But how can anyone ask you to do this? You have never lived apart from thought, and now you are being asked to go against the very thing that holds your make-believe world together.

We turn on the nightly news and hear of the bombing of a city with little regard for the dead. We hear of the murder of a small child and feel the pains of it for a day. We hear of the acquisition of nuclear weapons by a country developing its first atomic bomb and panic for a week, until we realize our little world is relatively safe. Death and destruction, then more of the same; and life goes on with little regard for anything other than ourselves and all things related.

Our world has become a fiasco, entertaining us with highlights of disaster as if to make our private domain feel a little better. We say, "They've got it bad. Things could be worse." We say this as if to inject ourselves with an anesthetic that deadens us to the pain we feel. More control over us is allowed simply because we tolerate what shouldn't be tolerated. We allow ourselves to be subjected to the whim of leaders who undermine human existence and say it could be worse. Is this good enough? It is not, and we feel the pain of it as it erupts within us at times as anger and rage. Most of the time, this pain is directed at the wrong people—our loved ones. Yet we even come to accept and tolerate this until it hits us hard and we are forced to look.

People are burdened. In our society, weakness is intolerable; survival of the fittest is the only game going, and you'd better win it or you'll be left well and truly on the side lines. Racial, political, and cultural differences are enough to start wars, because differences are a threat to our way of life. Another's point of view is not respected, but dismissed. We adopt a culture of being the strongest or luckiest nation on earth, but do we share our spoils or guard them at all costs? Scarcity is the cultural integration of the strongest and the luckiest, and any differences in regard to our way of life are immediately protected against with aggression.

We allow this life to be as it is, for it is the only path we see. It is what we have become by the system that made us accept it as all or nothing. We protect it, as we are fed horrifying stories of fear to reaffirm that might is right. If we judge others—regardless of right or wrong—they are killed, people who are perceived as weak are left homeless or starving, and we continue to do nothing to change it.

We accept unity unconsciousness over our own consciousness: meaning, over having to say we don't agree with the way our leadership handles worldly situations. We accept these philosophies, as it would be difficult to go against the majority. We know the consequences of disagreement with the norm. Our individuality needs to be accepted and trusted. We must learn to connect with it and have total belief in it. The world depends on each of us to change from unity unconsciousness to individual consciousness, where we follow our core values. We must be able to say no to things that we do not agree with. We must connect to Self and be fearless. The world cannot continue to be controlled by the minority while we sit idly by and allow the world to fall apart, people to be hurt, or children to go hungry.

Our Thoughts Are Not Our Own

Unity unconsciousness is a group manifestation of the combined thoughtless distortions we, as individuals, manifest into our reality. It is energy coming together *en masse* to manifest form: everything from racial hatred, to war, famine, and so on. Although this fact is hard to accept for some, we are all responsible for our current reality.

Change can only come from within each of us. We cannot change the system and the way our world is if we focus away from Self. Each of us has the power to change the world as we see it—and this literally changes the world. Try it. Perceive all people as good and use only kind words to speak about them. Pass no judgment for one day, and see what happens. You will start to see a completely different reality. You will no longer feel separated, but will feel united. You will act rather than react; perceive in love, not in hate; and you will see miracles happen in one day. This seeing is enlightening. The feelings are potentially life changing, and what you are seeing for the first time in a long time will be clear. This seeing is reconditioning the mind towards Self not away from it.

I know you are thinking, *How can I do that?* To see clearly, you must change your behaviors. You can, and you must. Try for one day to change a behavior, and then observe! The path we are on is destructive. Our children will pay the price of this complacency—just as we are doing now—if we continue to adopt the same thinking that has gotten us to this point in our lives.

You feel that something is not right, and like so many, you do nothing about it. There is enough for all. We must lose our fear of scarcity and begin to share and open our hearts. We must give what it is we wish to keep for ourselves, for sharing strengthens. Giving and forgiving are the answers to the world's problems. Give of yourself—in words, kindness, love, and where you can, in other things that will make another's life a little easier.

What we share or give, we receive. What we give, we strengthen; what we take and fear, we lose. It is the natural law of attraction. There is no escaping it. What we fear becomes our reality—a reality where loss is perceived.

Good news empowers us and gives us courage. The last thing our political system and leadership need is a whole lot of powerful, courageous, inwardly confident souls running around, freely thinking, and asking a lot of questions. Yes, bad news has its role, and its role is to control through fear. Let us start fixing the world by fixing ourselves. Find the answers to your uneasiness within; it is the only place that will never let you down. All the answers are at your very core of being—the place within where only pure love and all that is love emanates.

For each step you take towards inner awareness—each step towards releasing yourself from the chains of illusion you have created—your mind will become clearer. Two minutes replace two weeks, and two weeks replace two months. Each two-minute period of time you invest in yourself now—this very moment, the present moment—will exponentially create miracles in your life, people, and the world around you.

Yes, it's time for change and that change is in you, for that is where it starts and ends. Believe in you, and the cycle of healing will begin—the cycle that will surely lead you to complete peace and joy.

Rest Your Mind

Everything you ever dreamed possible is close. All you need do is the smallest thing to acquire it.

Rest your mind just for a moment, and be conscious of your feelings.

It is in awareness that changes occur.

Once the seed is planted, it will grow. It must, because who and what you are will feed it.

Your nature, your very being, has the sustenance and vitality to turn all fear into love. Your true Self is the very thing that will change your life forever in ways unimaginable. True freedom is only within you.

One of the greatest allies you have in the connection to Self is prayer. But you should not pray for something you want once and then blame your maker. That will stop you in your tracks from doing it again. Instead, keep on praying for the thing you want. Even when you think all is lost, that all has been said and done, keep going. You are praying to the greater being of all things—your higher power—and asking it, as part of that greatness, for a response. Do it. Don't be afraid of it, and keep the faith that your prayer will be answered.

In the power of your silence, you will hear the voice of God. You are not just the center of your world, you are, in fact, the center of the universe. You are it.

CHAPTER NINE

It Is in the Laughter of Your Children

"Once you have learned to love, you will have learned to live."
—Unknown

It is in your children's laughter that you see the spirit of creation. In their innocence, you see the love for all. Through their eyes, you see the beauty in the world. They give special meaning to life. Let's teach them well. It's in this teaching that we will strengthen these gifts in ourselves.

Have you listened to their laughter? Have you the time, or are you consumed with the daily function of doing whatever you do—consumed with stuff, any stuff, that ultimately is only a substitute for something you really need? Do you feel guilt—or worse, feel nothing—in their absence? The path you chose is the path they are subjected to. Our children don't need our path; they need a loving path. They don't need all the things outside them. They need all the things inside them. They don't need separation; they need unity. They need you!

What do we need? Let's teach them what we never had!

"If I meditate, can I stay up a little later?"
"Yep."

"Sit quietly, and if you mediate for a short while, I'll let you stay up a little later."

"Can I straighten my legs out, Dad?"

"Yep, if you are more comfortable,"

"Can I lie down?"

"Nope, sit up, back straight."

"I'm tired,"

"Well, then go to bed,"

"No."

"Okay, then meditate, and you can stay up a little longer."

My five-year-old and my six-year-old were being introduced to meditation. It was fun, and it always made me smile. They were fidgety and restless, but what was more important for them was staying up a little longer. I found a way for them to go within and feel peace. As a father, it's what I cared about, so I put up with the whining and discomfort they were expressing to help them find a means of going within and finding solitude in their little bodies and minds—a place I never had the opportunity to know or dwell in as a child. I did not get this opportunity until much later in my own life.

As I taught my children, I learned much. They relished the time with their dad, and they really started to enjoy the new feelings they were experiencing. Simple breathing techniques were all that were required initially, and I discovered that working in this way shows kids they can rest, be centered, and depend on their own feelings for solitude.

The benefits are extraordinary, and the results are almost instantaneous.

Haven't we burdened our beautiful children enough? They are burdened, like us, by the pressures of growing up. We are always concerned about our outer world while never really knowing our inner world. Look at our world; it speaks for itself. It is the result of unity unconsciousness—of our combined individual unconsciousness. We are not in good shape and need to change course.

Children are our eyes to the soul, and their innocence and inner beauty is evident and pure. We need to preserve that in them, not tarnish them with our grievances, judgments, or our social conditioning. Let's help them remember how magnificent they are—just like us. Maybe we have fallen from grace, but it doesn't mean we cannot get back up—and what better way to do it than to teach our kids?

Children are creative; they are our window to the soul. They only recognize the parts of life that are important, and they look for the joy in everything. This joy is their inner peace and abundance. The word *abundance* has a wonderful definition in this context; children have everything, regardless of how much they may have.

Children see life in everything around them—humor, laughter, and companionship. They are not defined by separation of any type—just pure abundance for life. We are the ones who see our abundance in things outside us, not children.

If we take away that joy in children, then we suppress them. If we expect too much of them, then we suppress them. "No, you can't" becomes the basis for soundproofed words, and they grow into adulthood believing in limitation and acting it out accordingly—just as we have experienced.

Children's Instincts

Show children love. Celebrate their laughter. Allow them freedom to express themselves and build their confidence. Encourage them to think for themselves. Hug them, kiss them, and allow them to feel safe. Allow them to be kids. Let them yell or have a tantrum. Be patient and laugh it off.

Children are learning about themselves and their feelings. Let's help them retain this vital knowledge, for they have it right. In the process, we will help ourselves. Remember what is important in life, and what (perhaps) we were deprived of: our feelings!

Look at your children, and talk to them. Do not condemn anything they say, but allow them the expression of Self. The world has conditioned us to watch what we say and do for fear of rejection or alienation. Let's learn to speak from the heart and do the things in life that just may be seen as a little odd or out of the norm for the sake of living life how we want for us and our children, and not how we are told to live and raise our children to another's standards that are contradictory to our own.

Our children need us to allow them the freedom to be who they are, to think for themselves, and to feel as they do. In this way, they will grow to add significantly to human consciousness. They are designed to experience all they can, and they do it in the confident, trusting, joyful manner in which they were born to live. Their lows or pains in life will not be the burden of wondering what to do next. Rather, those pains will be dealt with in confidence and inner knowledge.

Rather than place expectations and judgments of our learning on our children, let's place freedom of will, creative learning, self-reliance, self-awareness, and laughter at the root of their learning. Let us not stifle the essence of their lives, as was done in our lives. Rather, embrace it and feel the happiness in their language and laughter. Encourage it.

Listen to your children. They need you to do that. You will be surprised at the joy you feel if you can simply allow your own false needs to be removed. Those false outer needs replaced our essential needs, which were, for most of us, removed or forgotten in childhood, creating the attachments we interpret as "do-or-die must-haves" in order to feel secure. Those needs are demanding, and we feel the pressure of survival at the expense of life. We work hard to find freedom from the mundane and the feelings of not having enough, when really, we lack very little. Our world is full of natural beauty and beautiful things, but we just cannot see them clearly. Our children can, however, and they will find creativity, fun, and humor in most things. They can make fun from a fruit box or digging a hole. From anywhere, they can create fun from what we perceive as mere child's play. Maybe we should look at the mere child's play a little closer and see what we're missing.

Just listen to the laughter of children! If the laughter is missing, then we need to look at ourselves and ask why.

Our children are conditioned from their first years of learning in the home and at school to believe in our history and our past. Children are told to believe that our path is the path to follow—the answer to all. They are rarely given the time to express their views; instead, they are made to conform to our views and way of life. We never seem to devote enough time to our children. We always use the excuse of being too busy or consumed with other, more important matters than them. They feel a lack of love and display signs of it in their actions, which are far often chastised by us as well. Their laughter simply stops through our expectations.

We feel their lack of gratitude in making us feel poorly about their actions without any regard for the fact that we are responsible for those behaviors. Children need their parents to listen to them and have play-time with them. A little more is needed than the effort we give to them now. We do not have to devote our entire time to the task, for that would be as detrimental to you and them as no time would be. Children need their time, and you yours—but the time that must be found is quality time. Quality time is time when your children feel love, safety, and trust in you. More importantly, they need to be able to express themselves to you without criticism, without being told they are wrong, and without being told to be quiet. They need to be listened to and guided when needed.

The wonderful thing about couples being together or male-female bonding is that the yin-yang of parenting is shared and balanced. This does not mean, however, that we must stay in unloving relationships for the sake of the children; that is even more detrimental to them. Yet this should be considered more seriously when the challenge of a relationship requires healing from apparent breakdown. Both parties should be willing to take steps for healing together. There are wonderful lessons for children in this alone. Life's givens should be dealt with adequately by the parents! Children learn.

Our role is to help children establish inner strength and love of Self. This can only be done by guiding them to the place of inner knowledge—a place that exists for us all deep within us. It is done with love and respect for them as little people, rather than as objects of possession where children should be seen and not heard or obedient to the point of being stifled. Talk to your children, and teach them the values in life they can come to rely upon as important—in fact, vital. Their greatest lessons will be learned when we teach by example. Teaching by example will reinforce what they have experienced at home. What they see, what they hear, and how we act.

When our view of the world is distorted, then our children's view of the world will become distorted. There is no greater joy in life than seeing your children happy, joyful, and at peace with themselves. However, what we search for in them is often veiled by our own insecurities—and then we have the gall to blame them for their behavior.

During the time of my obsession with all things in life—and from the distorted view that eventually imploded my reality—I believed that like me, little boys needed to be brought up tougher. My son did not get the same loving, nurturing treatment that the two girls received. In hindsight, my healing began from that single-minded past thinking, and my son was one of my greatest catalysts for doing so—luckily, while he was still young.

Prior to my healing, there was a period that I felt enormous guilt for this thinking. I was almost proud to explain to people how my son—like all boys—needed to be tough in this world to survive, raise a family later, and withstand the ravages of a modern world, as if being tough is a prerequisite for success. This thinking was distorted!

It was after my realization of this wrongful thinking that change with all my children began. I began building love and self-confidence in them, respecting their views, laughing with them, listening to their wonderful and often hilarious conversations between each other, and seeing the joy in their eyes with almost everything they see and do. I respected them as little people who have amazing creativity and intuitive thinking. They need nurturing in all aspects of their lives, from love to creative thinking, to spiritual evolvement—the centeredness of Self.

The difference between now and the time prior to healing is profound in terms of the relationship between my son and me. We both enjoy a healthy father-son relationship. His needs are met, and I feel fulfilled. It is incomprehensible to me now to think of that past thinking and attitude. What I was taught as a child was a distorted reality, and it was detrimental to the betterment, health, and wellbeing of the family.

A father-son relationship is an amazing bond. The love and connection experienced is a blessing that one can only pray exists with all fathers and their sons. Fathers should teach their sons leadership through love—the love they learn at home. We must give all our children the confidence and inner awareness to discover a cure for any ailment that they may experience in life—the ailment of not listening to Self. The only cure to our modern, fear-based world is awareness of Self through Self-love.

Now is time to help our children heal and grow in life and love. If they are minors and infants, it is easy to start their lessons of love through yourself. Your healing is the best way to teach your children. The good news is that it is never too late to teach them. We just need to come to terms with our unease and deal with it. We must be honest with ourselves about our unease—and be honest with them. It is an openness they will understand, appreciate, and learn from. They will then be able to experience their own awareness through this.

You are teaching your children honesty and openness. These two attributes will allow their defenses to be dropped and their openness to be forthcoming to face their own realities—as they are, and as they will be. Their realities will not be influenced by our misguided, selfish teaching or by what they have learned and experienced from our past conditioning.

To start the healing process, we need to be aware of, and open to, the things that we have suppressed. We just need to face our truths. This will take courage—real courage. To face the truth is to seek more of life—much more—and to find the path to peace. We have to ask the hard questions about our past and the actions that have greatly contributed to our unease. Do it for yourself, and do it for your children.

Our children are the future on this planet. How we treat our children will impact their lives for a very long time. This is not to say it takes greater effort to teach them—it just takes greater awareness. In the awareness of Self, we will find it more challenging at first, but the rewards are great—not only for you, but also for your children.

Look at what they look at when they come home from school. Often, children see the news—which is all bad, of course. We tell our children, "We're okay. See, kids, aren't we lucky we weren't born there?" This separation makes us (and them) feel a little more secure. They start to develop the separation from Self and life. We need to teach them about unity—unity as a family, within relationships, and with our planet. We should not give children the teachings or visual experiences of separation that we are exposed to on a daily basis.

Bad news is again a talking point in the house—usually of a negative nature. This is only one of a number of nightly topics all for children's viewing. This attitude, then, usually stifles any goodwill and cheer in the family, and the positive, peaceful moment is awash with more of life's conditioning pool. Do we do this to avoid how we really feel?

In hindsight, when we were children, many of us were perhaps not as happy as we would have liked. We may have had feelings of abandonment, not being heard, not having our needs and wants met, or of forever needing fixing. We need to recognize that separate, other self we created to survive the pain we felt and later disguised to become our survival mechanism. Having learned this, we express pain, self-pity, and self-grandeur, manipulating our distorted values as to how our family should run. Often, that is exactly what we do—run and never stop running, expecting everyone else to keep up and shut up, including our kids.

It is not to say we don't love our children—we do, greatly. We simply don't know any better, as it is how we have been taught by our parents, teachers, or authority figures. We must recognize the truth of our healing and separation from Self. Before our healing, true love was lacking in us. We knew this love was ego love—the false self that believed conquests, acquisitions, or attachments would bring us joy to replace the love that was lacking. In love, there is joy. Without love, we look for joy elsewhere. We must recognize how to show love—real love—by detaching and accepting ourselves first. Be open and truthful about your reality, and identify your true feelings in relation to it.

Look in the eyes of your children. Listen to your children. Will they speak openly, with laughter, unafraid of criticism? Do we know what it is they need? Do we know what we need? Are they able to express themselves openly? Do we disguise everything with humor, silence, demanding behavior, or over-protectiveness? Do we think that this expression of self will make everything right and show them we love them?

Will we be accepted in the eyes of our children and be able to show them the true meaning of love they can feel deep within them and not display behaviors to cover up our guilt or shame? Does a laugh or a humorous comment justify our lack of meeting their real needs? That is how my father justified his behavior—with humor. It was years before I saw through this veil of shame—the shame I lived with and carried most of my life.

Children need time, our love, and to be allowed to be children! This gives them the confidence in Self to deal with their lives.

Moments after being beaten or a violent abusive episode during my childhood, there was quiet in our home. The next day, there was humor and laughter, as if the moment had never occurred. My father was quick to anger and quick to forget. After all, who would want to remember an insane moment in one's life and have to look in the mirror and face the truth? Humor made it all okay to the attacker, and the children learned the same message.

Is this love? When you speak to your children, do they answer with humor and fear? The fear is easy for them to disguise. They want love and feel as though they have it at last. "Look, my dad is so funny," they say, as his shadow dances to all those who visit. The humor is on show. Dare they know the truth? They wouldn't believe it anyway. After all, how could anyone disguise such violence and self-hate and be so entertaining and humorous?

Do we really know what our children think, feel, and believe? We will blame them if they attack their sibling, verbally abuse their parents, act out their anger in the street, or vent their feelings of insecurity. This behavior mirrors the lessons they have learned by example.

Are we prepared now to truly look at our children, listen to them, be honest and open with them, and then love them? They deserve our complete love. What better way is there to love them than to start to love our Self? Heal, and the world heals with you. That healing is first felt by our loved ones.

Perhaps it was a bad day at the office that we experience in our busy lives or one of another hundred reasons to feel dread. We hide our discontentment and suppress those feelings. What we need is love. Although we are at home and we are surrounded by love, Dad is in one room, the kids are in another, and Mum is in yet another—where is the love? Where is the appreciation for what we have? How do our kids learn the meaning of love and contentment and develop the inner confidence to make positive changes in the world? What are we teaching them? We have the hide to blame them for bad behavior when all they are looking for is a little bit of love, just like everyone else.

Saying, "Kids, do your homework, then bed," is the quickest and easiest way to deal with them, and Mum and Dad usually don't talk much anyway. No, we are teaching our children well. At the rate we are going, our kids will be lucky to find peace of mind in their forties—or much later in life. The fears we have grown in them will reflect our own and our way of life. Our attitudes and actions will be passed down the line, and not only our generation will suffer, but also those that follow, as generations have done for thousands of years.

Why can't we face the simple truth and bring to the light our unease? What part don't we get—that the world is not in good shape? Fearing the few over the many, we are afraid to speak out or simply content to ride the stream of complacency and lacking, because we don't feel connected anymore. We are shrouded by our constant conditioning, which numbs us to life's behaviors. It is this fear that is keeping us fixated on acquiring outer things. Our peace and joy are lost to a world we no longer know or have a say in.

No, it is not good enough to ignore our children! They are our future, and they have their lives. They need us to sit up and take notice of our Self—our deep, inner Self where all the answers to life reside and all the love radiates. They need us to appreciate them for what they are—beautiful little creators who will create a perfectly imperfect environment if only we give them the confidence to feel within and ask what is not okay about things. Isn't that worth the effort to your salvation? Think about that—your salvation can literally change the world. Just you—forget everyone else, for they are about to all benefit by your healing. The healing occurs the moment you connect to your inner stillness—the silent place of all knowing. You have it within. Stop telling yourself you are not worthy. You are more than worthy—much more! Are our creations and our children less than worthy in our eyes? Should we ignore them? I don't think so—and neither do you! They are more than worth it!

Instead of watching the news, try talking to your kids. Involve the whole family. Ask about everyone's day. Take them for an ice cream, go for a walk or a quick swim when you get home, and forget routine for a night. Let them jump on the lounge for a while, have a pillow fight, let your little boy beat you up awhile and then teach him to control it—put the necessary lessons in place. Get down to their level when you want to connect to them. It feels strange at first, because it didn't happen for you. What is there to fear? Do it anyway.

Let's stop telling our children about our day. Let's stop the blame game and stop letting them hear about the complain game. It's tough, at first, to undo bad conditioning, but it will not be long before you and your family are laughing together. The effort you put in fearlessly will be proportional to the time it takes to create real change.

Real change for our family was noticed about six to eight months after the decision to become consciously aware of the need to heal self; however, things literally got better for us all from day one of that decision being made. We regress or fall into old patterns of behavior less and less as time goes on. Trust in Self and stay on course. The wonderful dividends for your family are extraordinary. Talk about what you are attempting to do. Tell your family the truth, and let go of your fear of falling off—or worse, not doing it, because you think you will look silly. Have you really looked at kids and seen the way they go on? They redefine silliness, and they love you being silly, so fear nothing. You will not look silly—and if you do, good on you! You need be congratulated. Just go for it—you deserve it, and so do they! Play with it. Talk about it. Go out for a burger or ice cream regularly. No, you are not too tired!

It was amazing the first time I did this and actually spoke to people about it. They were really interested and thought about changes themselves, particularly when they saw me doing it. It is a powerful healer when people start saying, "You are the best dad I know." I'm doing more with my kids now than ever before, and I wouldn't have it any other way. I still have time for everything else—in fact, they love seeing you have time for everything else. They learn to balance their lives, just like you are balancing yours. It's great to see, witness, and experience this change in the family and in your Self.

Your children are your eyes to the world. Watch how they play and laugh, and you will start to laugh again. They really are funny little souls, and they just know how to find the joy in everything. We can't take that away from them, because it is what they need. Our world desperately needs more joy, love, and appreciation for all life.

Imagine a life without prejudice, hate, or discrimination of any kind. Kids don't care about what someone wears, although they might have a little laugh if they are not used to it. They laugh without malice. Nor do they care for the color of someone's skin or what religious beliefs others may have. Nor do they discern themselves as to different lifestyles; they accept things as they see them.

No, we teach them the lessons of discrimination, racial and social prejudice, and standards of living as separate from another, and religious or political separations. We do it out of fear, and it is what we believe protects us and our way of life. We blend in to the all-too-common beliefs of the masses, because it is easy; it's fearful to speak out. It is ingrained in us from a young age to believe in the past as a means of security for their future. We expect children to learn from our lessons. This is a distorted perception at best!

New thinking is needed, and our children have the answers. They have the answers inside them, as we do. Unlike us, they do not have to be taught our lessons, which have led the world to where it is today—a life consumed with fear and anxiety. The same lessons stem from the knowledge that has burdened us for centuries. Yes, a new thinking is required, and the thinking needs to be nurtured in our youth; their inner knowledge needs to be respected and supported. Allow our kids to think of solutions; their creativity will astound you. Give them a chance to express themselves. Encourage your schools to do it. The amazing thing is that far more schools are realizing the importance of this already, and it will spread as the world consciousness grows, as it is currently. It is growing at a rapid pace.

Allow your kids to express themselves through confidence—the confidence you instill in them. Allow them to speak their minds and follow their souls. It is the way they feel that we should teach them to follow. Their feelings are vital, as ours were important to us before we lost them to our lessons. We cannot expect to do the same thing time and time again and get a different result. We need to find the power of creative thinking, not the incessant thinking that is based on survival and ego control. Creative thinking is readily found in children.

Every cell in your body has the answers to life, and these answers are accessed through inner awareness and silence. We need to help our kids find that place within and develop their skills in expression to allow them the opportunity to find the answers to their questions and feel the peace that comes from this expression. It is expression of the soul—their soul and their journey.

Guidelines to Develop Healthy Young Minds

- There is no greater joy than freedom of the soul; it's in the laughter of our children. Be more aware of your children.
- Preserve their innocence. Recognize their age, and let them live it.
- Nurture them. Allow them to express themselves. Celebrate their laughter—do not hinder it.
- Talk to them instead of demanding things of them.
- If you want them to listen to you, occasionally act silly with them. Act their age (have fun).

- Encourage their creative side, and allow them to be Self-reliant. Don't do everything for them. Let them help Mum and Dad.
- Listen to them—this is big. Nurture them, and they will hear their wants and needs. It is not as demanding as some would believe. It is actually a beautiful realization. The simplicity of their lives is, in a way, a connection with our own (long ago suppressed).
- Make the time you have with them quality time. Listen, laugh, and play—get on the swings; play baseball or football.
- Never judge, criticize, or belittle them in front of others. Give them confidence in Self. In fact, judgments and criticisms of them will suppress their self-worth.
- Help them understand their feelings. Allow them to feel and to trust in their inner Selves and the instincts felt within their bodies. Encourage their instinctive knowledge. Allow them to learn what we were deprived of.

CHAPTER TEN

Relationships

John Lee's definition of co-dependency:
*"I will not tell you what I think and feel for fear of what
you may think and feel; therefore, I will say nothing."*

*It was a reasonably peaceful night at my home. My brother, sister, mother,
and I were sitting around the dining room table, enjoying dinner. Our
cleaner was tidying a few things and had most of the kitchen plates and
glasses out on the side bench next to us, doing a bit of a spring clean. Dad
wasn't home. I remember it was rather enjoyable. I felt relaxed, sitting
with my brother and mother that evening. I often felt like that whenever
Dad was not at home.*

*That feeling quickly dissipated with the sound of the front door
opening. Nervousness just seemed to fill the air, as usual, on his arrival.
I just wanted to hide or disappear completely, because as was culturally
common in those days, the approach to life was that children should be
seen and not heard. What mood was he going to be in? Did he win or
lose? It was too late—he was all smiles and loud.*

*Mum got up from the table and walked to the kitchen sink. He asked
a question, and she responded halfheartedly, with a touch of sarcasm.
Feeling put out, he began with a nervous laugh and his own sarcasm in
return. You would think the ledger was now square—nope, not so. He'd*

press one of us about something. Our response was generally poor from nervousness, not anything else. This would enrage him further, for now the ego was feeling self-conscious, not wanting to look like a fool; the fool was born.

With the sweep of a hand, every plate and glass from the spring clean and the bottles of soft drink that he'd just brought home were smashed all over the kitchen floor. Mum swore at him and went straight to the laundry to get a broom. She cut her foot. His embarrassment further enraged him. Now out of control, he followed her into the laundry. She was swearing at him. Moments passed, and she exited with her head down to cover a swollen, bleeding lip.

He turned on my brother, asking him a question. My father felt that his answer was inadequate, and he raised my brother by the head, his hands on either side of my brother's ears. He picked him up high and shook him ferociously. I feared for my brother's safety. His neck could have easily broken.

You have a chance now to forgive yourself for all the wrong ever done to you.

We carry the pain of these images in the cells in our bodies for years after. The decisions we make often relate to past moments like these. Attack to defend or control becomes the common response, and we wonder why we cannot relax, feel peace of mind, or have successful relationships. If anxiety governed much of our childhood, we unfortunately grow up feeling at home with it. We constantly look to the future for a better way without realizing. We look for relationships to help us feel complete and give us what we desperately yearned for as children—love, nurturing, and safety. Yet when we find these things, we haven't a clue how to manage them and often go on to other relationships that are less fulfilling. We say we are in love but do not know the definition. What are we in love with? Is it a part of another we feel missing within us? When we find anything that resembles goodness and lovingness, do we nurture it or destroy it?

Growing up, my feelings and my sibling's feelings didn't matter. We were just kids—what would we know? Our parents and teachers knew best. We had to look, be quiet, listen, and learn. We masked our behaviors with judgments and smiles to hide the many forms of disappointment we experienced. Repeatedly, we were told to keep these things to ourselves. We repressed our own needs for fear of upsetting our teachers, hiding our truths, needing to be validated to feel worthy.

We disappointed our parents or teachers when we acted out or could not give anymore. No adequate reason was given. Life, in essence, became not our own.

We allowed ourselves to be controlled and manipulated, although we really didn't have much choice as children. As time passed, we projected the same onto others. We suppressed images and were constantly anxious. The more we allowed life to continue in this way, the worse we felt. Un-ease was a constant companion. Dis-ease was a condition of aging, while we never really understood why. We didn't have a choice. We knew no better; we were too young. We weren't allowed to express our feelings—and when we did have a choice, often it was too late—we were conditioned.

Conditioned, learned responses were being expressed through fear of not being accepted and feeling separated from Self—and as a consequence, everything and everyone else. Our search for a remedy begins—a remedy felt deep within us in the place of inner knowing. Yet we know not where to look. We start the search for things outside us. Now there is want, feelings of never having enough, and feelings of scarcity, incompleteness, and discontent. The anxiety which we have come to know so well is playing parent in our lives through our adapted, other self that is now in control.

Identifying with the mind, we feel unworthy and fearful. We start to look for relationships and people who like us—people who will fit our mold and appear to accept us for the image we make of ourselves. Is this love? We feel it is. We jump from one relationship to another, again feeling unworthy; we are quick to blame, criticize, or attack. We mix with people who we try to fix, prop up, or complete us to give us our sense of worth, as we feel little worth within.

It is easy to mask our true inner feelings. We are loving, excitable, adventurous, and talkative, for this is how we have been taught to be. We seduce and manipulate to find the "other half" of us to give us our dues. We are good, aren't we? Show no one your pain for fear of rejection—the crumbling facade we hang on to so tightly. Attachments become our obsession, and our obsessions become our way of life. Any attachment based in obsession is unhealthy. The drama of life begins—the drama we all know so well and on which the illusion of our lives hangs in the balance.

In her book, *Facing Love Addiction,* Pia Mellody uses the term "love addict" to identify a needy soul. This person is addicted to love primarily through childhood abandonment or feelings of growing up with other siblings and feeling left out. Perhaps too much responsibility was placed on you as a child and your needs and wants were not met, or perhaps you were abandoned outright. This is exactly what love addicts attract. They are attracted to love-avoiding people. The love avoidant literally avoids love. This person grows up in a needy or abusive household and is often the go-between parents absorbed of energy. Later, this person is attracted to needy people. Both parties are unskilled in intimacy, and both avoid love once within the realm of intimacy, because as children, it was drained out of them.

Our reality hits home—we can't be intimate. To start, we have no knowledge of what to do. Our mentors were supposed to show us, but they did not have the skills to teach us. As children, we are abandoned, overly loved for the purpose of fulfilling another's lack, or abused emotionally or physically in some way. We are supposed to know true love and express intimacy, but simply don't and cannot.

We must relearn. It starts with our desire to change; then we must identify our pain and shame.

- Owning and expressing our feelings in truth is a wonderful beginning.
- Next, we must be prepared to change our behaviors so as to consciously create a new reality.
- Finally, take the time in silence to know and identify your true feelings—feelings you have rarely known in abundance or have only known fleetingly.

My wife and I were co-dependent, an understanding we acquired from our rehabilitation based on Pia Mellody's model of co-dependency. I was a workaholic and couldn't let a deal pass. My life was a reflection of my youth forever escaping and the residue of a hostile family environment. We were both living with what we assumed was love—but really, it was a case of the ego consuming our every thought as we battled to keep the perceived other half of us happy—an insane description of completeness that created control and anger issues. I was out of control, and my wife wanted me under control. We both lacked self-control and Self-love.

I didn't realize it at the time, but we were both living a lie. She would do anything to please me except ask for her wants and needs to be met. She would cook, clean, go out where I wanted, and see my friends. It was like my life was hers, and hers didn't matter, as she gave no mind to it openly. Her mind was seething deep within. At first, the adventure and all things she never had were wonderful, I'm sure, but it simply became too much. Resentment built up over time—slowly, over several years. She carried a lot of resentment, because her secret world could no longer be contained, and her truth needed to be realized. Her life was spent alone or with the kids, and she wanted more. She needed validation and feelings of worth, not expectation and control from a husband who was never at home and was always doing his own thing. Her feelings of worth had declined to a very low point, and she found it hard to function. Money couldn't fix her, but I thought that's all it took.

I had a compulsive disorder, which didn't mean I didn't love her. I just didn't love myself. I thought I was giving her everything she needed, and she thought I was dismissive of her and cared little for her. For me, nothing was further from the truth. I protected and financially supported her, and I thought that was what made a relationship. I just didn't know any better. The man provided and supported, and the partner looked after the house and kids—those were the lessons I learned. My life was absorbed in escapism from the past, and acquiring more was my excuse for the perfect life. I had her on a pedestal as the perfect wife. I also had no boundary. There was no healthy boundary to say no to things I didn't like.

I always thought my wife was ungrateful. I felt I was doing everything right. I too was living a lie. Genuinely, I couldn't find happiness in anything I acquired or had in my life. My wife took my self-issues personally, and I hers. Her expectation of me was that I should cheer up and do more—more with the kids, more around the house, more with her friends, and so on. I loved my family and her. I adored my kids, but like her, I expected too much and gave too little of what really counted. The expectation placed pressure on everyone. Control issues were based on unresolved past issues, and my wife's issues were based on attachment to her living a different reality than the one she preferred—that being a life where her needs and wants were validated. She could not express herself how she wanted, often allowing me to control her life so she could appear the perfect wife, as she was the perfect daughter. Her fear of abandonment was greater than her resolve to seek her needs; her past was reliving itself. She was living a life of not being able to express herself or her feelings and doing everything for everyone else. Simply put, she felt abandoned. It was only a matter of time before resentment set in. She was living a life in which she had to always be perfect. Her past had unresolved shame due to unmet needs and wants and was simply unsustainable indefinitely. The difficulty was that I didn't see it coming. She did.

Our relationship was tremendously passionate at times, and it was through this passion that our greatest challenges came to be. They say your greatest tests will come from your soul mate. If this was the basis of measurement, then she was definitely mine. We fought consistently, both needing to learn lessons of Self-love. We had fierce disagreements; then after the disagreements, we made things right—love and hate, they call it. The drama in our life gave us a sense of aliveness and wholeness—a feeling of being loved rather than having to face the truth of our reality. The truth was that we simply could not face our past. We must face the shame we carry; it is the only path to healing. We were told as children, to keep our heads up and smile—to let no one see our pain. Our feelings of discontent were dismissed—like most of our feelings. Don't they say that a family is as sick as the secrets it carries? What secrets are we carrying or going to continue to carry and pass on?

Our life became a game of survival. We were both looking for love in what we thought we had, yet we were deeply entrenched in our own egos and issues around it relating to abandonment or fear of intimacy. We both wanted control. We both had a fear of losing something, but we did not know what. She allowed me to have it, and I foolishly believed I had it, until the day she had enough. Her self was broken from living a life without her inner calm and peace with little validation or expression of love in the true sense. She had the courage to follow her conviction and leave.

Then my body broke, and later, my spirit came to life. My shadow didn't dance for some time.

I imagine one of the hardest things anyone has to face is fear of the unknown with kids to raise and a life of financial uncertainty. There were legal and personal issues and feelings of dread and tiredness. I had to find the strength to reclaim life from a past of allowing others to control it, or vice versa. I was not in touch with what they needed or wanted. This was all for the sake of no longer pleasing another and having the courage to seek Self-fulfillment, yet not understanding what that is.

Do you hold everyone in high esteem? As the great friend and lover, you are always propping people up—putting them on a pedestal, so to speak. The abandonment you felt from your family or society growing up is now being remedied by the mask you place on your partner, friends, family, or loved ones. Our material possessions show the world how lucky and fortunate we are: "Look at who I have in my life. Look what I've made of my life." We place them on a pedestal until even they feel worthier than us. It is a dangerous cocktail of poor self-worth and future resentment. One gives all, and the other takes all, often reversing roles as the love-dance continues. The giver feels unappreciated, and the taker feels a low self-worth from always being propped up or rescued. Resentment is the only conclusion.

Our lives are being played out through our past fears. We are afraid of being close, because we fear being hurt again. We are unable to express our true inner Self—the vulnerable, gentle, wonderful Self—and are afraid to leave the relationship for fear of abandonment. We are reenacting another's life—perhaps a parent's, a teacher's, or a caretaker's life—because we have been taught well.

In our relationships, we are neither ready to face the real truth, nor would we believe the truth just yet. The truth is that the love we have is not actually love. It is synthetic and made up for the sole purpose of feeling validated and complete. Without Self-love, sustainable, true love simply cannot exist. Mutual love and acceptance, equality, friendship, sharing, healthy boundaries, mutual validation, trust, openness, and vulnerability, without these attributes, what do we have? We have control, enmeshment, ego-based love, and manipulation, false belief in ideals of conditional love, expectation, anxiety, and fear-based communication. What we don't have is harmony, joy, and bliss through acceptance and openness.

What is love? Love, we think, is a thing outside us, like everything else. We think, *I want love, I deserve to be loved, I would like to give love, If only they would show me more love,* and *We were physical, so she/he does love me.* Our world represents our often deluded reality that we were born as anything but love. Love is represented as an acquisition or a trophy.

Love is, in fact, a sense: the sixth sense. It is inherent within us and is the source of all life. Everything is constantly changing, yet the one thing that never changes is the source of creation: love. It is our natural state of being. It is a constant. That is why we seek it from the state of illusion which we have been conditioned for and why we suffer or experience pain when we are separated from it. We must always return to it, regardless of where we think we are in our lives. It is the source from which we are made and created. It is the physical, spiritual unification of physical form, so we cannot escape it. It is the master plan of creation itself.

If we are loving, we find the "perfect" mates. You are the materialistic, adventurous one who comes on like a whirlwind and seduces your partner off his or her feet. At last, he or she is rescued. You love the connection you have not felt for a long time. The ego dances to keep you in tune, and life is seen through rose-colored glasses. It is all wonderful. This celebration of newness carries on for a short time until the facade fades and reality bites. Then it is all too much. Your unloved self simply rejects the notion of love. It deadens the feeling—the same way we did when we were growing up. The dynamics of the relationship change, and drama begins—the drama that is all too familiar. We attack, feeling the resentment of our past, use guilt and criticism, and then blame to control or feel validated. The drama helps us feel alive. Just like we did when we were kids, we are testing love. What is love? We cannot trust it. The person our partner fell in love with—the wonderful part of our inner Self, the amazing soul that revealed itself for a short time and gave our love a chance to shine—is now no more. The fear of intimacy is too great. Our past is running our life. Words of fear run riot in our head. One is avoiding, and the other is fixing. Both are trying to control. Both hold the illusion of self together.

The ego is now playing its primary function: control. Fear and pain are the solution, and its only end is death. Is this the death of an old way?

We live in our private little worlds, oblivious to our feelings, believing everything we see is to be believed. The center of our world is not us; it is everything outside us. Reality hits home at last. What is the purpose of this relationship? How is it serving me? What can I get out of it? Your partner will make demands, and you will give and expect a return. Yet you will not feel the return, for your wants and needs have never been adequately expressed to your partner, nor has your partner expressed his or her needs to you for fear of upsetting you. Your partner prefers instead to keep the peace, and without realizing it, allows resentment to blossom and take foothold instead.

The ego will now play its role and express itself through your body in the form of anxiety, discontent, boredom, or whatever way required to achieve its means. It cannot live in tranquility; it was created by you to protect the wounded part of you from the pain and trauma you experienced in childhood. It is the adapted self, and it is there to defend and protect you against anyone who doesn't understand you. The reality is that no one knows what we need, because we have not discussed it for fear of what people may think and feel about us if we do. Instead, we act out and react, feeling misinterpreted and misunderstood. Wasn't this how we were taught? "Say nothing. Don't tell people our secrets. The family is always right. What would they know? They are different from us." We were taught to choose to react instead of discuss. The adapted self cannot have a relationship that is sustainable or permanent. Yet we think the relationships that we are in are wonderful, sustainable, rock solid. Such is our attachment to our partners, and such is the pedestal we have placed them on to show the world everything is fine. Let's stop fooling ourselves. It is time to face our truth.

From very early in our lives, we had developed poor skills in Self-awareness, Self-expression, and appreciation of Self. We are not taught feelings of wholeness and connectedness within. We are taught that relationships are frail, hard work, and not permanent. Subliminally, we were taught not to trust and to believe everyone is out to get whatever they can. This teaching starts from our earliest years and continues through much of our growing-up years. When we recognize that our feelings are telling us a different reality—that it is not okay to hate, condemn, blame, and so on—we try to change our reality and fail, because we simply do not have the tools to do so. It is generational. One generation passes on to the next the same fear and shame that will continue until we stop it!

What suffers? Our relationships, of course.

Therefore, the ego has a purpose. Its aim is to keep you in the pain of your incessant thoughts until you have simply had enough! Its destructive powers are actually the catalyst for your return to true Self. Self-realization and Self-love are created from the life in pain and suffering of an unloved self. There is no choice; it must bring you to a place of realization. It will be then your choice as to how much you choose to change and learn—and in so doing, create a different reality.

Our relationships are our catalyst for change.

We were conditioned as we grew up, because we were so innocent; then, throughout our later years, we were unable to set boundaries, say no with confidence in our point of view, trust, or act on our own feelings. Instead, we chose to live life the way another person demands through their control over us—or our control over them. Whether we are conditioned to fear early in life or later, the effects are no different; the pain we express by our words and actions is felt in every corner of our lives. The effects on us are then expressed to others. Our pain is reflected in the way we communicate with those who are very close to us.

Our relationships suffer as a consequence.

When business is going well, we put up with the worst elements of people, because there is a benefit to us. As much as that benefit provides you in a monetary way, what it takes from you and your family pales into insignificance. We should be mindful of this and seek fulfillment in Self so all aspects of our lives can be balanced in harmony with the others.

The excuse for neglecting our relationship at home is often by excusing the relationships at work or the pressures associated with them. Who suffers—Mum and Dad, girlfriend and boyfriend, and who else? Often it is the innocent, our children—the beautiful souls who learn by your responses and are too often neglected and un-nurtured as a consequence, as we learned parenting from our parents and learned to carry on these same behaviors. Perhaps not to the same level, but each will carry his or her burden according to his or her genetic makeup and life experiences. Look at your children, as the signs of this reality are clear to see. Look at them, hear them, and speak to them—not at them. Most of all do not dismiss them. Give them your time if you dare. The signs are there. Feel your feelings when you do, don't get angry; just listen, and then accept totally and unconditionally. Do they express fear or anxiety? Just for today, listen and learn from them. Our relationships with our children are our most loving relationships, and our children will give and receive love unconditionally if we allow them to express and receive it in a healthy manner.

There is much to learn from them. Relationships with our children are the special relationships we too easily ignore. To stop the cycle, we must stop the shame from being passed down. Pia Mellody describes this as "toxic shame." You are being called to pioneer change, and what better place to start than with your children? The shame we carry growing up is the toxic shame rarely discussed or dealt with in any form or by any profession. We try to continually make sense of the nonsense and wonder why we are continually unhappy. The reason is that the people who hurt us are or were the same people who loved us, fed us, and took us to school. Many of us were shamed, and we felt we did something wrong. We were abandoned, abused, not listened to, or unable to express our feelings. It is no wonder we always try to please or fix others, always expecting something in return. We are always trying to be good, accepted, appreciated, or loved.

> *What was interesting to me was that when I was in rehabilitation for obsessive control disorder, anxiety, and other fear based-disorders, I saw other people who appeared to be relatively normal—school teachers, doctors, and lawyers. They were happy-go-lucky, and nothing was a problem except that life just managed to be intolerable or an addiction had gotten the better of them. The outstanding part that I witnessed was the complete unhappiness brought out in these people at times during those three weeks in this magnificent facility. They were perfectly happy people on the outside, but were extremely unhappy on the inside. These people had suicidal thoughts, Self-hate, anger, or grief. These were mostly childhood issues, and all had relationship difficulties—many with children suffering as a consequence.*

We developed beliefs about ourselves—that we were unimportant, unacceptable, unlovable, insignificant, powerless, and unworthy, that we didn't belong, or that we didn't matter. In order to feel again and in order to remedy our pain and shame, we must identify with our past, for it is in truth that we will consciously allow the light in. Truth is the light of wellness in recovery and the path to healing of an unloved self.

Try to imagine your Self as a beautiful, gentle soul, an all-loving soul that radiates love. This is exactly how you were born. Then life's lessons and experiences—as harsh as they were—encrusted you with a hardened, tough shell that cannot feel the pain, but continually hides that angelic soul somewhere within it. It is out of sight and out of mind. Now you are left with a mind-body connection—incessant thinking. Your life purpose is now in play. You medicate with drugs and alcohol, other psychological barriers, or walls for the instinctive purpose of survival, of surviving the pain of separation from this loving Self.

When we start to feel this reality—when we seek the truth—we start to heal the unknowing part of us. When we start to feel again, we start to know again. We realize that the all-loving Self is what we have always been searching for—yet never, until this moment, understood as our reality. A Course in Miracles refers to the moment of this realization as the "holy instant."

Each of us needs Self-love and Self-acceptance, and that love can only start when we identify it within us. Every time we speak our truth, we bring awareness into the illusion we have created and break through the barrier—that toughened shell born from fear. Eventually, the shame will disperse, leaving only the beautiful soul within you. Our senses will then feel alive, once again. It is your sixth sense that has the power to create the passion for life and bring all other senses to life. We repress the sixth sense until we are ready, and then it will appear.

Is a relationship we seek any different from a rainbow? Is there a pot of gold at the end of it? How exciting! We spend our whole lives in search of the so-called perfect relationship, the one that we imagine would complete us and provide us with some supposedly missing "other half" of us. It doesn't exist. There is no "other half" of you. There is only the whole of you. You have all the knowledge and wisdom at your disposal to love life to the fullest in complete peace and joy. The question is, when are you going to allow yourself the time in the inner silence of your Self to access this knowledge?

"There is nothing wrong with me!"

The first week of rehabilitation was very confronting for me. When I compared myself to others, I felt I was relatively okay. I would smile and try to be jovial. It shocked me when I was asked several times, "Why do you keep smiling?" When I was asked questions that related to love, I would change the topic or make a joke. The therapist was not happy. Her face would take on a serious look, and she would again ask, "Why do you avoid the question?"

I learned that we adapt the ego Self to avoid, and we go through life avoiding our true feelings.

No relationship can exist without love of Self. It can be a selfish comment if taken incorrectly—so don't. Your love needs you to love yourself—not from vanity, but from acceptance of Self, because here no judgment can exist. Judgment cannot exist, because to love your Self is no longer to attack or live in fear. In the absence of fear, there is love and light. It is a warm, radiating, beautiful white light that affects all who are touched by it.

We spend our whole lives looking for the perfect relationships, and we find them. We cross paths many a time—and when we do, we destroy those loving relationships, because we lack trust in them. We lack trust in ourselves. We lack Self-love and wonder how a person could love us or make excuses for how we could love them. We have become afraid of intimacy—or *into-me-you-see.* The people who loved us and fed us also ignored or shamed us—not intentionally, but from ignorance and their own thoughtless generational patterning.

I attended a lecture regarding anxiety and fear. It was suggested that fear is passed down through generations within our DNA makeup. This may explain why, in some families, two children brought up in the same environment turn out with completely different personalities—in fact, on opposite ends of the spectrum.

The same lessons are passed on to our parents by their parents or passed down by previous generations though DNA. We are afraid to show people our inner Self— "into-me-you-won't-see" —for fear of not being accepted. Fear of intimacy stops you from sharing yourself.

From the exterior, the world sees us loving. It is easy in public to express love as the perfect couple. Often you mean it. However, it is equally easy to switch and display aggressive behavior, because the wrong thing is perceived and easily acted out accordingly. The relationship is fickle. It is frail, like many modern day unloving-loving relationships.

Start to feel what it is to feel, and stop the generational patterning.

How do we see the signs to know our state of awareness or the truth of our reality when we literally don't know what we are looking for because we cover our feelings with all sorts of addictions? We cover our feelings with love addictions, sex addictions, work and money addictions, emotional addictions, psychological addictions, and drug and alcohol addictions. We allow things in our lives to violate and cover up our core values. How can we successfully identify the signs of our actual state in reality? Quite simply, you must trust in your feelings as interpreted within your body—the physical pain or joy expressed from your all-knowing Self via your body. It is how your instinctive, true Self—the soul—expresses itself to you. Our divine mechanism is to understand our true value system. For example, when we feel physical pain, as interpreted within Eckhart Tolle's *The Power of Now*, we are at odds with our core values and need to look within. Our feelings will always tell us the truth! We must learn to feel again!

Trust your instincts, for your instincts are guided by your spirit and your spirit is your greatest connection to your healing. Your physical pain will guide your feelings if you can learn to trust your Self again.

This is the benefit of physical form and why accepting our pain as a means of learning is appropriate. Our body pain, expressed through emotion, is telling us that things could be better. It is entirely up to you whether you deal with this in a positive manner by making the decision through your intent to change your reality for the better or stay caught in a rut until the reality you experience becomes almost unbearable and unmanageable.

This is the power of choice and free will. It will be totally your decision to choose your path and the appropriate lessons you wish to discover. For example, if it is forgiveness your soul requires to learn, then your subconscious—knowing this requirement, often without your mental awareness—will manifest thoughts within the mind. The mind, of course, belongs to the soul, and your soul purpose creates a reality of sufficient pain from your thought until the lesson is learned. What better, more efficient way is there for that lesson to be taught than through an unloving relationship? Therefore, according to the old saying, "What you resist persists." Your subconscious is now subtly taking command over the ego. It is not the purpose of your soul to dominate, as the ego does. The soul is based in love, and love accepts and guides only—and only when you are ready to receive its gifts will it be given.

Your ego believes it is in charge of your body, and it uses the mind for this purpose. However, the divine secret is that it can never be in control indefinitely. The ego is merely allowed to operate to create fear. The fear creates the experiences or the many avenues you may take to discover the true knowledge of all things love-related. In this case, your unconscious reaction to creating a reality is to provide the answer to the question, "What is forgiveness?" Forgiveness is a loving state of being—a direct connection to your sixth sense. Your chance to forgive is now!

Why do we stay in unloving relationships? The answer is quite simple—we haven't learned what we need from our relationships, and we don't love our Self sufficiently enough to change. We remain content to forego our own needs and wants. Your fear is not a random act of life paying out on you, like some unlucky soul who always seems to be at the wrong end of the stick. The sooner we accept our feelings and own them, the quicker we spiritually advance and find peace and joy within.

> *I stayed in toxic business relationships for eighteen years. I believed my needs and wants were in material possessions. I decided to forego many aspects of love in my life and thus reenact my past. That was what I believed to be totally real. I wasn't ready to change or face my truth. I thought I had everything, regardless of my constant unease. I knew no better—it was what I was taught to believe. I had no Self-love, and I needed external things to prop up my false sense of self.*
>
> *I was not prepared to let go of my fearful illusion until my real needs and wants came crashing into my reality. This all happened in an instant!*

We cannot sustain a truly loving relationship based on commonality, understanding, compassion, and forgiveness without love of Self. Relationships are the highest form of learning—and we are learning, as the divorce rates reveal. The pain created by the act of divorce makes us all look at our relationships differently. Yet more of us can learn, salvage what we have, and appreciate and enjoy all we have. We can also teach our children valuable lessons of love, intimacy, unity, gratitude, and Self-acceptance from our own healing. We can literally slow down the divorce rates by making a conscious effort to look at the signs and heed the warnings. We can start to feel our truth through the power of silence by observing without evaluating and opening ourselves to the truth of our reality.

What have you to really share? Have you asked yourself? If you have asked yourself this question, would you not know how to discover the answer? The answer is in the silence of your inner Self. Yet we rarely (if ever) go there, for the silent bliss within is a threat to the ego self we have created. We believe we have too little or too much to offer the relationship, and the relationship quickly turns sour. We feel insecurity about someone taking or consuming us or leaving us again. Feelings of abandonment or abuse keep us alert and busy so our wounded child selves are not hurt again.

It is funny how we continually search for what we already have in abundance!

What would happen if we were just being content without having, realizing we have enough? We could find the joy in being together with nothing or everything. You can have everything. All we need do is be grateful for what we have, and relationships will take on a whole new meaning. We will feel love instead of regret and discontentment. When the time comes to move on because the soul needs to experience something else, then do so with grace, dignity, and gratitude.

What is a healthy relationship? Do we know? We learn about relationships from our parents. How did your parents show affection? How did they resolve conflict? Who teaches you to get in touch with your feelings if not your parents? Have you ever been taught to listen without evaluating? Do you still believe children should be seen and not heard? Do you need approval from others to feel a sense of self-worth?

An intimate relationship consists of two people who each have their distinct, different lives. Each has his or her own sense of Self, friendships, work, hobbies, and interests, and both people have an unquestionable acceptance of each other. They are trusting and supportive of the relationships outside the two of them. In loving, you give part of your Self to another intimately. You have common interests, friends, and values. Your loving and nurturing Self is illuminating in this state of acceptance, and so is the love within the relationship. You will always have your differences, and acceptance of those differences will be dealt with in truth and with containment of Self-expression, not with resentment, blame, attack, and the like. It is important to remember that the relationship is outside the two of you as two distinct, loving people.

Healthy relationships are few and far between. The attachment created by one or both within the relationship is merely the ego wreaking havoc in your lives; lessons are still unlearned. The person who no longer displays the love that started the relationship becomes the attachment for the other to control and remedy. Again, the ego self maintains a sense of self-worth by trying to remedy the past. We live through another instead of with another. We entangle our lives in another rather than face the truth in our own lives. We are attached to another, thinking another person completes us. We do not realize we are complete in every way already.

Do you see the frailty and lack of foundation in our relationships? Until we love within our Self none are sustainable. The place of love can only come from within—the silent place of knowing all there is to know. This place is where wisdom, joy, and bliss reside permanently. It is who you are!

To access this place of knowing is the greatest quest a human being can make. It is the destiny of the soul. There is no avoiding it, for it is why we were created— to experience all we can in order to feel life in those experiences so that we truly know it.

To know love, you must know fear; yet love has no opposite. This is the divine contradiction to creation. To know anything, you must know the opposite. For anything to be understood, it must have an opposite. Have you ever managed people and felt, after some time, how much of yourself you needed to give away to manage well? How much compassion, understanding, forgiveness, passion, and consoling was needed? At the end of it all, did you feel you had learned more than you taught?

The same goes for intimate relationships. We need to look at them not as a means or device for completeness of self or have any expectation on them. We need to realize what joy we have in them; learn gratitude, appreciation, and acceptance; and develop a sense of sharing and complete caring in order to materialize the sheer bliss and love possible within it. It can only come when each person within the relationship has his or her own wants and needs met. This is vital to the health of a partnership. Each person supports the other, accepts his or her values, and accepts how that person likes his or her needs met. If we do not have expectations, then we are not attached to the replies they may give us when we discuss our wants and needs. Instead, we are happy to meet our own wants and needs and are happy to share them with our partners, if it suits them.

Light over Darkness

Think about how knowledge can alter your relationship.

Probably for the first time, you are fearlessly going to not care about what your partner thinks of your needs and wants and discuss them openly, regardless of your partner's reaction.

The openness is liberating. This will be your first taste of freedom for a long time.

Obviously, it would be a hard pill to swallow for a partner who was always in control to suddenly feel he or she was losing some of that control. Keep remembering where that person came from, as this will help you patiently work through any negative response you may get.

Remember, it is important to start somewhere.

Healing must come without fear. If fear becomes a component of a relationship, then the structure of the relationship will break down. At least one person must be willing to release or speak with the other without the ego attempting to control the outcome to the situation. This is the only way to live without fear and in total love. Love starts with Self, and the Self makes its boundary known—what you will accept and what you will not accept. Healing is to understand the difference between ego control and manipulation over another; being able to set a healthy boundary, and refusing to accept another person's fear or control. This definition is an act of Self-love and love of another.

Light Illuminates

Set healthy boundaries that can be accepted as an act of love, love of Self, and then love towards another by rejecting that person's fear. In essence, with time, patience, and vigilance in Self-awareness, your needs and wants are met. Thereby, you will continue to stay in a relationship that supports you.

It would be wise to consider leaving a relationship that ultimately does not support you or holds you back from evolving consciously.

Your life is your journey, so ask yourself, "How do you want to live it?

"Am I truly happy?

"Are my needs and wants met?"

Are you currently in a relationship in which you feel abandoned, lonely, afraid of what your partner may think, anxious from fear of expressing yourself, or one in which you are not spending adequate time together, or your partner is always too busy for you and not for everyone else? Do you feel you are not showing enough love to the children or yourself? Is your partner continually caught up in his or her own head space? Are you never going out? Is every request met with tiredness and excuses? Do you feel your partner is too demanding, too critical and judgmental, or has no time for you, though there is time for friends or even strangers? Do you feel your partner is needy, unsupportive, or places too much expectation to keep everything happy and in order? If so, then you have probably guessed that your needs and wants are not being met. What is being met, however, is a brick wall, and it is coming at you fast, regardless of what you think you may have acquired on the outside. These are some of the signs. Can you see them? They will turn into anger and resentment if you aren't fearless in expressing your needs and wants. Ask your partner to spend some time for both of you to discuss them. Often, the children carry the pain and shame of these unresolved issues.

Relationships are the greatest experience for learning we can have. They are the physical manifestation of wholeness, yet wholeness cannot be found in another. It can only be found in Self. The balance of wholeness is made easier in physical form through a relationship. Relationships express elements of the soul that are the very essence of the soul. They express love—particularly in intimate relationships. To have this, we must understand love and intimacy. A relationship is the opposite of the physical you—male or female. It is the ingredient of the completeness or oneness of spirit, your soul.

Relationships allow you the opportunity to give, forgive, and accept, and teach you humility, compassion, and understanding. When, and if, the relationship breaks down, you are given a chance to really see through the veil of grey that constantly obscures your vision of love. Perhaps you will have an opportunity to do the next relationship differently or change the dynamics of the current relationship so as not to be obscured by the fears you have come to normalize.

When did we last appreciate who we have in our lives? Why do we let it get so bad before we do something about it? Look at what you have, and if it serves you well, be grateful for it—truly grateful. But if it does not, deal with it now, for to not do so will take from you more than you will ever receive. You will see the signs when you recognize and can identify with the emotional pain you are constantly living with. Depression and anxiety replace having to deal with our reality. Depression is a modern-day disease. It is said that depression is a choice you make—a choice we can also heal, in most cases, by coming to terms with the truth. Is the relationship costing you more than you are prepared to give to it? Are you not giving to it and making excuses instead to compensate?

Depression is common, for in its absence, we would have to face our realities. We would have to face our feelings—anger, guilt, shame, loneliness, fear, and pain. We would prefer life to be easy, not difficult, as having to face our feelings is something we have repressed for so long. We live in a world of fantasy and illusion so that we don't have to face our realities. If we faced our realities, we may actually lose a relationship. We may actually feel abandoned, lost, or guilty. We may feel we are no longer feeling in control and at the whim of those around us. This is a past within our childhood we no longer wish to face.

Instead, we allow others to treat us with unkindness and act out our childhood trauma in adult form. We hurt as we are hurt—not intentionally, because no one wants to really hurt another. It is fear of being hurt that causes us to react as we do—react to the fear and experience, the same things we have experienced previously. We prefer to not identify with our wants and needs and instead satisfy another's wants and needs to please them; then we feel a lack of gratitude and disappointment from trying to please another. Once again, we neglect Self and allow abuse or neglect to continue for fear of losing that relationship and then facing abandonment.

We react then to life. We become better than most. We become invulnerable, without feelings, and live in a state of illusion—or we play the victim, act needy, and seek constant validation. Our lives become automatic, rigid, or limited through fear. We no longer accept our imperfections or those of another and become critical and judgmental. We may even prefer to accept negative control over ourselves and allow someone to change the way we think, feel, behave, and look. Both are caught up when both can operate successfully and accept one's own feelings, wants, and needs, but unfortunately, not know how to achieve that goal. Control—the instrument of survival—is often expressed through anxiety and fear.

Trauma is described as anything less than nurturing! It will be carried in your body as shame until you identify and deal with it. It will manifest as shame years later and create reactions—reactions to past pain to an unsuspecting loved one. We will pass the lesson on to our children, as it was done to us, unless we deal with it now. Children will only respond to nurturing parenting; the rest of the time, they are just reacting and adapting. To ensure we survive emotionally or physically, we react to a past condition. Children learn to react! We must be able to identify with trauma—in particular, our own. What was it that was less then nurturing? When you identify the truth of it, you can actually stop it. Generational conditioning ends with you!

At fifty-two, I went into a rehabilitation center, as I was suffering from many addictions. At eighteen, I replaced chemical addictions with psychological addictions. At fifty-two, I was suffering from depression, anxiety, obsessive-compulsive disorder, and co-dependency. The funny thing is that I didn't even feel I had an addiction, because like most of us, I stopped feeling. Nothing is a problem until it is a problem—until life becomes unmanageable. I was reacting to life rather than feeling my way through me.

I was successful in business, had three wonderful children, and could virtually do anything, have anything, and go anywhere in the world I wanted, yet the one thing that didn't seem right was that I could not be happy or at peace. I was plagued by incessant thinking and the need to control, and I was living in a constant state of anxiety. This highlighted an understanding I had that it was time to act. I was attached to my ex-wife, regardless of how many times I tried to tell myself I was detached. I knew I was attached when most of my thoughts were repetitive and constantly looking for damage control—what I needed to say or not say to please her. It was bordering on insanity.

Through many lectures, therapy, rehabilitation, and meditation, my life changed. I was given the tools to trust my Self and experience life through the value system I felt within myself, not from things outside me. This learning helped me feel, and feeling became my freedom. I started to like my Self, and then I started to really appreciate my Self and the wonderful people in my life: my children and the very few remaining friends I considered my inner circle of loving relationships. Chance meetings in the street were given time—time I once never had. Liking my Self was enough, and healing was progressing. Healing was based on feeling. I started to say no to abuse and the expectations of others, and I realized my own needs and wants for the first time in my life. I gave myself time to sit and listen to the inner quiet of my mind. I was free from incessant thinking—the poisonous constant thinking that creates distorted perception, anxiety, and fear.

Those are the same distortions that ultimately destroy relationships.

I started to realize what I didn't want and realized my attachments were part of my unhealed past. My ego was not letting go.

Say no to abuse, for love of Self necessitates creating boundaries. It is not okay to allow someone to project his or her pain onto you or your loved ones. By your acceptance of this projection, you give these people permission to continue. The most important thing you can teach your child is to have boundaries. Healthy boundaries will assist them through life. Not saying no to abuse creates shame within you and robs you of your ability to have boundaries. A child learns "no" as one of his or her very first words. Our reply as parents is often, "Don't say no to me." Children learn to bury their feelings and instead manipulate to get their needs and wants met. This is their creative way of surviving. Can you see a pattern of manipulation and how easily it can be created? The child grows up acting the victim or persecutes in order to get his or her needs met. It is dysfunctional communication that society accepts as normal.

A woman goes to the bus stop and says in an angry voice, "My bloody husband—he makes me so angry. He's a bastard."

The woman sitting at the bus stop replies, "Yep, they are all the same, aren't they?" Society considers this normal, because the majority in the population are co-dependent. Co-dependent people say, "I will not tell you what I think and feel, because I'm afraid of what you may think and feel, so I will say nothing." These people prefer instead to criticize and be blissfully unhappy. They live their lives without boundaries and teach their kids the same. Not being able to say no to something that upsets us and not being able to express our feelings increases the level of anxiety within each of us, and reactions replace responsible actions. We don't mean to teach our kids these things; we do it unintentionally, because that is how we were taught. We know no better.

"My well-being starts with me" is the greatest lesson you can give your children. Own your feelings; they are a gift to you. Your feelings are a life force—an energy that flows through you. Your feelings will tell you if you like something or not. Learn to identify with your own feelings, then express them openly and set a boundary against things that displease you. Be fearless in this approach to life, and your life will flourish—even though, at first, you will feel the pain of letting go quite severely.

People will not identify with this new you. They will look for the old you, for they are limited by their own fears. Change will scare them until they face their own truth. They will find it difficult to identify with your healing and expression of your feelings. Therefore you must be vigilant and strong. Mix with other healed souls to make your journey easier. Seek them out.

You can change your entire life—and subsequently, the world you see will open up. Your world will be energized, revitalized, joyful, and abundant. Freedom as you have never known it will be assured. It can happen in an instant. The moment you choose to change your life, the path will open to the beginning of new reality, and awareness of Self and your feelings will be acknowledged and accepted.

A partner of mine once said to me, "You will not get rid of me; I make you too much money." For the first eighteen years, I would have agreed with him. In a healed state of consciousness, I would have let him go rather than fight, resist, and keep him as a partner. During that period of self-denial, attachments to outer form forbade boundaries from existing; abuse of others was readily accepted so as to maintain a position. Manipulation and control were the answer. Trying to fix the other to satisfy all things financial was my addiction. I would not have continued chasing after him or patching up the destruction he would leave in his wake.

I found the courage to say no to the cycle of abuse. It was easy when I felt I had lost everything I surely loved—my family at home was the only thing at the time that was worthwhile and important to me. Within the week, I had paid him for his share of the business and moved on to an unknown world. For the first time in my life, what I had and did had a new meaning, and that meaning was to embrace love of Self and deny fear. It was my first taste of freedom.

In hindsight, the decision to sever my relationship with that partner should have been made much earlier, but I did not make it; my ego would never have allowed that decision to be made, as I lived in fear of the unknown. It relied on the perceived monetary gain and benefits as an overall objective of power, money, and external things for happiness. I believed this perception was an acceptable state of my reality. The ego within me was so dominant, I didn't realize I even had a problem—anyone conscious did, and those who were not conscious could laugh off my incessant, driven behavior. Can you see how it is possible to fear expressing your wants and needs to another when egos are butting up against each other—all for the purpose of survival or to receive the support of another person? Survival or support is so important, we cannot see our truth, nor do we want to. It would mean the death of the false self we created to protect us and give us our sense of worth. Without it, we are exposed, as we were when we were young.

In essence, we simply don't know there is a better way. There is, and it is full of abundance, love, joy, and bliss—all the things your false self strives to find and yet is unable to find.

I made the decision to change my undesirable business situation because I no longer felt good in the company of such negativity, and afterward my world changed completely. The people in my life and the business partners I have attracted are amazing people. The focus is away from money and is instead on relationships of like attributes, love of Self, and confidence within. Radiant energy has culminated in more abundance then I ever dreamed was possible.

Relationships should not be feared, for to fear them is fear of Self and of intimacy, and a sign that all is not well. Fear cannot exist where you deny it—and you deny it where love exists. Where love exists, no attack can occur. Your life becomes loving and fearless. Without fear, the world becomes your oyster.

In a way, dealing with your demons is a little like something that happened to me on a walk on a beautiful, bright, sunny morning. I had really missed my wife—or ex-wife, at this moment in time—and I found myself praying with sure intent. I asked God to bless me with a miracle. I asked God to show me the path away from the pain I was experiencing—the pain created from attachment. This pain, in all honesty, was a regular pain; it was just excessive on this particular day. Do you know the pain of a feeling of dread or anxiety when you wake and you constantly think about how to solve something or a situation with someone? Often, these problems are self-created and born from the cycle of negativity—from one incessant, negative thought to another— through unconscious thinking.

Well, on this day, I had enough of it, and I prayed for the path of light. I had awareness of what negative thoughts were in my mind, and I wanted out; at least, I wanted a solution. Solving my negativity would be hard to do, I thought at the time after reflecting back on the previous twelve months of turmoil. I asked for a miracle to occur and show me the way.

On the walk, I would often stop at a magnificent tree that represented divine energy. The tree had a large green canopy and a white solid trunk, and whenever the sun shone through, it seemed to sparkle with light against the sizable, oily, waxed leaves. It was really a beautiful tree. On this particular day, I even prayed when I walked. I was feeling vulnerable and needed strength. I stopped at the tree, and that's what I asked for: strength and the means to help me. As I asked, I looked and saw little starlings darting from the top branches to the trunk and then back up again. I thought nothing of it until I saw a huge blackbird spring from behind the thick trunk. With one hop and then another, the blackbird sprung a meter at a time away from the attack. The starlings continued their attack, one after the other, ridding the danger or the blackbird away from their home. To compare sizes, the starlings were the size of a ping-pong ball, and the blackbird was the size of a soccer ball. That, I thought, was courage. This is the same courage we need to be mindful of and rid our negative thoughts.

Then it dawned on me that the universe was talking to me. My message was being answered, because I truly needed an answer that particular day.

The universe talks to us all the time; we just don't listen. We need to. We need to ask for strength and guidance and then just watch and listen to the next words of the next song or what somebody may say to us at the gym or in the street. There are many ways the universe will talk to you. As you notice the signs, your powers of perception will strengthen, and the signs will become even more obvious to you. Ask and be aware.

We need to be ever-mindful of the big, black, negative thoughts and be constantly on the lookout. These thoughts will throw us back to our past, create anxiety and fear in life, and then cause reactions to the simplest triggers that stir in us the shame we carry. We must be vigilant in awareness and our healing path. We must identify our feelings, know the truth of where those feelings originated, and know what thoughts created them.

We must own our feelings and express them. Do you feel fear? Then say it. Do you feel pain? Then say it. Do you feel love? Then say it.

Letting Go

In the silence of your being, you will find the answers you are seeking if you ask for them, and then rest your body and mind.

Keep the negative thoughts away by being aware of them. Keep them away from your home and your family, because they are damaging your happiness and peace. They are damaging to the well-being of your partner and children, and your relationships. If negative thoughts are left to their own devices, they will consume your every positive thought and action and give you no rest.

Stop negative thoughts by your acknowledgement of them, and the relationship will flourish, as will the abundance in your life. Miracles will occur; universal support will not fail you.

Allow all to be. Concern yourself with your Self, not someone else—regardless of whether they are a girlfriend, boyfriend, husband, wife, or other relationship.

Control your feelings and behaviors, and accept life. All others will gravitate to you. The meanings behind words you once could not adequately deal with will no longer affect you.

Life will offer many totems if you are mindful in observing life. On the day I noticed the blackbird and the starlings, my awareness changed me, and I looked for those blackbirds from that day onward. I found them often and chased them away. Five weeks later, my ex-wife and I were laughing together. The lawyers who we allowed to savage our lives were finished. We faced our truth, removed the negativity of people pollution, and settled the separation without them to their amazement and shock. We both started to chase away our demons and negative thoughts.

The only thoughts that matter are thoughts that allow you peace of mind, and when your needs are met, you will gracefully meet another's if it serves you or the relationship in a positive manner. Maintain thoughts of gratitude and abundance—love of the things you have in your life right now and love of the things and people around you right now. No matter where you are in your relationship, you can start over—right now, this moment, this instant in time—the moment you ask for help, healing, peace, and more love in your life. Maintain thoughts that allow you to face your truth, and do not be afraid; it will take strength to change, and you must be vigilant.

To love is to have boundaries and not control another, live by your truths, and allow people the opportunity to grow with their truths. If your values align with another's, be grateful for this opportunity to share your completeness together.

Too often, I hear this type of expression being used in a relationship, having experienced similar relationships myself:

"I'm leaving you."

"Go, then. I couldn't care less."

"I can't do this any longer."

"You won't go. Your life is too good, so stop talking about it."

It is easy to place expectations on a relationship—worst of all, your own family. When was the last time you looked at the beautiful world you have created and were truly grateful for it? When? Isn't it time? Is the relationship worth saving? How would we know? Who was the role model?

Loving relationships are fertile grounds for attack, as they become attachments created from our own sense of lacking. Often we perceive that what we feel is lacking in us can be found within another. If we lack something, we project it, and if it is what we have come to rely upon within another because it is lacking in ourselves, then as soon as it is no longer felt by us to be in the other, we attack. For example, if we find calm in another, and are lacking calm in ourselves, when the other is not having a calm day, then we will too easily fear and attack. "You be calm. I'm too busy at work all day. If you fall apart, we are all stuffed." Now we have control and expectation issues over another from our sense of lacking with the added element of expectation. Anxiety and resentment will eventually follow, and from this attack, blame and resentment will result.

What does it take to have a healthy relationship and start to change a toxic one to a healthy one? Too often we either take a relationship for granted, or are too busy or too consumed by other selfish emotional attachments to change and appreciate what we already have in abundance. It takes courage no longer to do the things you would normally do. All healthy relationships require gratitude. Find what your relationship needs—do it for you and your children. My relationship needed gratitude rather than resentment based on expectation, a thank you, a loving word, coffee together just twenty minutes a day, time to talk a little, and accepting all that is said, for fear does not reside any longer within Self and therefore resistance becomes futile. Expectation created by ego is dead. Let it go, as it cannot serve you any longer. Be mindful of what you think and say.

We think we know another's reality, but there is no way we can truly know. We never ask. We assume too often, control too much, and always expect. We rarely listen—and when we do, we perceive incorrectly most of the time. We must learn to feel again, trust our instinct, take responsibility for our self, identify our source of pain, and be prepared to bring it to the light of knowing. Express yourself openly without fear of reprisal, be vulnerable, and allow others to see you for who you are, not what you have made of yourself. Take responsibility for your life—own it, accept it, and move forward. Be honest and open. Be responsible for your Self.

Listen to your feelings, as they are the life energy of your values, instincts, and intuitions. Trust your Self, and this trust will open many doors for you—and keep closed ones that should remain shut.

What is it we have created? How do we feel in this relationship? Do we complain, expect of the other, or criticize our partners in front of our friends, as if to heighten our own self-importance or fit in, perhaps, with others who are equally confused? Do we judge our relationships or fear that they are not permanent or evenly weighted? Why do we not stop for a moment to look at what we have and how we feel about our relationship before it is lost to face the pains of our unappreciative manifestations? It will be lost in one form or another, no matter how perfect it may appear, for the world we have created is based on grandiosity, not grandeur—on fear, not love.

The key to a wonderful relationship is to have a relationship with Self. At the center of Self is forgiveness. Forgiveness is readily available when the Self is fulfilled, as nothing can affect a loving Self. To forgive is to accept Self. Forgiveness no longer requires attack, because to genuinely forgive is to genuinely love, and love accepts all things as they are. Accept all that is said and done without judgment, and your anxiety and concern will immediately dissipate. In this acceptance, your life's meaning will be met, and you will develop appreciation for it and the relationships you hold close.

Remember to chase away the blackbirds and be ever mindful of them. Teach yourself no longer to judge anything or anyone, but just simply to be and do. Love your Self through inner awareness, and appreciate who you are and everything you have. We all have the ability to start the cycle of creation from gratitude. Perhaps be grateful for what you are going to bring into your life from now on, and never stop believing it. Have faith and maintain it. Accept pain as learning. By putting new meaning to pain, you are actually creating a positive from something you always thought was negative.

Pain is my path to learning, and when I feel it, I know that I need to chase away a blackbird—and I will.

There are many other feelings we can identify with. By simply asking ourselves in the quiet of our minds what they are, we can truly begin to feel them: feelings like shame, fear, love, joy, anger, loneliness, or guilt. Teach your children to express their feelings often. When we feel any of these feelings and emotions, it's important to question the source of them. Sit quietly, and allow your inner Self to connect to them. The path will open for you to see the source of your feelings.

Boring Down

When you feel a mood change and when you feel fear come over you, stop!

Ask yourself what it is you feel, and then bore down in that moment to find out why you feel that way. Drill down as far as you can, and remember your earliest childhood memory. Try to discover what part of your past has caused this feeling in you.

When you expose the truth of this past, it begins to lose its grip over you.

Your path to healing now begins to accelerate.

Express the feeling to the ones you love, and explain to them what you are doing. Allow yourself to be vulnerable; you may be surprised how your loved ones will appreciate this side of you they rarely see. Regardless, this is about you and not them—but their acceptance of your truth will help you tremendously.

> *Unfortunately, for a while after my separation and after I found my path to healing, my wife did not identify with my truth or my feelings. Her ego was still controlling her behaviors and attracting others of like behaviors, making her path to recovery more difficult. Yet what I came to realize was that it didn't matter any longer. What I discovered and what mattered was my connection to my Self. It was the lack of this connection that had kept me in a state of non-acceptance and uneasiness all my life and allowed no peace and joy in my life. In short, I was miserable, even though by modern standards I had it all.*
>
> *What mattered was feeling my way out of the mess, for I knew somehow that my healing would heal many others—most importantly, my children. Through my lack of Self-esteem and Self-love, my life had become unmanageable. I could no longer accept it, and I didn't.*

Holding Grace

Here is a pointer to follow in the beginning stages of expressing your Self and attuning to your feelings: Tread quietly through life and observe. When you are feeling anger or shame, identify with those feelings. Sit silently and find the source of thinking behind those feelings.

Realize that your perception is yours alone—your thoughts are your perception. Bring this realization to the light of truth; then accept and forgive. Forgiveness is the most powerful tool we have for our healing. It is also accessible in an instant.

To forgive is to accept, and no longer be angry or fear anything at all. It is ridding yourself of the largest of the blackbirds: resentment. It is a conscious decision to empower yourself and never allow the grip of outer influences or people to affect your reality or to pull you into a vortex of negativity. Forgiveness is the answer to your salvation—and through it, your salvation within a conscious world.

Love will emanate from you as you heal, so ask for help and guidance to start you on the path, and then be aware. In your awareness, your life will change. Your relationships will improve as people begin to respond positively to your calm and nonthreatening approach. You will become the light on the path to their recovery.

No longer expect things from another. Accept others as they are or change your situation. Be fearless, for in fearlessness greatness will happen. It may be a little scary at first, but live it. Do not live in fear any longer; reject it. With love, fear cannot exist.

"There is no remedy for love but to love more."
—Henry David Thoreau

CHAPTER ELEVEN

People Pollution

Complexity is created from ego and goes deeper and deeper. The universal answer to all is calmness of the mind and peacefulness in our existence!

After my wife and I separated, I often received phone calls from a friend who was highly disturbed when I needed time out for myself. He would say, "Let's catch up." He would telephone me daily, and when I felt the need to answer his phone call and explain myself, he would say, "We were friends. Let's catch up, and we can talk about it. We all need to talk about it." What he didn't hear (or want to) was that it was "me" time, time for me to sit, go within, and find solace in Self. His fear of being alone was causing this reaction in him. He, in fact, needed someone to talk to. But a lifetime of being consumed by other people's lives had taken its toll, and I needed to recoup.

This is a delicate subject—or is it? We have touched on this subject throughout this book, and now it is time to delve into its meaning and look at it for what it is. *People pollution* is the world of egos battling for space, outer space, center stage space, and separate space—everything except inner space.

Separation, at the end of the day, is the root cause of all our problems. It's the cause of our pain. Separation starts with self and projects outward as a consequence. It is the state of our world as we know it; pain projected outward to others creates people pollution. People aren't generally happy, no matter what they've got or what space they have created, regardless of size or stature.

Many of us just appear happy. We believe we are happy, living with our unease and constant, incessant thinking, and accept it as normal—but we do not look at the signs.

Simply put, we project what we don't like or where we feel lack onto others, and this creates pain for us. Yet the pain is often not even felt instantaneously by the recipient; it is laughed off until later in the quiet of your time, and brewed upon until a completely different reality surfaces. This reality is based on defending one's vulnerability and attacking the vulnerability of others. As a consequence, grief, blame, and resentment manifest themselves, and all the while increase one's own self-importance as camouflage. Who knows by what cause, or when, our lurking shadow will bubble into life?

The ego is your shadow as separate from your neighbors, and all suffer the same ill fate. This is the fate of no rest or peace of mind and the need to opinionate to feel worthy. Too often, we involve ourselves in other people's affairs to appear to be their savior or take sides with whoever gives us the most ear time or appears to offer the greater benefit and dismiss anything of value we may have in our lives only to replace it with their value systems, needs, and wants, regardless of how distorted their views are. With laughs, they hide their truth and reality; they are often unaware of these things themselves. Ignorance prevails over wisdom. Their fear and lives are being played out through you. They have meaning in their lives, and it is yours. Although they are not intentionally harmful, often they just are.

We allow people to opinionate and make judgments on our lives, because we are too afraid to follow our individual truth—the truth we have long since abandoned in favor of group unconsciousness in order to feel part of society or what we consider normal. We allow ourselves to be subjected to what others say and hide among their words rather than subject ourselves to our own individual beliefs, which we no longer adhere to.

We are forever projecting our fears onto others. We give our opinion from our feelings of lack. Let's involve ourselves in other people's business and see if we can help, forever hindering their experience. We hurt others by our unintentional selfishness. How can anyone truly know the reality of another, be it your partner, friend, lover, or child? You cannot. You can only know your own reality in a given situation. We think we know another's, but we don't know, and that is a fact!

We are too quick to involve ourselves in other's affairs. Our need is to control, fix, or help out and validate ourselves by giving meaning to our own lives.

It amazed me that during a critical time in my own family's drama or separation, many people gave their opinions—people without children or people within our family. Long-term friends said to my wife or me: "He's a bastard. You don't need a man in your life." "The children are okay. They'll manage without a father around." "Let's go out and live it up." "Men—they are all the same." "Your wife—she's not worth the effort." "Move on with someone else. Don't do this to yourself." As they said these things, they would be planning the next weekend bash to live it up or dramatizing any gossip in relation to the matter to justify their own selfish thinking. The amazing—and often disturbing—reality for me was that practically no one thought of our children in all this.

Those who did think of our children—and perhaps gave an ounce of reality to us as a couple and the fun they saw in us many a time—didn't give their opinions. They supported us and only wished for the health of the family as a whole. Conscious souls are easy to identify, as they operate from the perspective of "What would love do now?"

The next time you are faced with a dilemma,
ask your Self, "What would love do now?"

We listen to other people's pollution to suit our present reality or whatever distorted view we may hold at that time. Perhaps the guilt, unease, or shame we feel is justified in other likeminded individuals. Someone that will not judge us, but rather accept and validate us for who we are, regardless of the guilt we feel or the actions we take—someone just like us!

My wife needed the support of others; she had left the home. She had no counseling at the time, nor did she seek any joint counseling. She found solace in friends who virtually lived in a state of drama. Often, she described the guilt she felt by leaving the home in brief during conversations. Her reasons are hers, just like her truths are also hers to come to terms with within her time. Yet the need for us to be accepted is almost epidemic. We feel so little comfort in self that we continually seek out souls who are like us and then attach ourselves to them—and they often attach to us. This now validates our decisions and disguises our truths. Yet deep within, this is impossible, for the truth must always rise to the surface— and it will. Then, with an ounce of wisdom, we will seek an alternative path to find inner Self.

People pollution is our pain and lacking projected to another, creating pollution to validate our own pollution. We don't realize our own pollution, because our minds are fixated on our past—a past unhealed.

The unhealed self thinks, *I need to be involved in your affairs to feel my sense of worth and so I am not alone. I need you to be like me. You must speak with me, as I'm your friend. That's what friends do.* Do these sentences sound familiar? If they do, we need to work on a few things—namely ourselves—and perhaps distance ourselves for now from the pollution.

> *A friend of mine gave me what he understood to be sound advice (and many others, I am sure, would have considered it to be sound advice). During the time of my immense grief and pain soon after my family split up, he said to me, "Why did you tell her the truth? You never tell the truth. Even if she caught you in bed with another woman, you deny it."*
>
> *I thought about what he said and realized it was not where I wanted or needed to be. The courage to face and own your own truth is not found by hiding behind your finger. The truth is the truth, and that is why it is so hard to face. The truth is not your fault; the guilt you feel can only be released by owning your own truth.*
>
> *The act is no different than any other act of shame that we carry as baggage. We then look for people with the same baggage to justify our worth and our acting out.*
>
> *Without the truth, we repress the feelings that caused us to be discontented and the need to act in ways that would hurt another.*
>
> *I found the courage to face my truth, deal with it, own it, and release myself from the grip of fear that my past shame held over me.*
>
> *Never have I felt so liberated!*

The world is short of many things—food, water, resources—but one thing it is not short of is opinions. Opinions stuff everything up. We just can't seem to let life unfold: to just accept, listen, find our place in silence, allow others to do their bidding in the privacy of their grief or burden, and allow others the right to express their emotions without having or offering them our opinions.

People get strength from other people's mishaps. These mishaps give meaning or support to their somewhat mundane lives. These lives are perhaps not mundane in reality, but rather in our state of thinking—the world we see is how we think, speak, and act, after all. How are we going to vent our fear if not through our relationships? Relationships are the greatest catalyst for learning and the center stage of many people's lives. After all, we don't seem to be comfortable within our own skin.

Too often, we allow people to come into our world and the world of those we love to form their opinions and state them openly. All too often, people opinionate their own distorted values on our circumstances—their lives and experiences now opinionating over our own. This is not accepting the responsibility for our own life and the reality we see, because it is another's reality, value, and opinion we are accepting to feel a level of validation for our reality. The very essence of another's opinion is not the inherent knowing of our inner Self, the silent space of our spirit and the place where we need to be to find strength and wisdom.

People pollution is another's opinion based on their life journey, experiences, and judgments, which often play havoc in our own or another's world—all in the name of friendship. We allow people pollution to happen and suffer the consequences due to our lack of vision and conviction about the truth of our lives.

Often we sit with friends and colleagues and have macho, chest-beating interactions on all sorts of distorted subjects, the least of which pertain to love of Self and family. Often if one of the friends were having a bad time in his or her relationship, then it would be largely expressed as a generic mishap that happens to all—that we should all manifest this reality and fit in. We love only superficially, for fear consumes our thoughts and our lack of willingness to let go and realize that every wonderful thing is already in our lives—right here, right now. Yet our fear of missing out on something else or losing what we have amounts to nothing more than Self-sabotage. We desperately need to face our truths and evolve. Have you noticed how you cannot stop doing something that ultimately must bring harm to you and those you love? Why do you think this happens? You are not clinically insane.

It is our genetic makeup. It is what we are all about: living, experiencing, and creating. We must face our truth. It is our soul's purpose to return to our inner Self.

Why allow idle talk to spoil the beauty all around you—the beauty and abundance that exists in your life now? It doesn't matter if you are in a poor part of your relationship right at this moment or whether you are suffering grief over some other event in your life, it is time to accept it. If you are in a loving relationship, then stand up and fight for it. Go against the tide, and don't be drawn into other people's pollution. Don't allow them to spoil your wonderful life or the potential of a wonderful life. Swim against the tide, and let others see you for who you truly are: courageous, strong, loving, and happy. Be strong in knowing the truth. Too often, we allow people to come into our lives and take over, and they do it because they get something from it. They get a sense of worth, while we get a sense of someone caring—a belonging or a loving connectedness against the hurt or uneasiness we are feeling. Sometimes others attempt to make us feel worthy so that they make themselves feel worthier—a fragile footing for any relationship!

Give me anything but the task of having to face my individualism.

After my wife and I ended our thirteen years of being together, people came to our rescue, choosing to spend part of the time with her and the other with me. Many of her friends were single or single with children and sided exclusively with her. Many hours were spent brewing over what a bad person I was. The more everyone talked, the angrier everyone became. Families got involved; so-called friends got involved—and everyone had an opinion! The masterstroke of the ego is opinion.

Eventually, I stopped the chatter. I realized things were just getting worse. It seemed that whoever was consoling me simply stopped communicating with me. You see, those who comforted me had no more to get from the relationship with me, so it ended; opportunity lay elsewhere. I didn't want to speak with anyone, as it was time to find my Self. I was lost in a sea of anger, hate, rage, and grief. I had suicidal tendencies, and any other emotion you can name, I had. My past was venting itself. Toxic shame, tremendous guilt, and self-loathing kept me in a state of depression. My ego sought retribution in any way it could—thinking and rethinking or going over the same things and just rehashing them in a different way, tone, or words, and the cycle continued. It wasn't healthy, and people were not making it better. My perception was that they were killing whatever was left to salvage. In reality, I was killing whatever was left to salvage. I had to forgive to survive—to help my kids—for I realized that in my healing, all others would heal. I found the path in this utter pain.

Is life—our world—just a mirror of the pain we experience and the feelings we experience as individuals? Don't wars start because of misperception and lack of love, lack of forgiveness, or the expression of one's own pain, lack, or lust projected onto another?

In pain, people do all sorts of funny things. We allow so-called friends into our lives to give opinions about our families. We allow their words to console us about our actions, in whatever form we choose to take action. Are our beautiful children able to defend the fact that they may want a mum and dad together? We allow, perhaps, through the guilt of our actions or the grief we have caused others by our actions, to accept counsel over our lives and children from others with no professional training, even if those people don't have families or children or have suffered the same fate. It amounts to insanity feeding insanity.

Individually, this happens to us all the time—at work, at the pub, in a boardroom, at the courthouse, at a cafe, on a girls' night out, on a boys' night out—and we laugh while the seeds of destruction are planted. Unhappy people look for other unhappy people. We don't even know it until we are forced to take a good look. Then we realize what we had and lost, and we enter a new reality that now offers us the seeds of opportunity to grow, heal, and help others.

We should ask ourselves some relevant questions here. Where are our boundaries to protect ourselves? Where is the love? Why are we so afraid of love? Since love is what we have all become separated from—as individuals and as a society—would showing it publicly be unacceptable? We fear we would not fit in. We fear we might appear weak or wimpy. Would you be ridiculed? We fear being rejected, as we did when we were young.

Why do we have to listen to other people's opinions or speak obsessively, going over the same thing time and time again, as if attached to the outcome? Perhaps we need the opinions of others to feel validated, thus proving ourselves right. Perhaps we need a different result the more times we speak of it.

Not many of us were validated when we were growing up, thus every opportunity we get is an opportunity to feel validated, however the means. But it is important to remember that the only validation we need is our own!

Choose to sit with your feelings instead of having to defend a position or the need to speak of an occurrence with many for support. Others will gladly give support to fulfill their own need for validation or worth. Sit with your feelings. Own those feelings. Seek no other validation outside of your Self. If it is pain you feel, then allow yourself to feel it. If it is grief, anger, or shame, then also sit with that feeling in the quiet of your knowledge. Seek no other opinion. Go within to the quiet solitude of your inner Self.

Stop other people's pollution from intensifying the cycle of negativity within their Self or your own reality.

Own Your Feelings

Here is a simple technique for when you feel yourself upset, needing another's opinion, fearful, or alone: Stop! Sit quietly, and feel your true feelings, which you may recognize as pain.

in your body. Then observe the thoughts that created this physical pain or anxiety

Next, in this moment of realization, bore down to the past and ask yourself, "Where did this feeling first originate?"

Often you can see the place in your past—and when you do, you are in touch with your truth. It is here you can learn to release the fear by forgiving this part of your past.

My world had collapsed. All that was left for me to do was forgive. I had to learn to forgive all those who sided, condemned, and judged. I had to forgive myself for the same aliments. Even close friends, who were instrumental in the boardroom chatter, ran for the hills when the trouble began between my wife and I, perhaps for fear it would get too close to their nests. We certainly are good with the advice—and even better at seeking out souls who will listen and justify any guilt we might feel. We listen to everything other than the truth, for ego cannot know truth. Fear cannot know truth. Our past cannot know truth. All three cannot know love!

Pollution, it seems, is all we have to talk about. If we stopped the gossip, what would we have to talk about? Think about it, and answer the question from observation.

To say we should be careful who we keep as company is an understatement. We should seek out conscious souls who are on the learning path to enlightenment, inner peace, and love.

An old saying, "Show me your friends, and I'll show you who you are," has relevance to a healing mind. We often fail to accept wisdom that comes with history. If only we learned from it rather than repeat the thinking that creates the same mistakes of our past.

Wisdom comes from our elderly—if only we would give them the respect and time necessary to hear their words. Ancient philosophies or cultures abound in wisdom—if only we would seek them out. We fail to accept wisdom, because wisdom poses a threat to the illusions we create in our lives. Wisdom means we would have to face the truth of our lives and our past.

Only love knows truth, and love can only come from within the silence and stillness of inner Self.

Those who make me laugh are my enemies! Pollution comforts their unease. They cannot cry with you; they will laugh with you and let you know it's okay to be like them.

Laughter, in the context of this meaning, comes at a time when opinion does not suffice. The truth remains unrevealed, and truth concealed is judgment over another. If we sit in judgment, then the real issue at hand—the truth of the painful experience—is replaced with the illusionary issue of one's opinion. Their fear is now center stage and projecting itself into that life; their ego separates whatever it can to pacify its own feelings of separation. To separate another is to justify your own separation from Self-love; this separation is often selfish and ignorant by design. It reinforces the belief that you are right, for any unity would destroy that concept you have hung onto and depended upon for so long in the belief that your very survival depended on it.

In the light of our consciousness, we will see the truth for what it is. Unhealed souls will be easy to see. Healed souls even easier.

Of course, during the time of my divorce, there were those who listened in the silence of their minds and gave no opinion. They gave simply their shoulders and support. They expressed love for the children. Some were so dear, they cried at a love lost. They felt the love was deserving of more—a chance, perhaps, to make things right. Their tears were testament to their genuineness.

These friends would sit and listen or call. There was never a burden expressed, just a call to say hello and send messages of their willingness to be with me if needed. Their silence was validation of their love for us and the family. There was no opinion—no sense of lack. These people were content within their own lives and families. They respected life and family values; they understand friendship. They do not compete, control, demand, fix, or fascinate over our affairs. They were there in support, ready to assist if asked. They always gave an ear, but never a judgment.

It is easy to judge and bring our own life derailments onto others, and this has caused all the separation and hatred in the world—sixty countries at war and one hundred million people murdered during the twentieth century. These events don't happen as global events without our participation as individuals. We allow this to occur, and it is our group unconsciousness that allows our governing bodies to do the damage to others—and thus ourselves. We create our reality, and together, we create the global reality. Unfortunately, it occurs from the absence of love and the expression of fear.

Our minds are polluted by the power-hungry, and this power seeps into the fabric of our society, communities, and families. It manifests itself through each of us until the end means no longer serves anyone. It is destructive, and the fear of this destruction begets more fear. In that fear lies the need to acquire and attach to external things. In such neediness, many concerns arise, and anxiety breeds mass health, social, and family issues. The lessons are not learned; the fear is simply passed on from one generation to the next.

We wonder why everyone has an opinion. It is there because in the absence of love of Self, the self needs to glorify its existence with self-importance. The important self needs companions and others to validate it—to feel worthy—and there is no better companion than someone in pain.

Recognize these people, for they are the ones who need consoling. Forgive them, for they know no better; their lives are unfulfilled. Mostly, they don't realize this and would scoff at this suggestion. Don't give them permission to continue— they will, and when you tire of their opinion, they will turn and blame you for all sorts of reasons. Most notably, they will blame you for abandoning them when they supported you. This is incorrect and illogical, of course, yet true. They believe they provide real support for you in time of need without looking at the complete picture, yet their lack within themselves gives them a sense of security in your affairs until you no longer seek their opinion or see it for what it really is—their past acting out inappropriate behaviors.

Your energy, for now, is very important to you and the ones you truly love. It is time for you to seek your inner Self and be free of these outside burdens. Be a burning log, and seek out other burning logs. Judgment and criticism will be absent from their support. They will not look to derail you and take you down an alternative path, which is often detrimental to you and your family's well-being, but rather allow you space to heal—to determine your wants and needs and those of your loved ones. Only if asked will they offer an opinion. Let's forgive the past. What has been said and done is over. To reside in the memory of the words and actions that brought you to this point in your life is to condemn yourself to the same pollution of the mind-body identified state of being. We must start to look for the spiritual container that can take our pain and offer comfort to empty that past into. The comfort of one's soul is the greatest comfort we can find, for it totally supports the physical you. In this state, your healing is assured without any doubt of any kind.

Living in the past has no relevance on the journey to freedom. Learning from the past, however, is important. Forgive all those you thought were causing you harm. Without forgiveness, we relive the past, and we don't learn from the past!

Ignorance over spitefulness, in most cases, creates the need for drama, and to be drawn into the same web of confusion is to trap the mind and blind ourselves from a truthful reality. This keeps us in a state of illusion.

Each of us operates from fear or love, and we have the choice to go within and find only love or live outwardly in fear or become disconnected from Self and trapped, as have many others in our past who cannot serve our greater cause. To be free of this affliction is to forgive all the wrongs we ever thought were done to us and allow these people to find their own path.

Let's not cast judgment over anyone. Drop it as you would a hot coal, for what is prescribed is truth! Our own judgment is just another extension of a false reality. Do not go there. Be vigilant against it.

Look at truth for what it is. Look at what we need to do to grow in consciousness. Be with souls that are on the journey within, will face the truth of their life experiences, and will better understand what it is that makes them think, say, and do things that have brought them so much unease. Being with people of like minds and participating in group therapy are powerful healing functions.

In the healed light of what you will become, many others will be healed. Climb to the top of that mountain, and then throw down the rope to others to help them. Do not try to carry everyone to the summit on your journey there, for the ego will try to take you to the path of helping others so the burden of it prevents your arrival. Your ego will demand that you are above others, that you should be righteous and give your opinion and advice. This is the fate we must avoid. This is a course we have been on for too long.

Healing is Self-love, and there is no need to preach or be grandiose with our new lessons or our understanding of finding the path of healing. Try not to assist anyone, regardless of who they are, as you are the most important part of your life now. To help others, you must help yourself first and completely be on the path of your own healing.

Do not be afraid to venture away from the need to be validated. Be content to own any feeling you may have—feelings of fear, loneliness, grief, or pain. The path to truth is only difficult at first. We also must be courageous to face it. This is the only way you can help all others.

Miracles will occur. Your peace is assured. Give yourself a chance to witness them.

Stop idle talk and people pollution. Do not listen to it. Distance yourself from it. Choose to sit with your Self, listen to your Self, and start the process of trusting your Self. We have learned to not trust, for it is trust in Self that was taken away from us. We trusted our loved ones when we were growing up, we trusted our friends at school who let us down, we trusted our community and our leaders, and we got hurt.

The pain of others is accepted because it is that pain that we feel we can associate with.

There is no choice in pain. There is, however, a choice with suffering! Suffering is a continuation through choice of the pain we experience. We associate with it, because we feel comforted that others are choosing to suffer like us. We allow others' opinions to keep us from conscious creation and from experiencing all the love, joy, and bliss this magnificent life has to offer each and every one of us.

Sit with the inner you. Own your pain. Feel the feelings associated with that pain. In accepting it, you will release it. It will be the end of idle gossip. Reasoning will play a conscious part of your reality and put an end to people pollution that will no longer have an appeal for you. This is choosing against suffering—suffering exacerbated by people pollution.

CHAPTER TWELVE

Forgiveness

"The highest form of human intelligence is to observe without evaluating."
—Jiddu Krishnamurti

There came a point where my wife (now my ex-wife) and I had simply had enough. Worn down by time and the pressures of separation, she had decided to finally do something about her emotions and deal with her pain. She booked herself into a self-help retreat for three weeks and dealt with her relationship issues that she felt needed attention.

This was something I really had not considered a possibility only a few months prior to her going. The time comes in all our lives where we can either accept the truth of our reality or go on in life feeling less than complete. It was time for her to face her truth and do something positive for herself.

I married her for her loving nature as well as her strength—an inner strength I did not believe I had at the time. I had the bravado and the outer strength, and she had inner calm—or so I thought. It certainly appeared like that to me at the time. Yet it was the lack of her inner calm and the fact that she had not dealt with her past or feelings of abandonment that caused her resentment to escalate and eventually derail the very life she longed for—the life of comfort, family, and a loving and accepting relationship. In fact, it was a mirror of my own derailment.

She decided to forgive herself, and I too decided to forgive myself. It was at that point our friendship actually had a chance—a friendship which is very important for the children and our own sense of Self.

For her to go to the retreat or therapy clinic was an expression of Self-love—something she had been separated from for a very long time. Her need was to evolve and use her strength and courage no longer to accept a life of turmoil, unresolved anger, pain from constant unease, suffering from constantly thinking about how she could get her life back, the children and the hurt they felt, and the shame associated with decisions of divorce or separation. Instead, she chose the path of peace and love.

Self-love creates courage. Each time we hear or see someone actually doing something about his or her pain, depression, anxiety, or addiction, know what he or she is doing is an act of Self-love. Support that person; don't criticize him or her. Instead, be aware and appreciate his or her effort. This person is healing his or her past experiences and has the courage, inner strength, and wisdom to do something about them. I have a great respect for people in rehabilitation. They are an inspiration, and they show real courage!

Many of us choose to do nothing—to conform, to accept what is not acceptable by our own values and standards—yet we do not stand by our inner values, for it is the path of least resistance; we allow other's values to dominate our own. This is not freedom. Freedom is living by the path of your highest good—the path of evolving—and being able to express love and connect with it. It is in the pain of the past that most people are willing to take action, and those who take the path should be praised for their initiative and strength. They are the strong ones—the leaders who can and will make a big difference in other people's lives.

Forgiving yourself is taking action, not staying within the unsatisfactory conditions we subject ourselves and those around us to. Life conditions are created by our unresolved pasts. It is the courage within that enables us to take action—a higher soul that demands more. Your highest good is being supported by your willingness to act. If only people could realize that the act of Self-forgiveness is the commencement of a moderate and joyfully blissful life. To self-forgive is no longer to carry guilt or shame of our past. To release our guilt and shame is to free our self of these fear based afflictions that create our false reality. Too often, however, we do not forgive, because we simply don't understand what it is we are forgiving.

In essence, we are forgiving our self for not feeling that we were good enough and carrying shame—often other people's shame that was burdened on us over years, not realizing the pain it created. We do not realize we were later caught in a rut, going over and over the same things, just expressing them differently and expecting a different outcome. An unforgiving self is caught in the trap of a mind-identified state that had no understanding of forgiveness to self or anyone else. We are unforgiving for all the wrong we thought had happened to us.

It is now time to rest and forgive our self. In the spirit of Self, all forgiveness is possible, and our connection to Self will fertilize the ground for complete forgiveness.

Would you criticize a drunk, a drug addict, a person with any addiction, a person who can't seem to hold a relationship, a gambler, or a person with any phobia? If so—and I would say many of us have criticized these people—would you judge if you knew they judge themselves even more harshly? Would you judge these people if you knew that they could one day be members of your own family? Would you then criticize them if they sought help and did something about it?

Judgment is the separation that has divided us all—in particular, judgment over the willing, the courageous, individuals who speak out, the elderly, and those who've been made wiser by their life experiences. Where, then, is the wisdom for change? The wisdom is found in the fearless and time-laden individuals who are unafraid of change. These people are too willing to share if given a chance; often, this is a chance they never get. Our opinions and judgments are more important than listening to and acquiring wisdom.

It is not a loving act to stand above others in judgment, for the problem is with the judge—our self. All of us must seek new paths—the paths where unity replaces separation. Our whole existence is about experience and learning for the purpose of evolving. The people who decide enough is enough are connecting with their souls and their higher Self; they are connecting to wisdom born from past experiences. Most of us fail to learn from history; instead, we repeat the same mistakes, because we simply fail to forgive the past.

Could you imagine the depth of knowledge these souls that connect to wisdom could share with us and the wisdom they could pass on if only we would listen? Listening to them would instill confidence in them; allow them to come out of their drama, shame, and fear; and allow them to speak and heal through the insight that many of them possess. Having been in rehabilitation with many fearful, unhappy people, I learned very quickly how incredibly insightful they were once they were given an ounce of confidence. At the end of my time in rehab, many of these people I could call friends and rely on if ever I needed a word or an ear for support or love.

These people have experienced more in one lifetime than others often have. Yet without acknowledgement from us, their wisdom will remain contained. We all need to appreciate and express loving awareness of each soul—particularly the souls who choose a higher path.

Should we give excuses for our pain by covering it with self-grandeur and do nothing about it other than criticize and judge others? You see, it is easy to see this sign in ourselves simply by catching the criticism or judgment as it occurs. You will be surprised at how often you actually criticize another for the benefit of making yourself feel better. If you judge another, you are really judging yourself. If you attack another, you are really attacking yourself.

Face your past. Be truthful about it. Seek professional help to assist you to start, and then have the courage to forgive yourself. Have the courage to stand alone in this world and say enough is enough, fearlessly swim against the tide, say no to things that you no longer believe in, and say no to people who continue to keep you in a rut. It's a scary thought, isn't it? Why is it scary? Because we have all been so separated for so long, everyone and everything around us become our support mechanisms. Without these, we feel lifeless; the drama helps us feel alive. All is an illusion, and all arises from the feeling of being separate and our sense of lack.

Next time we see a soul reaching its higher state by doing something about its pain, let's love that soul and hold it up as a role model to others and ourselves. By that person's wisdom, ours will be met. Do not look to another's misfortune as your gain, regardless of the urge to lift your mood, satisfy your ego, or be right. Stand out—stand alone, if you have to—for unity is peace, and all of us need to work together to change the path we are on. Forgive yourself, and your entire world will change. Forgiveness of our ego self and others will become a way of living—the path to freedom, complete happiness, and peace within.

The life you desire, dream of, or want derives its source from forgiveness. Forgiveness is the key to happiness, joy, and peace. We live by the concept of attack and defense, feeling separate from all else and others. The world appears to be based on solid foundation; yet we are forever attacking every aspect of it in an effort to have it succumb to our way of thinking or living.

The hardest period in the time after my separation from my wife was when her family members decided not to support the marriage. It was hard, considering the affection and trust I held for them. They decided no longer to support my wife and me in the marriage; instead, they chose to condemn it. Often their condemnation was verbal abuse. In short, no professional help was sought by them. Forgiveness was too heavily laden with resentment and self-centeredness. Ego control was for gain—not for the children's gain, but for their own.

The losers in all this, as I saw at the time, were our children. It was devastating. They only wanted their mum and dad together. They weren't given that chance.

It was apparent that in the drama, others became enmeshed in our lives. My wife could not see it; her pain, guilt, and resentment were too great. It was a chance for her parents, perhaps, to be the supportive family to her, having been separated from their daughter for so long, as both lived in different countries. Perhaps they had fear and guilt for not being able to provide for my wife the way they would have liked to have done earlier in her life. My wife was the eldest daughter, and the expectation was on her to be perfect and to look after her siblings. Her family did not provide her with the loving and nurturing she required. This was perhaps a means to make amends and the reason for their support of her leaving the marriage. Regardless, it was about them and not about my children, and that made me terribly angry.

Eighteen months after our separation, my wife and I attended one week of full-time counseling. My wife was afraid to tell her family about the counseling we were undertaking, and they were devastated at our renewed friendship, which they assumed by our seeing each other each day. The hostility continued eighteen months later; it amounted to insanity! This was not about reconciliation of our family. It appeared their lack of support was more about their mistakes in life—their guilt and lack— and I felt they were using my family to vent their frustrations stemming from their past. I had no choice, however, but to forgive them—grievance was keeping me a prisoner within my mind. It was an exceptionally hard time for me, as I had witnessed the pain of our children and the anguish they endured over this time. Forgiveness was the last thing on my mind! It wasn't coming from my wife's family. Forgiveness had to start somewhere else for the sake of my children. I desperately needed an answer. I had to look within.

Idle gossip and people pollution does not stop outside the family. It contaminates the family, in many cases. Growing up as a child from a well-to-do family prior to my family's massive financial loss, I saw the devastation first hand of what outer form, material possessions, and money can do to a mind conspiring for gain and creating judgment, which is then followed by criticism. This causes an attitude that no one is good enough and that our self is worthier than others.

The escape of a sorry past will find an avenue for release wherever the opportunity arises. The seed of discontent is easy to grow, and the easiest avenue to find a release is in our own guilt when we're among the people that we say we love. Who do we really love? Perhaps our egos are the centers of our love, disguised in any way they can to feel wholeness, right, justification, or validation of self after spending so much time searching for acceptance, validation, and approval of one's journey. The more distorted the journey, the more, it seems, is needed.

Our lives are based on drama, and drama helps us feel alive. Drama helps us do something about the poor state in which we see ourselves; yet most of the time, ignorance prevents our seeing. We are so accustomed to drama, attack, and anxiety, we believe these things are normal.

We blame ourselves for the wrong we feel we have done; this blame is quickly followed by guilt. The blame and guilt are then projected onto others, as if they were the cause of our indiscretions. Yet we cannot seem to forgive ourselves or others, and we often keep on doing what makes us feel guilty—the indiscretions that we cannot seem to let go, regardless of our cries for help to be released.

Why do we not forgive our self? Why do we keep on doing the indiscretions, regardless of the fear we have of the consequences to us and our loved ones? How and why would you really stop an indiscretion that you are apparently enjoying, such as drugs, sex, or food? Is the enjoyment in the control you haven't felt for a long time? Now you have had enough! Medicate to placate for whatever your reason. Now you are in control. You are in control until it controls you—and it will!

The answer is that you are not ready to spiritually evolve at that moment; however, the moment you are ready, you will bring into your reality circumstances and events that your physical being may not like. This is the purpose of life. The feeling manifestation of spiritual growth will begin with pain and end with forgiveness. It all ends with forgiveness!

Therapy has taught me that most likely you will not stop until your life becomes unmanageable and it is in control of you. Until it does, there will be no forgiveness of self or others. For what reason would we need to forgive? We convince our self and others that our lives are okay. The good thing, however, is that the action of medicating will create the environment for pain, shame, and change! Change opens wide the door of forgiveness.

Medicating suppresses, and whatever is suppressed will create anxiety within. Anxiety will create all sorts of reactions and unwelcome responses.

It comes down to feelings. When our feelings are no longer tolerable due to whatever emotions are caused by our unease—guilt, jealousy, resentment, grief, or fear—the anxiety created by these emotions will cause uncontrollable behaviors of attack, emotional or physical abuse, anger, rage, or depression. All these things feed the body more pain. Then the mind will seek to evolve automatically and create thoughts appropriate to manifest a different, more peaceful reality. That reality may have come at a costly physical price—divorce, a loved one leaving home, a nervous breakdown, loss of a business, a partnership dissolving, or illness from disease.

As I was editing this section of the book, I actually noticed my feelings of uneasiness through the anger and resentment I was experiencing toward a young man on the shoreline speaking loudly in conversation with two older women. In fact, he was so loud, I could not hear myself think to edit.

My reality was that he should have consideration for my writing and either speak quietly or move away. I noticed my behavior when the anger I felt welled up inside me and caused a tightening of my muscles and a knot in my stomach.

I stopped, went within Self, and identified the thoughts. Within a few moments, I traced the origin of those thoughts to my childhood. I could hear my father telling us to shut up and go to our rooms so he could sit and read his newspaper.

In that moment, I released my body pain through breathing techniques and replaced the thoughts.

To ask for alternative life answers to our unease is simply a matter of connecting through awareness to the inner Self. It is simple, yet we initially find it quite difficult from all the years of poor conditioning applied to us. We build layer upon layer of hardened ego self. The inner Self—the home of all forgiveness and love—will guide you through your intuition to seek answers that will benefit you in the highest order. Truth is the only medium for penetrating the hardened shell created by our past. It is then that we are able to face the past, own it, and decide what to do with it. Staying in a state of ignorance and denial will simply keep you in a state of unease.

Think thoughts of a preferred or desired reality for you. Meditate on them, and act as if you have already created this reality for yourself. Imagine this reality in your life. Would you be happy or sad? Of course you would be happy and grateful. In this state of having, would you attack or forgive? Of course you would forgive. Recollect your past, and look at the state you were in. You came from a state of fear and pain. Now you are asking for a new answer to your unease as you spiritually evolve. In that pain and at the moment of asking, there is the seed of forgiveness and love.

In every action detrimental to your physical form is the seed of forgiveness and love.

Now, through positive thought, we are in a forgiving state. We are no longer ready to pass over our responsibility to others for our actions. Until we are triggered by the reactions of others, of course—which must happen a number of times—this is how we learn, apply what we learn, and cement its affects. The ego took layer upon layer to create; now we undo it by the same process in reverse. We must be vigilant and continue to practice this positive alignment. In time, you will get the connection and be quick in awareness of connection to Self versus separation from Self. When we attack, abuse, blame, or point the finger, we are separate from Self.

When we align to Self, we can state what it is we need and want and stay connected to Self, because it is only about you! Your Self is expressing your needs and wants perfectly—but we must go within and really listen to what those needs are!

You cannot undo years of bad conditioning overnight; however, if you are aware of each time you attempt positive alignment and regress into past reactive states, then each time, you will strengthen your awareness and ability to sustain Self-control and Self-awareness. To access a state of forgiveness and acceptance, we need to access the inner silence of Self, the positive alignment of mind, body, and spirit. In acceptance is forgiveness, so as they say in rehab, "Fake it till you make it."

If you are not ready to connect to a loving Self, you will simply not search for a different path to the one you are on. You will instead choose to continue on the path of self-destruction in whatever form that is—it could be anxiety, fear, depression, grief, drugs, sex addiction, food addiction, workaholism, alcoholism, and so on. These addictions come from a place of feeling little self-worth within; they are medication to our true feelings.

We learned when we were children that it wasn't okay to express our needs and wants. We learned responses which suppressed our true feelings and developed our wounded child within us. Often, low self-worth developed as a consequence. We believed that our self-worth was directly related to acquiring false needs and wants to make us feel worthy. As the years passed, we kept busy. We were afraid to identify with our insecurities and projected what we feared was lacking in our communication with others. We allowed others to control or manipulate us for fear of being disliked or offending anyone. Then we made excuses for the way we live. We hid our pasts and did not own up to them. Guilt and shame are now playing major roles in our lives.

We end up not meaning what we say or saying what we mean. We are indirect and live life with resentment instead of speaking our truth. We allow others to take advantage of us; we do not express our needs or wants adequately.

> *My friend on the shoreline was speaking so loudly that I couldn't hear myself think. When I returned to my book, it seemed as if his tempo had actually increased; obviously, the sound of his own voice was pleasing him somewhat.*
>
> *It was time to act! I simply excused myself into his conversation, and once I had his attention, I asked him if he wouldn't mind quieting his pitch. I told him that I found his stories interesting—and in part, the stories were interesting—but they were affecting my own.*
>
> *He pleasantly agreed, and he did quiet his tone. The cordial approach between us resulted in smiles and a pleasant exchange. There was no room for resentment, and therefore, no need for further judgment on my part or resentment that may have resulted thereafter by him. The exchange of smiles was an excellent gift.*

Choose to react no longer. Choose to accept all for what it is. Enjoy the process of witnessing the experience, and just forgive. If you feel a reaction coming on, leave the experience; move away, and find your friend—your inner silence. Give yourself a moment to think before you react. That one act of moving away is often enough to contain and protect yourself. Choosing to act in a conscious approach with boundaries will keep you centered and give you the power to see clearly instead of reacting or reliving your past.

Forgive yourself. Stop the blame by being direct. It is okay to say no! Listen to your feelings and act on them without fear of someone liking or disliking you. Just allow things to be and accept all that has occurred to this point. Please yourself, not others. Forget feeling responsible for others. Clear the negative thoughts. Learn to say no to things you don't want, are not happy with, and cannot or will not accept.

What Would Love Do Now?

Remember, being direct is being firm, rather than abusive or controlling. When in doubt about what to do, ask yourself, "What would love do now?"

Our greatest fear is feeling, and yet our greatest salvation is exactly that: feeling. We must learn to feel what we really feel. Ask yourself ten times per day, "What am I feeling now?" Learn to identify with your true feelings. Jealousy is not a true feeling, rather it is a sign that you are covering a true feeling. Perhaps you feel angry from fear of rejection or not being given adequate attention. Perhaps you are angry because your feel abandoned, unloved, or lonely. Perhaps your anger was caused by something your partner said or did or something you carry from your past. Ask yourself, "Why am I feeling like this?" Know what you feel, for then it is easier to discover the thought behind it: the why. Once you do this, you can discuss it or drop it. When you know your feelings, you start the stages of inner knowing—connecting to Self.

This is the beginning of true forgiveness and expressing love.

When guilt is the basis of our lives, the things we are doing are contrary to our inner beliefs and instincts, hence the reason we feel guilty. We hide these truths and cover our true feelings with lies and cover-ups. We are, in effect, living lives we do not believe in, resonate with, or would truly choose.

We live our lives in fear of feeling worthless, unloved, and separate from others, our Self, and God. Fear can be a very big motivator! I ran my entire life on adrenaline and fear. It was only when I cut the fear that I felt the overwhelming exhaustion from years of incessant doing and running away from my past. The funny thing is, in hindsight, I thought I was happy. Such was my disguise—my ego!

The cover-up of pain is easy; most of us do it. Unhappy individuals search for the same thing—lies and false laughter—when really, all we want is to cry. Drug and alcohol abuse, constant criticisms and judgments, false smiles, humor or anger as a means of communicating, physical or emotional abuse to others and to our self, idle gossip, neglect of our kids and partner, blame, non-acceptance, and searching for people who accept us, regardless of how detrimental our relationship with them may be—these things cover the pain, and we have come to understand them as normal.

We say everything is good with us. We refuse to feel or come to terms with our truth, preferring the uneasy comfort of ignorance over our fear of rejection in our truth. Often the truth is suppressed in us. We continue to repeat the scenario: the unconscious leading the unconscious, with no one giving in, each fighting for control—in whatever form—to be recognized, appreciated, or loved, and yet no one hearing any other's call. This world offers little forgiveness. We have become so separated from Self that forgiveness is replaced with expectations. Expectations are creating global anxiety and depression. The good thing is that we are starting to notice.

It is in our observation of global pain that consciousness is lifting throughout the world.

We are starting to realize change is needed, and we are starting to sit up and take notice. We are willing to change, for the feelings of separation from Self and others have kept us unhappy for long enough. The world we see is in crisis. Superficial happiness is tied to external things and cannot give us lasting peace or joy. We are learning this and starting to search for greater fulfillment in our lives, and this path can only exist in a journey inwards to the spiritual Self, the all-knowing Self.

Look at the state of our planet and the lives we systematically destroy. Can we really say we are compassionate, all-loving, and generous of soul? No, in honesty, to say this would be a travesty. We have no tolerance, and love is a mere illusion, for we are all disconnected from Self, and there is little forgiveness in the world—but we are beginning to take notice and demand change. Change can only come from each of us individually. This will create global change.

Do not continue to blame yourself or others or feel guilty for what you have done. This is the secret to life, and your life is in your experiences. You must have hope and replace guilt with a loving acceptance of Self. The pain and problems you have experienced are the reasoning behind your return to Self, the return to love, and loving our own Self and others. Through forgiveness, we return to our loving Self—forgiveness through those experiences. In the awareness of this, the change within you begins. Forgiveness becomes your salvation.

Love starts at home. We must go within and find solitude. It is here that we are called to unite once again. It is in connecting to Self that love can be truly felt. This is where all love will emanate, and the support of the universe will gather force behind you and give you your every desire. It is true, and I have experienced it over and over. I am blessed to have realized this truth.

> *The first time I made a conscious decision to detach from partners and material possessions that I had hung onto throughout my life, I felt awkward and afraid.*
>
> *I acted courageously on the knowledge that I needed to do it!*
>
> *The next morning, when I woke, I felt completely liberated and at peace. It was the first time in a very long time I felt this way, and I knew my decision was right!*
>
> *I had connected to my Self—my inner knowledge and true values—and I had trusted my Self!*

True love is forgiveness and acceptance. True love cannot exist outside you—only within. It is from here that we connect to all that is, the essence and very nature of who we are. This is the connecting point to the matrix of all life. Our connection to Self is complete, and we do not—from this place of being—look anywhere else for it. What we choose instead is to share our love rather than look for what is lacking.

We cannot look to another to complete us, and the realization of this will dramatically alter your concept of love. The love we understand is an illusion. Love has no opposite. It cannot, as love is what holds all things together and all things in place. Fear destroys. Love binds and expands. Anything offered to attack is not love. It is simply a means of control to satisfy an internal fear of disconnection and separation.

Forgiveness is the path to our salvation. True salvation is where only peace and joy can exist. Forgiveness must start with our self, we must learn to nurture our adapted ego self, not condemn or criticize self, and then the connection to our inner world will be open to our outer world.

Forgive all the wrong you felt was ever done to you with awareness, and look at life through forgiving eyes. This does not mean we dismiss what was done to us; hence the need for our awareness. We, however, must find a way to forgive and release our Self from those perceived wrongs. The peace you will find in this learning is beyond anything you have ever felt. It is in forgiveness that you connect to life. Attack is no longer an option; thereby anxiety no longer keeps you in the prison of your mind. Peace replaces anger, and joy replaces heartache and despair.

You will no longer judge another, but accept that person as he or she is and realize that the meanings behind life's adages are in fact true:

- It takes all kinds to make the world go around.
- Live and let live.
- Be free of attachments.

Accept life and all it offers, and believe the higher power of all things will look after you. That's what makes life so interesting and exciting.

- Embrace life and all people within it; don't judge or criticize it or them.
- Trust and let go.

Problems are there for a reason, and the conscious mind knows this, for it is this path that leads us all back to the source from which we came. Experience life completely, with acceptance of all that happens. We have a choice to consciously live with peace and joy or react in fear and anger, for the feeling of disconnection is what most of us choose to follow.

Forgiveness means you no longer hold inner dialogue that is consumed by hate and fear; incessant thinking creates pain and unease. Forgiveness releases these thoughts and feelings, and allows us to trust in life. Trust in life, and it will reward you with riches.

> *Two years and one month after my wife and I broke apart, we sat together outside a little cafe in a quaint little town, laughing and wondering what the hell just happened. We both started to forgive. We accepted the past as the past and decided at almost the same moment in time to release it—to just let it go. We had had enough. What mattered to us now were our children.*

Forgive, for your joy and peace depend on it. Life is full of people who have a sense of superiority and grandiosity. They are conceited and opinionated. Their actions and purposes in life are wasteful, these people take and are selfish in their actions and with their never-ending wants. Forgiveness does not depend on your conquests and acquisitions. Forgiveness is inner healing and fullness of heart. It is the place we find Self-love and are no longer subject to the whim of outer influences or opinion.

Remember this—nothing you will see of anger, fear, or hate in another can be anything other than a call for love.

Love can only permanently exist in all of us, and its lacking will create an intentional, hurtful, and purposeful reaction from its host.

Choose an action that will move you away from a possible trigger or reaction until you are centered in Self.

If we did not have pain and fear as master teachers, then how would we know our capability of the power we possess to recreate our self anew and be wiser by the experience? If you are the all-loving Self that is capable of complete forgiveness and love, then to know this must stem from the place of not knowing this. The opposite of something brings it into knowing; hence, pain and fear are our guides to love and forgiveness.

Let us not look at problems as problems, but as chances to rediscover Self. If you do not do this, then you are accepting that you are insignificant and without purpose within the complexity of universal intelligence. How can someone like you—someone who is complete, capable, and complex by creation—be insignificant? It doesn't make sense. We have just lost our way; that is all. We are all on the path of finding it again—and we will.

Reality is what we know is real. Yet only love and loving connection are real. Our purpose within this amazingly awe-inspiring universe is to remember these things and reconnect to them in physical form. It is time to have faith in the greater plan of life. Accept and forgive each other, for nothing else is more powerful then unity. In unity, there is unity consciousness. It is through this consciousness that global changes will occur. Consciousness is belief in Self and all others that are one source in creation. Forgive, and we will all experience monumental changes in the world.

Remember the peace that you will feel almost instantaneously when you start to forgive. Forgive for a day, as we discussed earlier, and feel the difference within your body.

Don't discard these feelings or give up on them because you fear losing control. Loss of control is a prerequisite to healing. Even giving up judgments, criticisms, and idle gossip will create that fear. In accepting and forgiving, you may feel you are losing control at first; the truth is that for the first time in your life, you actually will be gaining control!

Remember that in your healing, people will try to get you to react. The reason is that they are feeling uneasy that you are no longer connecting to their drama—the drama that allows them to feel alive, connected, or validated.

Our purpose is to be aware of these reactions and know they are expressing pain. Simply observe and be aware. In the light of your consciousness, the attacks of others will fade away. After a time, they will no longer be able to attack you, draw you into their drama, needle your support, or whatever means they go by. Your silence will be the mirror of their pain. They will have no choice but to look at themselves. Be silent and connected, and you will start the process of healing in others. You see, people need a reaction to feed their reaction; in a way, this justifies their position. Don't allow it. Simply don't attack, condone, or validate an unacceptable condition. Stop feeding energy to it, and it will not exist. It will cease to exist for you the moment you are aware of it and choose to not react to it. This is forgiveness!

Allow others to find their paths unobstructed by opinion.

By your non-reaction to another's pain, the negative energy being signaled at you can no longer be fed its own life energy. This negative energy will need to be vented in other areas of their lives until, through your continued non-reaction, they are forced to face their unforgiving self. The pain we all bring to our reality is the pain by which we learn. Forgiveness of self and others is the key to peace and prosperity. Forgiveness will enrich you, and love will emanate from your very being. It will be felt by all and eventually totally accepted as the only path by you. It is the path to your salvation—to total peace and joy.

In the light of forgiveness, you will heal many, and the feelings of love you experience will be like nothing you have ever experienced.

A Process of Forgiveness

1. At the moment you feel unease in your body, note where it is.
2. Be aware that you are not aligned to your true values; you are disconnected to your inner you.
3. Sit quietly, and place your awareness to your body pain. Say what you are feeling—grief, anger, resentment, loneliness, and so on. Simply drop the

feeling and be aware once again of the physical pain.

4. Breathe inward, and allow the breath to carry this pain with it. After a short time, your body will feel rested.

5. Now you have isolated the negative energy that fed your thoughts. Simply observe them.

6. As the thoughts come, realize what those thoughts are.

7. Continue to sit quietly and breathe.

8. Ask yourself in the inner silence of self, "What part of my past caused me to feel this way?" Remember that your negative thoughts stem from your past.

9. Recognize any resemblance between your feelings and that past.

10. Forgive yourself for your reactions—for carrying the shame of that past for so long. Recognize that you are now in control of your life!

    Use positive affirmations:

    • "I am now in control of my life."

    • "I forgive those I now recognize for holding me in their shame, and I forgive myself for carrying it for so long. I send them love and offer myself love."

    • "I am okay in Self."

11. Know that those who you reacted to have helped you recognize and release the part of your past that kept you prisoner within your mind and body. They helped liberate you, and you love them for it.

This is true forgiveness!

CHAPTER THIRTEEN

The Three-L Rule

"Life is too deep for words, so don't try to describe it, just live it."
—C. S. Lewis

What did I give . . . money?

According to my world, that was the answer to life—but what about according to another's reality? I obviously assumed I knew . . . but did I ask anyone their true needs or wants? And if they told me, did I listen? No, I knew better. I gave people what I believed they needed instead, and I thought I could make them understand eventually. Such was my belief. I would resist life in every way to achieve my goals, which were attached to my obsessions.

Could I just accept life? Nope! I could not. I didn't trust life to give me what I wanted. I felt solely responsible, and what I believed I needed for my sense of worth was to provide others with what I deemed important to give.

I was tormented by my relentless thinking and actions.

Could I love? No, there was no time for that. I was too busy resisting life, achieving, and filling my sense of lack with all things outside Self.

Learn to Give

Giving is my favorite subject. For years, I gave. I was very giving; yet in hindsight, what was my motive? What I learned was not to give to the point of exhaustion or as a means of control. Both are acts of low self-worth. This is very important in the act of giving. To become dependent on a condition of giving—to win favor, control, or remedy another—will take away from you; your action will give permission to the other to keep taking. Expectation is all too easy and is a path to resentment.

In a world of give and take, we often see the givers give too much and the takers take too much. Sooner or later, lack of appreciation by both will become a topic of concern. The receiver will feel disempowered, and the giver will feel unappreciated. Neither party expresses their true needs or wants. They repress their true feelings. Money fixes—doesn't it? In the absence of Self-love it can be very destructive.

The art of giving is to give either when the heart tells you it is time to help someone in need or to someone who genuinely asks for assistance that you are able to provide. However, if that person makes a habit of asking you—meaning, if they continually take advantage of you by regularly asking you to do something they simply do not wish to do themselves or if they choose to look after their needs and wants without consideration of yours—then you should simply refuse any assistance. Just stop, be polite, and set a boundary; say that you will not do this for them any longer. This will satisfy your creeping resentment, put an end to the guilt you may feel for not saying "no" sooner, and also teach that person a valuable lesson in learning to give.

Giving and receiving are both loving acts, provided they are genuinely felt with love within the giver and the receiver. If these acts come from a place of doing through expectation or guilt, then the reality takes on a new meaning. Now instead of love felt, the exchange is being compromised to cover real feelings, desires, needs, and wants. In contrast, from a loving perspective, there is a great deal of joy in both giving and receiving—and with them, validation, a sense of Self-worth, care, and nurturing. All are acts of love.

We need to be able to receive graciously as well in order to eliminate expectation so the loving act of receiving is felt as validation of the person giving. Now a sense of Self-worth and love is felt once again by the giver. Any giving and receiving by these same people will be deeply acknowledged, appreciated, and valued. The lesson of giving will be learned.

I heard a saying once that I never forgot: "I will dance the way you whistle." What I found relevant about these words is that when the tide turned and I experienced the abuse of my partner—when her resentment was being vented—it became as if I no longer heard the abuse. Instead, I felt worse. I felt even guiltier and blamed myself for her or her family reacting this way. This continued on, and

I allowed it to continue from the guilt I felt of inappropriate acts I committed during the marriage. Yet I should never have accepted abuse of any kind, and my silence should have been my reply instead of the likeminded thinking and reacting abusively. At this particular time, my Self-worth was very low. I felt like a complete failure. I looked at only the worst elements of my life. I allowed my assorted childhood pains to consume my life and dictate its terms. These pains ruled my life, thus allowing me to take the abuse and give permission for it to continue. I would give materially to compensate and when I did not feel appreciated; attack was my only reply.

These are the patterns my wife and I communicated by for thirteen years. We gave to compensate instead of giving to love. Lack of appreciation was the only conclusion. Our roles were reversed.

I didn't dance to her whistle. Her whistle was abuse, and my dance should have been silence—the dance of Self-worth, not Self-hate; the dance of not giving, as I was simply not receiving. Giving from love was not the recipe I was taught. I was taught, "I will buy my way out of this." This attitude simply kept my wife in a state of resentment, for how was her Self-worth improving? How was she being validated? I was literally manifesting and reinforcing an abuse-to-receive mentality, and for me, this lack of appreciation was followed by resentment. Negative energy was reinforcing itself in the other.

What you wish to strengthen within yourself, you must give away first. Do you want Self-worth? Then give another Self-worth. Do you want Self-love? Then do not accept abuse or any loveless act; give love, even if that means silence. Do you want fear? Then allow fear to continue. Do not fear that what you give will be lost; it is only lost by false perception, as this is how we were conditioned to believe. What you give will be strengthened in whatever form it is given. When in doubt, remember to ask the question, "What would love do now?"

> My wife and I spent our entire lives giving. She would give to feel a sense of worth that was lost to her while growing up. She was expected to be the perfect daughter—this was always expected! I gave to her financially within our relationship, believing this to be the solution.
>
> For both of us, it was exhausting.
>
> The workplace was no different. As time went by and more success was achieved, I reached a point where almost no boundaries existed. This absence of boundaries gave permission to the takers to keep taking and draining any emotional energy that remained. Little to no time was available for me or my family at the end of most of my workdays.

The personnel that I employed or partnered with simply kept taking without regard for anyone else or the financial affairs of the business. This was draining. Due to the "rather the devil you know" syndrome, I went on and kept giving. Simply put, I made every excuse why it could not be afforded, but it didn't stop the constant asking. First, one person would ask for something; then the other would ask, and on and on it went—people asked for pay rises and time off, followed by holiday liberties. The more I gave to remedy, the more it continued. I had made enough money; therefore, I was too complacent to retrain or lesson the risks by changing personnel. This became more obvious. I simply kept up appearances and gave in to the demands of my team. I stayed with the team that kept asking. It got to the point that each did less, delegated more and determined their worth to the organization based on pay rises and liberties.

Staff turnover was high. The unfortunate few who couldn't speak up or were controlled by the power-hungry, assertive personnel were silenced by intimidation tactics to quiet any perceived threat to the power players, hence creating internal pressure and loss of very good staff. Doesn't all life mimic, in some way, the macro level of group consciousness? All this is done for the most ego-driven and assertive, leaving a trail of despair for so many. There was always an excuse, as the managers, directors, and long-term employees fought for position because the CEO opted for the same path—complacency over creativity.

After twenty-five years in my role as CEO, I was spent, exhausted, and unable to break free of my unease through my lack of confidence to change my reality: the job, the pressure, the staff, the aggression and relentless doing, the drama, covering up my past but merely accepted more of the same. This was at the expense of the ones I loved; it was all from my fear of love. All this was done to keep my little world in place; all the while, I believed it was for someone else—my family. Perhaps this rings bells. Isn't this a snap view of so many of us and our modern world? Where is the love—the genuine, heartfelt giving and receiving? Where is the concern for the less assertive or the duty of care to the ones that could not or would not speak up?

Was I, as manager of so many, really giving? Or, like them, was I just playing a role—an ego role—all of us used to fill a void of despair with feelings of separation within all? No, this was not giving, for giving has to be heartfelt and well received for it to be a loving act. All giving should be a loving act or simply not given.

What are you teaching? Any act of giving for the purpose of control, manipulation, or deriving its base from your feeling of Self-worth or another's is not beneficial to either you (the giver) or the receiver. The only result will be resentment and lack of gratitude and appreciation.

> *Each member knew of remuneration given to another, and a few disgruntled antagonists (who should have been removed) started rumors of favoritism. The amazing thing is that few businesses have the courage to say no. It is a strong and very effective word in the art of giving and should be used more often—yet not from a selfish perspective. Giving can only be felt within. We know who should be given something and who should not, yet we rarely listen to our Self.*
>
> *I was exhausted from years of expansion and planning, keeping the team together, and dishing out advice and assistance to the ultimate detriment of my marriage and the business as I knew it. This was actually a good realization. I eventually realized that this business took much away from my time I had available for my family. I just couldn't—or perhaps wouldn't—find in myself the time to share quality time with my own family.*
>
> *My family members were the ones I truly loved. My past did not allow this quality of life to evolve. The need was to keep busy. I feared the intimacy I had been deprived of in my childhood.*
>
> *My wife, who fought hard to be the perfect wife (and to the most part was), simply had had enough as well. From years of looking after her siblings from the age of eight or ten to being the perfect sister and help for her family, she continued in life as she had been taught. She did everything for everyone else except spend quality time for herself.*
>
> *The perfect wife did everything for me and my kids, forever denying her needs and wants. She never spoke up; instead, she complained about issues unrelated to her real needs. She lacked appreciation in me for the lack of time and love I showed to her and the children. Yet it wasn't until late in our marriage she made this felt.*
>
> *Neither of us spoke up and demanded what we wanted until it was too late. The marriage collapsed under the weight of it all.*
>
> *We were both very giving, but neither of us was able to sustain everything and everyone within our lives. Our lives were effectively lived*

outside of us. There was precious little for us or the family. Effectively, we gave more then we received. The little leftover energy we had for ourselves meant we spent a world apart, even when together. Where was the love?

If we receive a genuine, kind gesture from another—a small gift—then the gratitude felt within leads us to a point of reciprocal acknowledgement. To not receive well is a clouded judgment of either control or lack of self-esteem: "I'm not good enough" or "I'm too good."

Sooner or later, this will play havoc in your life. You will feel the consequences of disempowering another, or the feelings you have of low esteem will implode and reach a breaking point. You need to look at your own self and recognize when to spend quality time with your Self.

Giving is a beautiful thing. To see the eyes of another light up in happiness and appreciation is the magnetism of giving for some of us. Is it inherent or taught? Either way, your boundaries must be maintained for the giving to be appreciated and reciprocated—otherwise you are giving an invitation to someone to keep taking. Boundaries are established when the giver does not compromise personal values.

We must learn the difference. To give to gain is compromise. To give as a means of control can only end in disappointment. In disappointment, the giving is lost to both the giver and the receiver! It is easily replaced by resentment and a lack of appreciation. In today's world, this is all too common.

It is time to look within and see the level of commitment you give or the generous gifts given and ask the very important questions, "What is my motivation for doing this?" and "Is it going to benefit or hinder the other person?"

Giving is a blessing, and it is time we learned to receive as well. It is not wise to teach someone to take, for thereafter, his or her life will be made more difficult—particularly if it is your child you are teaching or passing knowledge to. If your choice is to give and bless another, then accept his or her blessing graciously in return. If it is a charitable act and the giving is isolated to your feeling a need to help another soul, then of course no acknowledgment will be given in return, for none is required. The loving act is sufficient; the universe will do the rest—you can be sure of that.

Giving is one of the greatest joys in life. We must make sure it remains a joy and does not become a chore because we do not establish a boundary and ignore our own needs and wants, stopping others from attaching to our giving and us from attaching to our giving as a form of communication or control. The joy will be rewarded with joy, and if the moment is a small gift or a certain time with someone to help one in need, you are in the moment of creating joy for another and inner joy of Self.

Learn to Accept

Acceptance of life contains faith for the creation of peace and joy in your life. The missing ingredient that most of us would benefit from is acceptance of all that is and all that occurs. This is the missing ingredient when all you desire is a whisper away. To not accept leads to resistance, and resistance will stop a desire happening. Faith is acceptance. It is letting go, trusting in the universe and in yourself, knowing that you are being provided for, and knowing that only the best of what is will be served to you.

The inner Self is made of faith, and in it is complete acceptance. The access to the soul is a place within you consisting purely of love of all things, people, and species, and life in all its form. The soul is a place within you of great creativity, and in that creativity are your wellness, joy, and complete peace. There are no more battles to fight and defend here. Your life becomes yours for your choosing; it is not at the mercy of your thought, but in command of it. As you command, so will it be.

Acceptance is the key to this: meaning, a letting go of resistance, which is the mind-identified state that keeps us bound to material possessions and life attachments without the joy and peace of being who we are. The inner you is an echo of love, which is the basis of all creation. Wholeness is felt in this state deep within. It is here that separation can no longer exist. It is of love that thought manifests pureness and creativity. In this state, your attachment to the outer form is no longer relevant. Here you are free to determine all that is and all you desire as loving. Nothing else can exist, for here you are immersed in your true, deeper oneness, which is called Self. That oneness is one with all that is.

You were not created separate from anyone or anything. You are part of, and whole within, everything in existence. God did not abandon us and create us to hurt and feel pain. We decided our destiny for the soul's purpose of our realizing our greatness. Acceptance of life is being content with the faith of knowing that we are created in love. Yet we fear it. We often believe that love is nothing but a wish, and outside our grasp. Our search is for the meaning of who and what we are.

Our belief is that we were created as single, separate entities. We believe we were made to fight and struggle for our survival against all other single separate entities. Even to reflect on this thought now seems absurd. How can we be separate from all of the wonders of creation: the valleys, the mountains, the sea, the sky, birds, the water, the fish, species of all kinds, the Amazon, the Arctic, and the solar system?

Is there any logic to the thinking that God created the wonders of the universe, our planet, and us—the greatest of creations—and left us separate and to die without any connection or existence to all that is? Would God end it all finally with death and passing from this life to non-existence? If this is the cruel intention of his creation, no wonder we are afraid of God. I suppose he could have created us in a less than magnificent world and not gone to this trouble if we were so insignificant.

Absurdity has to stop. You are magnificent, as are all things in creation. Yet you are probably the most magnificent of all creation, because you can create. You do it every day in many ways—unconsciously, perhaps, but nevertheless creating. You are, therefore, like your creator. We may choose to create consciously, like him, or continue to unconsciously create, thereby making our lives more difficult.

Acceptance of all that is means living in the now—this very present moment in time where no time exists. There is no past—a linear description of time—and no future in the here and now. In this state, you are accepting, for you are not judging and consumed by anxiety of past or concerns of being somewhere else in the future. You are accepting of this very moment, and that is life itself.

Focus intently on a flower. Look at it, pick it, and look even closer at it. Smell it. Feel its petals. Just do it. Remember what it feels like to smell the roses. Take time to focus intently on a gift of creation and become aware of this moment.

In this state, there is no fear. There only exists a moment of complete acceptance. Acceptance is the key to peace and joy within, for the fight can no longer exist. There is no longer resistance unconsciously created by your need to defend or resist all you have, all you have acquired, or all you feel you lack. This moment in time may only represent a small window for you to feel a different reality to things, but it is important, in that this moment will offer you recognition of the greater benefit that lies within your grasp. This benefit is so great that all you have and all you perceive you are will change in reality so dramatically that life will have complete meaning to you, and your purpose will have complete direction.

Acceptance of all that is allows the means to live between the inner Self and outer world in peace. You are no longer subjected to the false perceptions you once held and lived your life by. There is no joy in your false perception. False perception is the ego state of resistance to all that is. Our ego depends on our attachment to things outside us; it is based in fear. Therefore, its life form cannot exist deep within us, in the place of pure love. This separate, other self—a disconnected and non-accepting self—pushes or pulls its way through life, acquiring things, and medicating to relieve the feelings of separation. Deep within is your loved-filled being, through which your past conditioning and teaching have separated your outer self from your inner Self. The adapted ego self now runs your life from your loving, inner Self—and here lies the problem. All problems are but one; all problems are based on separation. Separation is non-acceptance. Your shadow is leading the dance of your life.

To find the path within is to free your adapted self to your true Self. This is done by acceptance of your adapted self and awareness of your need to connect to your inner Self. The inner Self is the all-loving state of all within all creation— complete acceptance. We all realize in our deeper subconscious the absurdity of thinking we are separate from God, our higher power, or the life energy which created space and form. We have all doubted, at some point in our lives, that this cannot be all there is to us, our existence, or the path we have chosen. We believe that because of our lack of faith.

Our separation—born from non-acceptance of life and created by false teaching—has become who we are. Fear of losing what we have acquired or possess has become our false temple—our worship. It is sad that the world we live in is the world in which we now must bring up our children, a world in which we sit idly by and choose to do little about the problems. It is a world where death and destruction are readily accepted as a way of life.

Acceptance is now. It is time, and you owe it to yourself to look beyond the manmade self that has been created by your conditioning. You are capable of changing the world. Accept all things with faith and the belief that you will, in return, be abundantly looked after; this is vital for your salvation.

Acceptance is forgiving. Forgive all people and all things that have occurred in your life. Make that decision now. Look within, for it is a place where life will take on new meaning for you. Forgive, for love of Self cannot reflect a thought of separation. To forgive is to eliminate fear. Forgiveness is difficult, for the ego does not want to forgive. It is made by you to protect you from your feeling of separation from God, your neighbor, and life itself in all forms. The idea that you should take what you can and give little in return needs to be replaced by giving all you can and having no expectation of getting in return. Your faith will change what you get, for what you get will be given freely. What you give will strengthen you, and you will be given.

To want more love, give more love. To want peace, give peace. To want your children happy, show them your happiness. If you desire anything, simply give it. You must think about what you wish to receive and then simply give it. If you want more time for your wife, then give her time; if you want more money, then give money. Work out in quiet and solitude what really matters to you, for most of us only give this idea fleeting moments of awareness and then discard them as irrelevant when they stand to oppose the ego state of mind in acquiring things outside us. The idea that we have no time becomes our way of life, and our hostility, anxiety, or resentment protects this state of mind. This creates the drama we have become engrossed in.

The drama has become our addiction to life; we believe the drama is life. It gives us the false sense of aliveness. How dare we think of the things which truly would make us happy, because we don't deserve this life yet? We believe we simply haven't punished our self from doing enough to deserve it. Let us keep punishing our self as this will satisfy our thirst for feeling separate, not knowing we created this separation from false belief. If we knew this, surely we would stop doing it immediately. To continue would amount to insanity, or at the very least, a delusional state of belief in nothingness.

Let go of outer resistance, and go within. Forgive those you deem unworthy. Forgive yourself for the same affliction. Accept all that happens and all you experience. Let all be as it is, as all of it is universally supporting your evolution. Life energy is providing you the seeds for change. Resistance, for example, is as important to you at this stage of your evolutionary process as it is the means by which you are brought back to awareness.

So accept even resistance! Eventually, when you realize that what you resist will simply not go away, you will seek a different path and thereby create a new reality. Hence, in this stage of your evolutionary process, resistance has a purpose. Start to see this purpose, and you will start to accept life! There is no escaping the outcome, for the outcome is truth—truth born from love—and nothing will stand before your soul and its truth ultimately. Therefore, the sooner we connect to truth, the sooner life offers up its bounty.

We can continue to resist all that is all our lives. Prior to death, we can be aware of what we ultimately must know, or we can choose right now and right here to seek a new path. That path is the path of acceptance, which consciously creates peace and joy. Whatever you choose in this state is yours. Without outer resistance, we are no longer burdened by a world seen through blinkers or the tinted glaze of our reality steeped in the uneasiness of never having enough. The world as we see it is not real. How can it be real if we do not accept it? We do not accept it if we continually resist it. Accept resistance. Own it. Feel no guilt toward the behavior, and then drop it. Change the behavior.

Negative thought will feed and fuel more negative thought. This is the requirement of negativity. It is an energy within the cycle of life that requires more of the same in order to feed and stay alive. Like all energy, survival is its quest. Stop negativity in its tracks by present moment awareness and acceptance of all that is and all that happens, and the life force of negativity will dissipate. It will no longer acquire a foothold in your domain and thereby release you to create anew.

Negative thought can be stopped by replacing it with positive thought or present moment awareness and total acceptance of all that occurs. Do not beat yourself up for having a negative thought. Accept these negative thoughts, and then you will be able to release them. Each time you feel a body pain, you are feeling a sense of separation from Self. As this occurs, be aware and realize that you are no longer in the present moment. In fact, you will be living in a past moment or future time. Anxiety and concern will then rule your life. Catch the thought feeding the pain, and again, this present moment awareness will cut the link to a series of thoughts that are feeding on one another for their very survival. One negative thought will need to burden you with another and then another. The perfect day is ruined by a chain reaction of negativity or a belief that the world is against you. See how you react to a negative thought. There are many avenues of release from a negative thought; unfortunately, in an unconscious state, that release is with more negativity. Born from self-pity, resentment, and blame, your non-acceptance of what is occurring will manifest a poor reaction and an outburst of grief or emotional turmoil. The negative pattern will continue until you become consciously aware of it.

Once the light of truth is shown to this negative reality we have created, it stops. In awareness, we realize that the path we are on is not real. It cannot be real. It can only be a clouded, distorted view of a world shrouded in pain. Who wants pain? It is the very thing we try so hard to avoid. But through our lack of knowing where to find the solution, we delve deeper into it. It is as if the pain we cause and feel will somehow alleviate its existence. Anger, attack, grief, self-pity, blame, hurting your neighbor, taking, resisting life, winning over someone, control, resentment, and manipulation are all forms of non-acceptance. Yet we display these feelings and behaviors as if by doing so, we will win over, control, and ultimately be accepted. We cannot, because the other—regardless of how consensual it may appear—requires love and security of Self as much as you. Sooner or later, the reality of this must become their experience. You no longer will control or win an argument, and the result will be a breakdown in communication, which to you will violate the very core of who you think you are.

The resulting path will be one of despair in some form. Grief and depression will be all too common. Your reality will be seen as the center of your world, and little else will have any significance as you fight to protect the image you have created or hung on to—what you thought was lost. There is no easy path to non-acceptance.

The path can ultimately only be like the path of all life force: total acceptance. It is here—and only on this path—that permanency and fulfillment reside within complete peace and joy, its core centered from a loving acceptance. It is here that you will discover the true reality you have always searched for and never found.

Your acceptance will relieve your false belief in impossible burdens!

Learn to Love

Every emotion that we have either comes from love or fear. The five natural emotions of grief, anger, envy, fear, and love are different forms or expressions of love. In his book *Conversations with God, Book 3*, Neale Donald Walsch describes these five emotions as "natural" because we are born with them.

In essence, we are beings of mind-body-spirit. Being mind, body, and spirit means that we can create at three levels simultaneously. Creation comes from making choices and decisions about what we will to be. In choosing, the mind operates at three levels: the levels of logic, intuition, and emotion. The emotion felt in the body is a byproduct of the mind and intuition of the spirit.

All is linked to spirit, as the body and mind are housed within the spirit. The spirit is the dominant, balanced, and consistent aspect of the triune beings that we are. Yet it is here that we see and feel the fundamental difference of our creation and the way in which we can express or distort love. *Conversations with God, Book 3* wonderfully refers to the five natural emotions. These emotions, it says, in essence all stem from one dominant emotion: love.

Walsch outlines Dr. Elisabeth Kübler-Ross's teachings on the five natural emotions. If we allow these emotions to be expressed in a healthy manner as children, then they are dealt with well as adults. For example, if grief is allowed to be expressed in a healthy manner when you are a child, then as an adult, you are unlikely to experience depression. But in reality, the world is in crisis because we don't express grief in a healthy manner. Almost one in five people in western society experience depression, with enormous amounts of drugs—both illegal and legal—being used to combat the effects.

The etymology of the word "emotion" is the French verb "emouvoir," meaning to "stir up" and from the Latin verb "emouvere," meaning to "agitate." Emotion affects the body and is fed by the mind, thus reenergizing itself. Children experience grief to repel sadness or loss. It is normal and should be respected and lovingly consoled in the child, thus giving the child permission to grieve and pass through it as a healthy, normal experience.

The same goes for the each other of the four emotions. Anger in children is the means by which they can say they do not like something and say "no" to it. If anger is disallowed and the child is told he or she is wrong to be angry, the anger will manifest in the adult as rage. Repressed anger becomes violent, irrational behavior; rage is the consequence.

Envy in a child who is supervised and accepted will prevent jealousy as an adult, in most cases. Envy is a normal childhood emotion often seen between siblings for getting ahead. If repressed, jealousy in adulthood becomes apparent. Jealousy is a cruel, destructive emotion.

Fear, again a natural emotion born within us, allows us to anticipate things that are dangerous. It allows the child to understand caution. If repressed, the child grows to adulthood suffering panic attacks. Panic inhibits and limits one's experiences; it prevents life experiences and joys.

Love is the natural emotion. It is who we are, how we were created, what we came from, and what we will return to. If love is expressed to our children without limitation or conditions attached, then the children will grow up into loving adults, in most cases. Life will be well received, and life experiences will be accepted or responded to in a loving manner. However, if love is repressed in the child, then the adult will find it difficult to accept or give love throughout his or her life.

All emotions derive their source from one of the two main emotions: either fear or love. All thought is also based on the premise of originating from either fear or love.

The dominant and only consistent aspect of being is spirit. The spirit derives all power and energy from one source. That source is the source from which it and all things are created: pure love.

Therefore, love is the dominant emotion, and it triggers all responses of all other emotions, including fear. To believe someone wishes to live in fear is as insane as saying we were created for no purpose, which many believe. You cannot believe you have a purpose if the purpose is to be born, struggle, and die. Love is the beginning, the end, and the hereafter.

Fear, in its highest form, is only love that has been distorted. Love is the journey of every soul. Your spirit will always lead you back to the source which you know well. Knowing the source well means that you can be intuitive and always return to its wholesome, nurturing, healing energy, no matter what difficulties or pain you choose to experience. In fact, the more you choose to experience pain created by your resistance and non-acceptance of life, the faster you will return to it. You gravitate to it because you are it. You are the love of all that is; that is how you were created.

Relationships are the highest form of completeness—especially intimate relationships that we can experience in physical form. That is why we gravitate to them. It is the sense of completeness that relationships offer that makes them highly sought after.

Unfortunately, our love was distorted while in our childhood, and throughout our growing up years and the understanding of what we know to be real within—who we truly are—was lost in translation. The path to learning then becomes difficult, and the pain experienced from the separation felt is almost intolerable.

It is in relationships that our greatest lessons or greatest opportunities exist for us to find the balance of all that we are. The opportunity exists to experience enlightenment, which is the bridge between the physical and non-physical realms. The path to peace and joy is often referred to as heaven on earth.

Every thought either comes from fear or love, and all fear is an expression in its highest form as love. Love is the beginning and the end. Yet we have come to fear it, and in the fear, we seek answers. The answers are within you, and in the place of silence is the ability to gain access to the all-knowing, from which all is answered. Prayer, faith, and belief are all inner knowledge, and the prayer that is said with faith and belief will be answered. Love is the quest, and with love, all you desire can manifest into your reality.

It is made manifest and real, as the law of the universe will synchronize with your spirit and harmonize mind and body so you, the triune being, will consciously create. You will create in love from the all-loving Self.

Learning to love is about forgiveness. If the greatest experiences we have come from our relationships, then our greatest learning and path to Self-fulfillment is within the power of forgiving and freeing the mind and body of emotions that will limit your experiences and keep you in a separate reality from what you are seeking.

If you look at distorted love and see the world we are currently in operating in fear, then the lessons we teach our children and our attitudes towards our neighbors must change in order to positively acquire the lessons of love. How we react to our brothers and sisters will directly relate to the quality of our own lives. To judge, criticize, attack, and defend are forms of illusion, separate from and the opposite of love. Yet love has no opposite; this is a divine dichotomy, and forgiveness is the only way to access the knowledge of this. Forgiving is loving. Forgiveness is freedom—your freedom.

Love is all there is. Everything in existence is made of love. If love had an opposite, then what we are simply would not exist, nor anything else. To learn this will be to truly understand creation and your missing link to creating everything in your life you desire. It is pure connection to who you are and everything else that is.

Accept all things from all people, stand without judgment, and your world will be limitless, free, and abundant. This is the lesson we must teach our children, and by giving this to them, we will strengthen it in us. Learning to love must start with us. It must start within, and forgiving yourself is an intricate part of that learning. Forgive all those around you, and know that they are here with you in this journey to evolve, like you, and the path to your salvation is no different than theirs. We are inexplicably linked together. There are hundreds of people in our lives who are crossing paths regularly. Each plays a role in your life, as you play in their lives; all are on a quest to evolve.

We must always return to love and the experiences that will take us there. Love is all there is. We must return to it, as the spirit in each of us will seek only this path. We choose to separate from love for the soul's purpose of knowing what love is. It is our destiny, our journey, and our evolution. When you decide to return to love is entirely your choice. Let's not hand it to our creator; that choice was given to you because of pure love and trust in you.

CHAPTER FOURTEEN

Possibilities

"You and I are essentially infinite choice-makers. In every moment of our existence, we are in that field of all possibilities where we have access to an infinity of choices."
—Deepak Chopra

A world of possibilities exists in every moment of every event in your life. We must have belief in the eternity of all possibilities—the timeless zone where reality is not measured in time but in context. The actual event shall be as you think it.

This is a complex understanding. All your life, you have been led to believe that things only exist in time. We know that time is a human invention to account for movement in space originating from the natural cycles, such as length of time between dark and daylight, moon appearances, earth orbits, etc. We are so conditioned to this way of thinking that it is very difficult to shift to modern scientific and spiritual understandings of all things existing in one moment in time. Past and future no longer have a place, as they can only exist now.

In this state of knowing, what you think is exactly what you create. It cannot be any other way, because the past and future can only exist in this moment. Time as we understand it is linear and horizontal. Yet eternity, as we are coming to understand once again, is vertical. That is, all things occur in this moment; therefore, as you think, you create. Any thought—infinite in number—becomes the basis of all possibility. Based on the premise "as you wish, you shall have" is in an instant.

Eternity does not exist in time, for if it did, it would have a beginning and an end. The complexity of all that is would be hampered by the past and future as we understand them, and the world as we know it could not exist. The universe could not exist.

If we take a mere sample of our lives, and add the past to them, then more times than not we are adding judgments and fear of those experiences within them. Living in the past is living with our past experiences and the conditioning by which those experiences came about. They came about by other's fears being projected onto us. This is what time affords. It affords fear, deadline, expectation within a time frame, and anxiety as a consequence. Along the way, attack and defense become the attributes of our lives. "Do before you die" becomes our motto! Attitudes based on fear are created by the past—the anxiety these attitudes bring through judgment, and thereafter, the future hope of what might be and the concerns connected with constantly thinking of means to achieve that future. Any fear associated with desire or want will stop the desire or want from manifesting into reality. The universe will not support giving you something that is connected to fear, as fear does not exist in true reality.

The stories of our lives interfere with the natural, progressive order of our creative abilities, and many lessons are learned along the way. These lessons are there for the purpose of us understanding our capabilities as natural creators. In a way, this puts us on the path of remembering what we are and what we are able to be, do, and have, as it is and was intended by our very creation.

Time, in effect, breaks down creation or pure love into little bits in which we can experience something that is opposite to love, although in reality love has no opposite. Each little bit can be experienced with each other little bit of experience in whatever infinite combination in order to know every little bit of the whole—pure love, which is the infinite source of energy of all things. To understand this infinite source of energy is to ultimately infinitely create. In the language of eternity (eternal no-time) it is described as—you think it, and you create it instantly. However, to appreciate this creative power and evolve, we must experience each little bit in conjunction with every other little bit to know the entirety of all of it—creation itself, pure love—hence our reasoning to physical form—expression of the totality of our experiences. It is the path to complete understanding and awareness of who we are and who we wish to be. Is it complex? Not really. Work with this; just accept for the moment and allow it to come to you in little bits.

If we take this reasoning for a moment and think of all the drama we create or live with, which detracts from our own quality of life, then at the same time try to imagine the power and complexity of our universe and the stuff that makes it tick—universal intelligence—we surely realize it would not be possible for all to exist with an ounce of the same drama. How could such complexity and magnificence—of which you are an integral part—exist with the slightest hiccup of fear or drama? It would be too ludicrous to even perceive, for what foundation could exist in the overwhelming intelligence of life? Surely not a detracting energy force—a negative energy created within the drama of life. Drama creates the pain for us to choose alternative paths. This creates the infinite number of possibilities to choose from for a reason.

We must keep returning to present moment awareness and thinking if our purpose is to evolve or enlighten, existing in the field of all possibility for this moment—right here and now. This is the way universal intelligence works. It does not exist in time; therefore, it does not exist in fear at all. It just is. Therefore, your life—with the exemption of past and future—also must exist without fear. There cannot be fear if you are not thinking of the past or future. What is just is, and as you observe without judgment in present moment awareness, so it shall be.

It is in this state of "present-ness" that creative thought abounds. It is that state in which universal intelligence operates. Yet we do not remember it. We are so conditioned by time that our lives are full of thinking, planning, and judging because we are led to believe the end of our lives means the end—this is far from the truth.

We create a myriad of possibilities in which to live our lives. Those possibilities express all different forms of fear—self-created strategies to eradicate fear—yet we cannot think with fear to eradicate fear because the effect can only result in more fear and therefore more anxiety, concern, worry, pain and unease. It is through these experiences of fear that we start to look for an alternative path, and on that path we become aware of knowing who we are and what we wish to become.

We were created into perfection. It is not possible to know the awe-inspiring Self from that position of perfection, thus the physical form and life drama created specifically for human experiences unfold for the sole purpose of helping us remember our higher Self. It is from the higher Self that we are guided and ultimately remember and know what we are capable of. Our journey is to remember! The opposite must exist in any situation in order for the situation to be known—fear and love, silence and sound, forgiveness and hate, control and letting go, wisdom and ignorance, up and down, large and small, unmanifested and manifested, and nothingness and matter.

Perfection is love—pure love. To be born to it would be to not truly understand it—accept it, yes, but not understand it! Hence, we have the need to evolve by knowing and creating a greater aspect of it—the law of all life—and the need to understand through its opposite, thus creating anew. Forever expand loving consciousness by truly knowing and understanding love—the opposite of self-manifested experiences of fear!

In the complex and perfect creation of all that is, we were created. In that creation, we have the power to create. In physical form, we cannot remember this, because our lives are so consumed with fear, which stops the belief and faith in knowing the creation of exactly what we desire is possible and instantaneous. Time delays creation; therefore, we do not believe what we create was created by us. We think that what happens to us is from some outside force and random by design.

But it is not—it is exactly as you created. All things that occur to you and around you are what you have brought into your life at exactly the right time of its occurrence.

You may be hit by a feather, bowled over by a brick, or run down by a Mack truck, and then you are back on your path. It is in the drama of life that awareness of perfection is born. In every moment, the opportunity exists for our salvation; it is through infinite possibilities that salvation is born. What is it that you want from this moment? We must all come to the realization of our memories of our higher Self. We must connect within sooner or later; it is the only means by which the universe can unfold perfection. You are its creation. You are perfect, not less than perfect; therefore, you cannot be adrift for long in terms of universal consciousness. You must return to the place of all-knowing, as you are part of it, and life's dramas are the means by which we acquire access to this knowledge and wisdom.

What causes us not to remember our true Self is:

- Impatience, or putting time to things, creates anticipation and anxiety.
- Fear of loss, or the belief in scarcity, that there's "not enough to go around."
- The belief in separation, that we are "here on our own."
- Our conditioning and the teachings we learn through life that create our fears.
- The drama we act out through life, further suppressing those fears.
- Our anxiety and unease, which we have come to normalize.

There are many ways for us to block our desires and create the opportunities for seeking alternative possibilities, creating the seeds of opportunities to return and remember the higher Self. This is a reality that most of the time results from fear.

So what of possibilities? What are their functions and purposes, and what do all possibilities mean?

Your physical existence is for the unmanifested to know its Self. You are created like God to create like him and to be aware of your divine presence. The soul's purpose of divine understanding and evolution is accomplished by being born in physical form and experiencing life and the wondrous multitude of possibilities for it. It is your understanding and your evolution. This is the understanding and potential evolution that cannot exist without knowing who you are and what you wish to become spiritually.

We were created perfect, and we are here to experience things that are less than perfect. You write the tale of your life through your thoughts, words, and actions. Self-created ego assists with the process of what is less than perfect. Ego—the element behind all separation and feeling of lack—creates a world of experience for you to feel pain and fear. In this pain and fear, you have the seed of your salvation and opportunity to understand their opposites: love and joy.

The divine dichotomy is that love has no opposite; therefore, love simply needs to be remembered. It is remembered through the experience of fear.

It is the knowledge through experience and feeling of love that your soul seeks. Your soul's purpose is felt only in the subconscious connection to Self. Hence, it is felt in meditation as a state of bliss. The universe can only support this, as it cannot defy creation; it cannot allow anything other than this ultimate goal to exist in your reality. The purpose of life now has meaning and connects you to everything else in the universe—all people, all species, and all that is.

You write your tale to teach your self through your experiences what it is you wish to learn (for example, forgiveness, loneliness, grief, and so on). All fear-based feelings and behaviors are part of the greater aspect of knowing pure love. The list is endless, and the combinations of all experiences are infinite. The more we experience our many possibilities, the higher our soul's spiritual evolution will be.

Can you see logic in life with this understanding? It supersedes death and finality; an ending becomes a beginning. How can energy end? It goes on for eternity. You are pure loving energy!

All that is and all that will ever be is now; therefore, this moment in time is your possible realization of all you are—your higher Self. In every moment, there are many, many possibilities. In this very moment, you have many options. Those options will create an effect, anger will create resentment, resentment will create unease in the body and more pain, and a lack of forgiveness will create separation and feelings of low self-worth. All will create opportunity to knowing wisdom. In every moment of your existence are the seeds of wisdom. When will we choose to accept life rather than resist it? It is our choice.

If time is attached—which it is in human, physical form—demands and expectations are placed against that time. The field of all possibilities, which now exist by those demands, expectations, and controls to create sufficient awareness of the separation created by those possibilities, jolts us back into some level of knowing this. Time is the cause of fear. The past and future result in anxiety and concern. As a consequence, attack and defense become a normal cycle of daily events. Forgiveness, tolerance, and understanding are given only minimal persuasion and are quickly eliminated in favor of protecting self and our way of life.

Hence, we have created options through possibilities for the purpose of learning the opposite of what we are in an effort to comprehend more clearly who we truly are and what we wish to become. Our lives are nothing but possibilities, and the possibilities determine our outcome or experiences and give us the greater opportunity to evolve spiritually.

> *I considered the worst period of my life to be when I had been divorced for the second time. I had little children, age four and five, and my eldest daughter, age seventeen, was in distress. Even after my wife left me, I just couldn't let go with acceptance or the realization that if things were meant to be, they would be. No, instead I had to act on every rumor or innuendo I heard and verbally attack my wife. Instead of creating a peaceful, relaxed atmosphere for her to communicate with me, I actually created hostility, and that hostility erupted in her. Regardless of how we felt about each other, there was no common ground for communication.*
>
> *The possibilities we chose were resentment, anger, and guilt mixed together, plus shame and fear. Fear was the basis of all these feelings.*
>
> *When my wife first walked out, we would often meet at least two to three times per week and do a dinner or concert or just be together. It was pleasant, and in hindsight, had I not tried to control the outcome or control her in some way, then our communication would have developed a healthy foundation—something we never had. She couldn't forgive, and I resisted. Hence, our past learning was still in play. Even without fixing my Self, I had an expectation that we would get back together. In other words, the same person she was escaping from was the person trying to use blame, control, money, and guilt to win her over. It won nothing*

but hostility and attack in return. What I needed to realize was that resisting was futile.

There were a number of possibilities I could have taken, yet I didn't have the means or know-how to communicate effectively, and my wife lacked similar skills. What we created by the options we took were hostility, pain, and more hostility. Our communication over the course of the next two years went from poor to worse. Eventually, we couldn't even speak to each other. At the time, those years were perceived as the worst two years of both our lives. Our learning was created by our choices. Neither of us was aware of an alternative path.

Eventually, the lessons of forgiveness, acceptance, and letting go had to be learned—and they were.

We all have choices to make, and those choices will determine whether we live in peace or pain. Choices, if founded in peace, can only result in peace, regardless of what we believe at the time for ourselves to be the better option. For example, we may feel that retribution is a way of making others feel bad, thereby bringing them around to our point of view. Of course, this is a deluded perception that must end in attack and resentment. The universe knows better, and trust and faith will assure only the best outcome possible.

Unfortunately, most of us choose the pain option, and our choices and experiences are reflections of that option. You see, if you create drama, then drama must be returned—or how would you learn to eliminate drama and find peace? If we cannot find peace and love by our actions, then spiritually, we cannot progress. Taking this thought further, if you, as an intricate part of the whole, could not find peace and joy, then how would the universe and all that exists come to exist? It could not, because only in love and peace can anything survive and expand, otherwise it will detract or contract. If the universe detracts, we could not exist. Now do you see your divine purpose? To experience is to know who and what you are—to evolve spiritually to create more love, peace, abundance, bliss, and thereby joy to expand all that is.

It is in our infinite possibilities that we create the means by which we know and understand pure love. It is in this knowing that we create more. We create individually and together; our relationships are the greatest catalyst for knowing this. The field of all possibilities exists within those relationships.

Think of the best possible outcome, and never vary your thought from this outcome. Regardless of what perception your ego can create, dismiss it. Stop, and in the silence of being you, sit quietly and allow the perception of what you don't want to pass. Relax into the moment of now, and allow creative, positive thought to flood your body. The easiest way to do this is to be grateful for what you do have, not what you think you have just lost or that which you do not have.

What you are then doing is unconsciously creating a different reality. If left unchecked, your reality will manifest around the negative thought of not having—of the pain you are feeling—and the result will be grief, despair, and more pain. That will attract to it more of the same. The reality you are choosing now is looking for the same energy to survive. Attack becomes your defense, self-compassion is created from self-importance, and resentment plays out in every area of your life. The neighbor cops it; so does the partner. The children, as a side consequence, feel this, even if it is not directed intentionally, as does anyone else privy to that period of your life who happens to differ in opinion to your own. What possibilities have we adopted in this state?

You create every experience in your life. Your thoughts and words are powerfully and unceasingly creating. Every thought and every word is creating. Together, we are even more powerful creators, and unity consciousness can and will manifest exactly by the same means. Hence, negativity, such as fear of loss of a way of life, can easily result in war or economic hardship.

> *I knew, after a year of bad communication, that enough was enough and there needed to be another way. I knew deep in my heart I truly loved my wife. She was gone. The more I thought about her wrong doings—in hindsight, I can honestly say they were, to a large extent, self-created, wrong perceptions—the more I looked for a reason to attack. All my experiences became self-centered, self-opinionated manifestations that were incorrect, because we end up creating more crap than what actually occurs. There is no silence and rest to find the answers of Self, just more answers to things on the outside to fill the lack on the inside.*

We create drama in our lives, and that drama comes from not being centered in Self. We try to find answers in things, labels, and events. Relying on fear to conquer is a poor perception, and lacking awareness of the higher Self, the only possibilities are to experience more of the same. It cannot be any other way.

Anything that interferes with the natural and limitless expression of the Self will only end in despair. A breakdown must occur until the expression is allowed freedom through experience.

For every event in your life, there are a number of possible outcomes. Which outcome will be directly linked to your choices? Within the silence of Self, the truth of your highest path can be felt.

The destiny you reach will be inexplicably linked to the thoughts, words, and actions you adopt. So choose carefully your thought, and let your words and actions follow.

CHAPTER FIFTEEN

Swimming in the Sky

*"Reverie is not a mind vacuum. It is rather the gift of
an hour which knows the plentitude of the soul."*
—Gaston Bachelard

Dream—consciously dream—and find the place where your soul feels alive and your heart feels content. It is conscious dreaming that heightens your vibrational frequency and sets you on a path of creation. This is not dreaming of things you feel you need to sustain your life—the things you have clung to and thought of incessantly due to feelings of lack. No, this dreaming is your heartfelt, creative desire for people, special places, and things that bring you immense joy within. You desire places where your soul rejoices, your breath is taken away, and joy emanates through you and around you.

Life is there for you to share in abundance. Our thoughts are the first link to creative creation.

Give yourself this time to dream a wonderful dream, not an illusion based in pain. Listen to your favorite music and become engrossed in it. Dream, without fear, the dream the soul knows well. See your children as happy and content. See yourself, your partner, and your family in a loving environment, laughing and enjoying time together alone. See yourself and the ones you care for swimming at your favorite beach or on the shores of a beautiful island or perhaps drinking champagne in your favorite hotel. See yourself camping by a lake with friends and fishing for your food in a place you have always dreamed of going but never did. Imagine kayaking a river you have always thought of doing. Think of a passionate encounter and feel yourself there. See yourself being more accepting and tolerant, and think of the wonderful response you will receive from others. See yourself and your spouse or partner in a loving relationship, happy to be together, laughing, talking, and just being kind to each other.

Dream of what it will feel like to live joyfully, and hold those images for just a while, whether they are of a loving, kind, adventurous, or creative nature. Hold those images in your awareness. See yourself on stage, singing and dancing, because you have always desired that creative element of you be permitted to shine. See yourself helping others and the joy you receive in the look of appreciation they give through their eyes. See yourself meditating in a place your spirit has always wanted to go.

Dream, pray, and listen to music! Have we been conditioned to believe prayer has to also be a certain way? Why can't you pray with the backdrop of your favorite music? Pray for your desires, and allow the music to strengthen your belief for the added power you receive from the joy of your favorite sounds—music that strengthens your spirit. Try it, and allow yourself to experience the joy that will emanate from this practice.

Is there anything more positive than prayer or desire—the power of asking through word with the joy of your chosen sounds?

Yet all too often, we cannot stop to hear any sound—not the sound of nature, the sound of our favorite music, or even the sound of our children laughing. Nor do we take time out to imagine the beautiful things all around us as part of us. That magnificent part of life is a part we fail to see and hear. Instead, we choose "doing" and constant thinking to fuel the drama of our lives over peace of mind. We desperately cling to drama, believing this is our only reality. Without it, we fear we will enter an abyss. It is odd that we intentionally choose to ignore the beauty all around us for fear of missing out. That is all we ever seem to do—miss out on life!

Dream about your desires, as they are yours for the taking. But do not dream a mad, obsessive dream that pushes you and drives you to insanity. We are talking of a beautiful place that is yours for the dreaming. Visualize your place of joy, and whenever you feel the urge of pain creeping in to distract you go to that place. Reprogram your mind to think joyful thoughts and venture into the realm of possibility. We all need to dream.

Perhaps your dreams are of an abundance of material things, rather than of emotional and spiritual desires. Dream of your new home—the one you never thought you could afford. Treat yourself and a friend to a stay at a world-renowned spa center. See a loved one well and healed and in your arms as you jet off together for a week away on a secluded, exotic island. Dream of more money, a better job, or a promotion and recognition in your current job and how that will impact your life and the lives of your loved ones. Buy the car you've always wanted, and feel the feeling of leaving the showroom with it and driving off for the first time.

Most of us were told as children that daydreaming is not allowed and that it would never get us anywhere. Then we are given a clip over the ear. We are asked, "What are you daydreaming for? Get on with it." If daydreaming was prohibited in your household, you were made to feel lazy, hopeless, and limited.

In essence, our natural creative abilities were often dampened, dismissed as laziness, or called useless. Our visualizations were suppressed because of another's own conditioning to believe that the only way to achieve success is through hard work and constant effort, sweating to protect all that is yours for fear of loss itself. How can anyone dream from this point? We are all creative, yet many of us were simply conditioned out of this belief. We are creative, and we can create. It is how we were created. Our creative ability was repressed when we were children and replaced with logic and reasoning—logic which, for the most part, was illogical. Logic and reasoning replaced creativity and imagination, which are our two greatest gifts. Creative thinking is what this world needs, a radical shift in thinking to solve the problems of the world with far less fear and effort expended. This effort frustrates many and leaves them wanting!

We dream all day long, but the dreams we have are clouded with want and stem from fear. The purpose of these dreams is to escape our truth—the truth we are so afraid of, the truth of our past and our learning thus far. Our dreaming is of wanting more and fearing less. Anxiety becomes our friend, drama our obsessive belief that this is the nature of life. Instead, we need to reprogram our minds to positively visualize what is ours for the dreaming. Stop believing things "can't be done" or "can't be achieved," particularly if they bring you and your loved ones joy, peace, rest, bliss, and love. Ours is a fear-based reality, which lacks faith. Fear will prevent dreaming, believing in something, or being creative. It will create in you the same resistance and non-acceptance it has always done. If you resist, then your current reality will persist. Things will not be done, and you will not acquire what you desire—not how you want, that is.

Everything can be done, and everything you desire can be made real for you. We desire our heart's desires too sparingly, often giving up just before realizing those desires into our reality. Simply stop the expectation to the visualization and stop the sand clock to them. Allow all to happen in accordance with the timing suitable for your soul. Expectation and time create resistance, and resistance stops things from happening how you desire them to happen. As to timing, there is no time. It will occur the moment your faith and belief are aligned.

Quick Creation Tip

Know yourself!

Watch how you manifest the small things in life, and think about how you felt inside when you received those things. Think about how easily they came to you.

You will find that you thought of small things once and never thought of them again, and they manifested. Why? What happened was that you thought of your desire and then released it. You did not remember that you sent out your desire and so gave little thought or emotional attachment to the thing you desired afterward.

In fact, because you spoke no word that contradicted what you wanted after sending out your desire the law of attraction was able to do its work.

It is your choice to visualize and then allow, through acceptance, the universe to deliver your desire in the format that it knows will best meet your spiritual need. If we adapt a conscious pattern of behavior through positive thought processing or swimming in the sky—dreaming of heartfelt desires—then this positive connection will provide you extremely positive outcomes. It is negative thought processes that prevent you from creating something as you would like. We need to be mindful to get off that frequency!

Put yourself in a positive state, and then do your utmost to remain in that state by whatever means you choose. Choose visualization through daydreaming and positive affirmations, continually being aware and on the lookout for negative thoughts. React immediately to negative input when your awareness is in a heightened sense of knowledge, and replace those negative thoughts. With practice, it really does get easier. Miracles start to occur.

Do not blame yourself, anyone else, or your higher power for what you wanted and could never get before. We need now replace the want of something with the desire for something, dream our perfect lists of things we desire whenever we feel woe, remain in a positive state without expectation or a sand clock, and allow Self to manifest what it is we desire. We can manifest fear and drama, and now we must relearn so we can manifest the things that offer us love and peace.

If you expect a certain outcome—in other words, you try to control the event and who and what should be given to you—then you are resisting. If you put a time on its arrival, you are resisting. What does resisting do? It pushes away the thing you desire through your obsession or need to control or acquire it—two behaviors that need to be dealt with.

Therefore, in effect, the process of learning to consciously create will not be given until you can learn to let go. In rehab, there was a saying written on the wall of the stairwell, which I read every day: "Let go, let God." In essence, this is what we must have the faith to do. Let the higher power of all—in whatever form that may be for you—take control; then control your behavior and feelings and have faith that the higher power knows what is best for you and knows the most appropriate timing for its delivery.

We all need a spiritual container to put our negative thoughts in—as well as our positive thoughts—allow all to be, and believe in the outcome most appropriate for us at the time. The spiritual container has been lost to us by our teaching. It is time to find your higher power, your connection to the intelligence of all life. Find it, as it is the only thing that will sit above you. It will always be there, regardless of any circumstance detrimental to your reality. It will guide you and is accessed and communicated within the inner silence of Self.

Let us think for a moment and decide how often we would have a negative thought. You see, it's negative thoughts that virtually rule our lives, and one negative thought feeds another and then another—then on and on it goes. What protective mechanism have we been taught to remedy this onslaught? We have virtually no positive solution I can think of. We have been taught to judge, criticize, attack, blame, and so on, and this is an ego-driven, mind-identified state of being.

Our day starts with a hiccup and ends in a nightmare, for we were not given the tools to create a new reality. Meditate and you will feel peace, but as you may know, unrest consumes us in the beginning stages of learning or practicing meditation, because our world has been so consumed with unease. We barely feel this unease anymore; such is our lengthy and continuous conditioning to it or living with it.

Dreaming is a tool we can use to change our state and focus our visualization to a positive desire anytime we choose. If we now take the power of dreaming and visualize ourselves in a joyful place, the art of meditation must immediately start on a softer footing. This positive mental experience becomes easy through practice, because your soul will always gravitate to joy if it is given the opportunity to do so. The soul and spirit are love, and love will not dominate. It is your choice that will allow light in or keep light out. A positive mental experience is joy and love.

We don't daydream, because we were told from very young to stop dreaming. We were told, "You can't have that," "Don't be silly, get those thoughts out of your head," "How could you do that?" and "Get on with it—stop daydreaming." What were we daydreaming for—a better life, perhaps? Was this the envy of those who taught us—who suffered at the hands of not creating their dreams or not living the lives they most desired? The people who told us to stop dreaming then passed this lack of belief to us.

Let us stop this cycle, for in a positive dream state, creation will occur. Dream from belief, and then have faith in your dream. Start believing, be positive, believe all is possible, and it will happen to you! Once you have accepted this, feel how it feels within you. Don't be afraid because you were told it was silly. Think about this. Is it silly to have everything you or your children have always wanted? How would you feel if you could click your fingers and what you wanted was there for you or them? Let us try this state change. We know already that a positive state change emits a higher electrical field of energy—as in the state of joy and bliss—and can only return to you the same like-energy with constant belief through thought, word, and action, creating matter or form.

It's all too hard, isn't it? We have been conditioned for over half our lives or more to believe that life is resistance—and where has that gotten us? Look around—the answers are all around us! When are we going to condition back? When are we going to teach our kids and those around us of a better way?

We are not talking here of one shot at this and then giving up, because throughout our entire lives, we believed it was easier to give up and suffer the pain in defeat—the defeat of not realizing our dreams. Do you know it is far easier to have a positive mindset than it ever is to have a negative one? The reason is that negative energy consumes everything—it takes away from you and leaves you wanting. Positive energy expands and gives life to you. Negative thought takes enormous effort, but it is an effort we are at home with and find easy. Love and positive affirmations are by their very nature effortless, but something which we have long forgotten. Energy is wasted when we hold negative energy. Life becomes a grudge—resentment the center piece and blame and self-pity the consequence.

How good does it feel to read a positive message or positive affirmation from a friend? Then why do we not choose to do it more often?

If we daydream positive dreams and feel our Self absorbed by them, thereby creating the continuous stream of positive thought anytime, our reality must manifest in a positive experience, as the higher vibrational state in which we are now aligned universally must attract to you the experience most appropriate for you.

To create what we desire, we need the thought.

Three Steps of Receiving

1. Daydreaming is a process for positive thought or visualization.
2. Word is next in the process—prayer or positive verbal response when you speak of it.
3. Action is the final step—a positive attitude and outlook that what you desire is imminent and that you need to be grateful for it prior to receiving it.

We must believe in the outcome and not give in to fear of not having what we want. We just need to let go and have faith.

This requires faith that you are being supported by the universe. Faith is the key. It has to be, because if you think about it, how many times have you attempted to create the world you desired and been disappointed it didn't eventuate? We fail to believe, because our control behavior said to us, "It's not here yet; therefore, it's not coming." What's not coming? We couldn't tell anyway, for if any little miracle did happen, we would miss it because we are fixated on a specific thing. If we don't look for the signs of what is being delivered and remain fixated on a specific thing, then of course we will miss the support or gift given.

This is your key to manifesting. We need to dream incredibly wonderful dreams. Have a list of things to do and a list of things you desire that will give you joy, more love, and rest. Think of things that replenish your soul and those you love. Place no expectation for its timing, and allow no anxiety to form part of receiving your desire, for this is negative and resisting. Resisting simply stops you from realizing, as it has to date.

No, this is conscious dreaming and believing in the abundance of life that awaits you when you choose to accept it.

This is the primary difference between having and enjoying all you have, all you have created thus far, or all you will ever have against the constant wanting and waiting and lack of gratitude that we are currently fixated on that makes up our current perceived (often ungrateful) reality.

As for people and things that really make you happy, go there whenever you need an energy boost, a hit of love, joy, bliss, or a positive experience; just do not allow yourself to dwell on things that will bring you pain. Know the difference by realizing your truth—the truth of your past and the truth of what you should be grateful for in your life versus the pain clearly visible by your behaviors. Do not overlook the addictions that we may carry around as baggage in our lives. These may be addictions of food, sex, drugs, alcohol, control, anxiety, love addiction, or any other addiction, for they are simply medicating and obscuring your current pain.

Let the light of truth guide you through your feelings and behaviors, and then have the courage to show gratitude for what is important to you and your loved ones right here and right now. Then dream your heartfelt desires. Become absorbed in that state, and be grateful for your creative gift—the gift given to you at birth, which is the creative power of manifestation. In likeness to God, you were created, but it seems too big a pill to swallow for most. Why is this? Do we really believe we were abandoned by even him? Look for the faith, have the courage to seek love, see the possibilities that exist for you, and believe in your worth and who you are, for you are as you were created. It is your choice to change or not.

Powering up

To power up positive mental energy, sit quietly and go within, in silence, and feel the new sensation that will emanate from spirit within your body.

Consciously breathe, and exaggerate the breath for at least five or more times to relax the body.

Consciously choose a desire, a best possible outcome. Bring the desire into your awareness. Go there, and yet do not become fixated on the image of it. Allow it to come to mind, and experience the journey of the outcome, and then release it.

Sit in silence and just be. Surrender to life. Let life flow through you.

Pray if any negative thoughts crowd your thinking. I say my favorite prayer over and over, applying it as a meditation mantra.

Allow your silence to return whenever you are aware of the peace and serenity within.

Trust that your desire has been sent. Remember that a thought is energy. Energy cannot die. It travels universally, never ending.

Now go on with the day, and have a great one!

Practice this method of swimming in the sky prior to each meditation. Desire. Release. Then sit in silence and breathe. Meditation that starts well often ends well!

Also, when you feel your day is not on track or you are uneasy, sit quietly for a moment and daydream, feeling no guilt in it. Sit, close your eyes, and go to your favorite destination or desire. Imagine yourself there. Play with it, and let your imagination run wild.

(If you'd like to receive a free audio of a guided version of this meditation, go to my website: www.epsilonhealingacademy.com)

CHAPTER SIXTEEN

Sunshine

———————

"The power of imagination makes us infinite."
—John Muir

The center of our world is bathed in light. It is the home of all that exists. It has warm, radiant energy that protects, nurtures, and gives life. It is warm and comforting. It brings peace and happiness by its very existence. No darkness can dwell in its presence. It is eternity and life energy, and it is within the essence of all that is.

All things in life are energy flows, and all are connected to a central consciousness. The energy that gives life to everything else is the sublime energy that has come to be termed the matrix of all matter and non-matter.

The energy flows through this matrix, giving life and sustaining it. We are connected to this energy matrix, as are all things and non-things. It is the nothingness between, around, and within all forms. It is the space by which energy is transferred and communicated. It is the power of the manifested and the non-manifested. It cannot die or be destroyed, as no energy can die or be destroyed.

It continues into infinity and beyond, and its source is the ever-present and all-powerful fullness of creation. It is what we are all a part of. It is how we connect to the greater consciousness, feel its presence, and know it exists. It is felt in the nothingness from which it came and is as much a part of us as the air we breathe.

We come from the light, and we will return to the light. The dark is made by us, and in the knowledge of the dark, we understand and love the light. The unconscious behaviors are often referred to as dark and dense energy, whereas conscious, happy, joyful thoughts, behaviors, and words are referred to as light, high vibrational energy, which is similar to the energy that gives life to all creation.

When we say, "Let's be silent and go within," we are actually physically connecting to a non-physical mode of connectedness or the essence of all life.

It cannot be seen by the eye. It is felt in the body, as it is the source from where we came. It is pure energy: light, high vibrational, universal energy. All of us are connected to each other and everything in existence through this energy. It is the consciousness of all matter, whether a stone or human being.

The purpose of this light is connectedness and life itself. It is as sunlight and has purpose in our physical existence—a light-giving, all-nurturing, loving energy. It is the place of pure happiness and joy. It is the source and sacredness of creation. It is the holy ground of existence where only love can exist. It has no opposite; it is pure love. It is love in which the universe and the universe beyond the universe express themselves. We are talking about the light of creation. Creation does not exist in dark. Don't think of sleep when you think spiritually, as without a body the spirit is free to be all it is—a part of the whole and a part of everything in existence.

All matter is made up of some degree of consciousness. Human form is the highest of this consciousness and vibrates at the highest frequency. Even a stone is made up of consciousness. All consciousness is made of life-sustaining light. It is the light that vibrates as energy of creation.

When we vibrate at a high vibrational rate, we are actually tuning in to pure energy. Pure energy is love energy. We are actually tuning in to and being a part of the light energy of the universe. However, when we are feeling heavy and dark and our thoughts reflect this attitude, then we are not tuning in to the high vibrational energy, and a reality different to what we desire will often occur.

The reason is because the universe will only support your spiritual growth and evolution—what is best for you at the time of your experiences. It is said that when you tune in to positive, happy thoughts, you are being supported to create what it is you desire. This is your reward for connecting. Yet when we choose a different mindset—one of illusion that is based on poor perception—then the energy is as its host: dark, slow, negative energy.

You will receive more of the same until awareness replaces the poor perception. It is your choice whether or not to become aware. Changing your state from the fear or pain of the negative thought will reconnect you to the positive, higher vibrational, joyful energy, and the rewards that you desire will be brought into your reality.

You see, the universe will always support you, whether or not you believe you are down on your luck. Your luck is determined as you create and experience. The purpose of being in human form is for us to know who we are and what we wish to be. That is evolving spiritually. For example, if you wish to understand forgiveness, your purpose in human form will be to have something happen that will give you the opportunity to forgive. While we may understand forgiveness as a concept and even talk about it as if we are forgiving souls, the reality is that the world shows itself to be anything but forgiving. To experience forgiveness—an essential part of expressing love—we must experience the associated pain to be able to have the opportunity to forgive. Our spiritual purpose is to live physically—to be able to break down the many facets of love and experience through feeling all aspects of that love. Hence, through the manifestation of feeling, our creation is able to know itself.

Yet in physical form, the distorted reality we create when love is lost for periods of time allows us to experience every negative element associated to love lost. It is your choice, then, to return to Self and Self-love, thereby being able to express love more deeply. The day you are born is the day you forget from where you came and thereby experience the many aspects of life, love, fear, and pain; your body's death (physical death) is the day you remember creation itself, your return to pure love, and the energy which you are—the spirit as part of the whole. Your remembrance day is full of love and appreciation for the life experienced. With it, you have a better spiritual understanding of who you truly are from those experiences!

The evolution of your soul through your complete understanding is made a reality by your experiencing and feeling each part of creation, of which there are many parts. This allows the evolution of your spirit and the heightening of your God-energy. It is the evolution of life itself through complete knowing.

If we take this concept of understanding and apply logic, then we must find good reasoning to know that a spirit of creation being one and the same as the universal energy of all energies must be far more than a static or non-evolving energy. As we are starting to realize, all life and non-life exists for the purpose of further creation and expansion. If it did not expand, it would contract. But our science confirms that our universe is an ever-expanding universe. We mimic, in physical form, the expansion we are a part of in spiritual form, hence we are forever evolving, growing, and expanding in physical and spiritual terms. Ultimately, our purpose in knowing this (knowing all there is to know) will be remembered.

It is our physical makeup devoid of spiritual awareness that has us doubt this reasoning. Our teachers have told us that we live, then we die, and if we are lucky, we are rewarded in the hereafter. Wow! It's no wonder we fear. The universe is never-ending; one universe blends into another. There are millions upon millions of solar systems, billions upon billions of planets and stars, and then more. Our teachings tell us we are so sure that we are here for no other reason but to be good, then die at the end of our days, to be no more. Is it really possible to be part of this magnificent universe as a separate, fallible entity with such an unimportant role?

It is time to look within and to connect to the light of consciousness. It is done in the silence of the mind and peace in the body. We must feel, break old patterns of behavior, and reconnect to Self, as part of the whole.

It is time to open the portal to this inner world, for we are the center of all that is, as is everyone and everything in creation. We are connected and must now choose to stay conscious, to remember from where we came and to where we will return. It is in that connectedness that we evolve and play our part in the evolution of all consciousness. The purpose of creation is to expand love through truly knowing love. Experiencing every facet of it!

How do we know it? As in the words of so many, we do this by being God's greatest creation. Experiencing its fear is to truly know love.

The greatest plan in creation was to give each of us individual consciousness to express through free will. The will and way we chose to create life for our individual consciousness was left entirely to us. Our choices shape the destiny we have come to experience. The unmanifested or God-energy of all there is experiences itself in this way. It is the purpose of our existence. That is why each of us is so important to the grander scheme of things.

We choose to live separately from this perfection, as we were created to do. To not remember is to create a life—to feel the many differences that exist outside of perfection and pure love. At any time, we can choose to return—not easily, of course, but this choice is available to each of us any time we choose to do so and set ourselves on the path of remembering, to return to it, and to do so in an enlightened state of being, which is a state of love, acceptance, and forgiveness.

Enlightenment is the bridge between the physical and non-physical realm. It is found by living in the physical realm, with all its fears, and with a connectedness to the spiritual realm and all its joy. It is living within it—in Self—without fear of any kind. Acceptance and forgiveness replace fear.

The entry point to this state of being is within the peace and stillness of inner Self. Through this connection, the light of presence can be felt within—not the fearful self we have created, but the true Self as we were created. The light of this consciousness is so powerful and peaceful that fear simply cannot exist. It is the sunlight of creation, and it can be felt and accessed with practice.

You are the light accessed through the power of your silence. The energy strengthens each time we go within. The light of presence grows stronger; people will feel it. It is the path to unity consciousness and the connectedness to all life. It is your path to freedom and peace of mind.

We all make up the light of creation, and we are all connected. We cannot be disconnected. To be disconnected would be a flaw in creation. Creation, at the magnitude we know it to be, could not exist with a flaw, could it? Wouldn't a flaw destroy it, as it does most things? Look at our physical world; it is full of flaws. These flaws are not created by our creator, but created by his creations through free will to experience the opposite of perfection. They are created by us!

How would life expand if creation stopped? If it didn't expand, what would happen to the energy? Everything is energy—even a thought. If it doesn't expand, then wouldn't it contract? Your evolution is as important as all life that exists. You are the expanding universe.

Let's access the all-knowing Self and re-connect for the purpose of evolving spiritually. The world we know needs it; no one will argue with that. We seem to be in a spot of bother. People are unhappy; their lives are without meaning. People unrelentingly do, acquire, condemn, punish, attack, defend, lie, and live in despair without knowing why.

Don't you deserve love, joy, and peace? It's not a science or an unachievable task outside your possibility; it is within you. You can literally have all this and all you desire. The reason you can is because what you are is made of the same stuff as all things are—perfectly connected. You are the greatest of creations and have the power to create.

All you need to do is believe and remember. Remembering is in the inner silence of you. The feeling of warmth you will experience within when you learn to reconnect will take away your fears and comfort all your concerns. The happiness you will feel will resonate from a deep understanding—the understanding and wisdom we all possess.

A Simple, Effective Meditation

Sit still and breathe. Close your eyes. Feel the light of your consciousness descend upon you and cover your entire body.

Let the light bathe you. Feel its warmth as it covers you and takes away your worries.

Breathe it in and out, and as you breathe out, let the darker, dense, negative thoughts be breathed out also. You are mentally creating a cleansing process to adjust your body, mind, and spirit connection.

Consciously connect to your breath, and the breath will take you within.

Slow your breathing as you proceed until the breath is a silent, soft, effortless whisper. Any negative thought will disrupt the flow of no-mind; just be aware and take your consciousness back to the breath.

Don't panic or be alarmed if you feel uneasy when consciously slowing yourself down and going to this place of inner silence and peace. Just be aware and allow all emotions and feelings to happen, and then simply return to the breath.

The more you practice, the stronger your connection will be and the quicker you will be able to access the inner realm of no-mind or peacefulness and rest.

Practice this for a few minutes throughout the day whenever you get a chance, and trust that the place we are returning to is a place forgotten, but a place we know well. In it there is more peace and joy than you could ever imagine possible.

In this state of meditation, allow the sunlight to filter down and cover you. Breathe in the light and relax. As you do this, the senses and the mind will be liberated from daily concerns. Practice will heighten the awareness within and strengthen within you.

Inner silence is the foundation of peace and tranquility.
(If you'd like to receive a free audio of a guided version of this meditation, go to my website: www.epsilonhealingacademy.com)

CHAPTER SEVENTEEN

The Power of Conscious Creation

"There are two ways to live: you can live as if nothing
is a miracle; you can live as if everything is a miracle."
—Albert Einstein

In the last two chapters, we have lightened our vibrational energy to positive affirmations and powerful, high vibrational light energy.

It is now time to gain techniques and specifics that will create miracles in your life and give you the life you desire and the power to consciously create.

Know this of yourself: You are powerful, incredible, a light to the world, and wonderful in every sense. Love is all you are. You were born as love and will pass on as love. The game we play in the middle is to remember this and to appreciate it: to heighten our awareness of love, the matrix of all that is, the glue that holds everything together. Life is there to support you as your reward for remembering, for to create is your birthright. It was born in you as your gift, and so it is that you create your world according to how you will it, do it, and then have it.

How do you wish to see it? How will you be it, and then how will you act it out? It will manifest exactly as you think, say, and do. Most people believe they must have something before they see it a certain way and thereafter believe. In reality, to enact the law of conscious creation, you must be it before you receive it, then do the things you would if you had it already, and finally, with great conviction and faith, know you have it.

Our perceptions create an unreal world. It is our perception of the world we see that is separate from our true reality. In effect, the world we create is the world we see through this distorted perception. If we see it, we believe it. This is how our minds have been trained to think. We first see something or have the thing available. Second, we believe or act out the things we would when we have it; third, we enjoy or appreciate the things we have. This poses a problem, because we often do not believe we can have something and rejoice in it until we have it. Because the thing you want is often left wanting—in other words, not received, but valued and then wanted—it remains always wanted. As most things that we want are slow in their arrival or not delivered within our time frame or in the manner we want them, we simply give up. Seeing didn't occur in the manner we would have it, so we believe we created nothing. This is very far from the truth. We never stop creating!

Conscious creation is about belief, faith, and no expectation or determination of the thing you desire.

Let me explain further. Expectation is control. Control is resisting, and more often than not, it will lead to disappointment. I came to believe expectation was vital to survival and a form of making sure my control was being met. What I found within my life and subsequent readings within all types of literature was that expectation erodes the foundation of desire.

Remember that the universe knows all there is to know. You are one with it, as it is with you—conscious energy. It will support your every desire, and it knows what things or experiences you require at each moment of your life. Let it choose!

Experiences will come into your reality according to your level of awareness and physical and spiritual evolution. The universe will support you, so trust and have faith that it knows best and will deliver what you deserve (or better) to suit your soul's path. To control an outcome will be to continue to resist, and what we resist will persist.

Expectation will only be met with resistance. Expectation will lead to disappointment.

I heard many times in therapy sessions: "Let go and let God. Make your desire clear, and release it without expectation!"

Your desires must be left to the universe. In effect, it must be left to the higher power of all. It is done in the inner knowledge of and connection to Self, and must not be shared with all unless conscious themselves. Other people's judgments and criticisms will undermine your desires if they are not in a conscious loving state.

The "Be, Do, Have" Principal

In order to consciously create, it is important to reverse the practice of seeing first, and we must learn to practice often. The more you practice, the stronger your power of creation will be, and then the greater your belief will be. The rest is a cycle of attraction.

In simple terms, we must:

1. Be or believe we have the thing we desire before we have it. For example, a better friendship, a loving husband, wife, or girlfriend, a new car, more money, a holiday, more recognition, and so on.

2. Next, we need to have a positive mental attitude and do the things we would do as if we have the thing we desired already—even before we have it.

3. Finally, we need to have faith that the thing we desire is here already, to accept that it was created in this moment of desire. Rejoice in it, and be grateful for it. Have no expectation. Just have faith!

It is our perception of the world from our learning that creates in us anxiety and concern. Our perceptions are based on our judgments, and our judgments are based on our past experiences. We believe we must acquire a certain thing; therefore, we expend great effort in the acquiring before we see its reality and believe in it. Yet this is incorrect.

If you wish to simplify your life, remove anxiety and concern and learn to accept and appreciate the creative power you have at your disposal. In essence, doing far less achieves far more.

Creation at an individual level is constantly taking place in your life. Every positive thought and every negative thought become your reality. You can choose to consciously create or unconsciously react to life. You create nonetheless but are unaware of it. Each of us participates in creating. We create good experiences and also bad experiences. In the true sense, no experience is bad, for we are here to experience through feeling the effects of our thoughts, words and actions within those experiences. Ultimately it is through feeling that we are returned to the memory of who we are.

The world we see is a world where each of us fights for our survival separate from everything and everyone. It is taught to us at a young age and continues through life. We do not tolerate the weak and give little mind to the homeless and underprivileged for fear of becoming like them. Our society has conformed to the law of scarcity for centuries. Fear is the order we follow and a way of life that privileges the few at the expense of the many.

It is here our individual thoughts, words, and behaviors cater to the mentalities that tell us to think and grow rich, survive at all cost, fight for every step, and take what you can. It is here that we react and conform to much of life, rather than create anew.

Thought that is invested in past experiences will manifest in your reality as separation and this is what causes you pain expressed as anxiety and fear. Yes, you may acquire what it is you seek and survive many battles, but where is the joy in being, doing, and having? Where is the rest you need that is free of the affliction of incessant thinking or the wasted energy of manipulation and control? The constant chatter in your head never ceases until the thing you seek is acquired, and then you move on to the next conquest.

Thought invested in present moment thinking is thought no longer burdened with the layers upon layers of judgment from previous experiences. It is here that all thinking is fresh and creative. A thought born in this moment is liberated, for it contains the essence of your creativity—an inner attribute of all of us. It has no judgment attached to it, for it has no past.

Knowing that only the past carries the judgments we have all come to rely upon for our very survival, do we now react as we have always done to life experiences, other people, and our relationships, or do we learn to create anew what we truly desire? It is a choice we must each make alone in order to unite together.

Do we react from our past? Do we act out a previous response to a similar set of circumstances or create with new thought patterns based in positive awareness and creative solutions in the present? Those states come directly from your inner being—your soul.

Remember, as we react the thoughts associated with that reaction are manifesting as a past experience being acted out. How can your reaction find a peaceful solution with the same thoughts that created the event in the first place? It cannot.

The past thought resurfaces as your reality. The world you see is now a reactionary one from previous experiences. You cannot expect a poor experience which did not serve you well in the past to be met with the same thought pattern and improve the outcome. It will keep repeating itself, because what you resist will persist.

When my lovely wife left me and ventured down a path I considered undesirable based on my evaluation of her, I reacted with anger and hurt. That anger created the same reaction in her. Both of us were operating out of past experiences.

I had no regard for her hurts and feelings or the anger she was feeling. Simply put, I could not see over my own anger to notice the cause of her pain. I simply attacked the problem. My wife had enormous issues with me that I never saw coming. For example, she did not feel validated or important. She did not feel important enough even to look after the home, and I was dismissive of her opinions about our finances and matters relating to the home or family. I believed I was always right—a control issue that had haunted me since childhood.

I have no excuses. There was no mentor to explain these important bits to a relationship. It took my wife leaving for me to search for answers to see the truth. I am not saying it's one-sided, for we all come together for a reason. You attract into your life people for the very reasons of growth and awareness. It is the law of attraction—the universe looking after you, even though at the time, it doesn't feel like it.

My wife did not live her truth; in fact, she tried to fit into a mold for me and allowed life to unfold in a way that was less than perfect for her. Life was easy for her, and she let me make all the decisions—in fact, she wanted me to. She didn't speak out, even when a decision may have bothered her. She carried her own childhood issues and never dealt with them. She was easy to anger instead of talking. She did not validate me; she only thought she did—and vice versa.

We were constantly fighting each other; looking for love where it could not be found and reliving our past histories, which were being played out within the relationship. Were we afraid of abandonment or not being loved? Our egos played on a stage. We tried to inflict pain on one another in an effort to gain the moral high ground and control the other. There was no speaking out; there was anger, then making up with one another, and then anger again. It became very tiring. We were living in make-believe, and it was a nightmare.

Who teaches us these things?

The perfect life—family, kids, and the whole shebang—were in total disarray. We were both trying to fix our past through the other while neither faced their truth—not from malice, but from ignorance.

Pain and fear created more of the same experience. I attacked my wife for the wrongs I perceived, and she committed herself to those wrongs to create more pain in me. Her resentment of an unhealed past was my inheritance. Our relationship ended the way it started— with love and hate. My wife did more damage to herself and to us, in defiance of me, and I perceived that tenfold. My world was collapsing, and I was effectively fighting an uphill battle, which I was surely losing. Her world was collapsing also, and neither of us could see through our own issues to see the other person's issues. What we saw was exactly the reality we perceived! We did not own our issues; we denied them and blamed each other. It did not matter what happened to us; it mattered that we simply could not debrief our own individual pasts, which had great impact on us.

Six months after we broke up and she left the home, I needed answers as to why it wasn't fixed. It then dawned on me that I could not control or impose my will on another person. All I could do was heal myself. This became my quest. I searched for the Holy Grail: peace within. My spiritual evolution began in earnest.

I had to do it; my kids were hurting. The thought of their pain drove me to the books to learn and to attend hours of counseling. I finally concluded my inner battle some two years later, and I continued my new journey after attending a rehabilitation clinic.

My journey of conscious creation began at the very moment I questioned my current reality. I couldn't fix my current reality until I healed myself. It was then that I knew that no other thought could infect the new thought of this moment. There was a kind of peace at that moment that I felt deep within. I hit on something at the time; I just didn't know the severity of change that was to follow.

The first task was to show an act of love to my wife, and I did. I stopped almost all communication with her. This allowed me precious moments to be in the present and not be consumed with self-pity, anger, and all the other emotions and sensations I was creating. The *past kept visiting, and each time I regressed, I learned a little more, so I decided to make my pain my awareness of another lesson that needed to be learned.*

I started to allow the knowing of what I felt to come to me through the power of silence. No words could aptly describe anything I was experiencing or serve me in any positive way any further. It was words that prevented my healing. I allowed the judgments of others to interfere with the reality of positive conscious creation. From all the books I was reading and the numerous counseling sessions and lectures I attended, it was obvious that talk was cheap. I wanted to feel my way through my body. I wanted to feel—manifestation to the ever resourceful, all-knowing Self—the place of all knowledge. I just wanted to trust and have faith in the power of Self. Feeling was to become my conduit to the inner Self.

Next, I required my thoughts to be new thoughts. I thought without judgment. I would eliminate any negative thought immediately and replace it with a thought of the perfect outcome I desired. I would desire what I wanted, and then, through feeling my way into my meditation, I would live the moment completely and fully in the silence of my inner Self.

As negative thoughts arose I could feel the anxiety, feel the unease within, and therefore I was able to become aware of them. To release them, I took this awareness back to my breath and the silence within.

After each meditation, I had thoughts of incredible insight, almost as if I was being given a road map. I found myself living the roadmap—following the path without fear, for often now the path was of loving actions rather than negative reactions. However, since I had spent my life preparing for all the negative possibilities and allowing anxiety to rule such a large part of my life, diligent awareness of eradicating negative thoughts needed constant monitoring. In a way, the process of tricking the mind into reaffirming positive affirmations needed such vigilance.

It was necessary to recognize negative thoughts and replace them immediately with positive ones, literally tricking the mind until it became habitual. Through awareness I could now feel the unease and anxiety within and instantly know that a thought needed to change. I no longer looked for the "bullets" (the negative thoughts of what might happen) in every aspect of life.

The question I would find myself asking when in doubt was, "What would love do now?" To follow this reasoning or to reason is the purpose of the mind until you are made aware. I found that asking "What would love do now?" took away negative thought patterns or doubt. What would love do now? Love doesn't get anxious, attack, worry, resent, and so on, and if you really think about this question, then the benefit of asking it in the power of creation will become obvious. We must remove our intrinsic, deep-seated need to question and doubt. I left my thought with my higher power.

All my life, I feared a higher power, because I felt any higher power never stood by me. Like everything else, I separated from it. There was me, and above me I put everybody else on a pedestal to replace my higher power.

Now let's look at this logically. Our thoughts, words or actions—often a reaction—follow each other. We allow other unconscious people to use words or validate themselves against the backdrop of our life. The problem with this method or belief system is that when the going gets tough as it surely will—a life given—who is left to pick up the pieces? You of course—and are feeling alone again!

You see we are not connected to our inner Self—instead we are connected to everything outside Self. When we are not connected within we cannot resolve problems within. Instead we constantly need to look outward, and the answer can never be found there.

The higher power became the power that guided me. Faith became a goal—faith in a higher power and faith in the law of the universe. The law of the universe will support your every thought, loving or unloving. An unloving act will be supported by more resistance, causing a greater unloving impact on you until you change. Change can only come through connection to Self. In biblical terms, our higher power gave us free will as a gift for us to use in whichever way we choose to create our world. The reason is that each of us would truly acquire spiritual evolution—this is your soul's purpose on earth.

Remember, the universe will support your every thought, good or bad. You need to know the bad to know the good. For example, if you are a bad communicator—always having a go at someone or someone having a go at you as a consequence—and all you really want is to be liked, you just don't know how to be liked, which causes your reaction.

How would you learn to be a good communicator if everybody agreed with the way you communicated and let you get away with such poor behavior?

The reality is that your natural, evolutionary instinct derives its source from your soul. It does this so you can experience a greater aspect of life; hence, it supports your evolutionary purpose. It is your will to experience all aspects of life. Eventually, the pain created by your perceived or adapted will becomes your realization of the change needed—your instinctive knowledge of the need to acquire peace within. The instinctive knowledge is that which comes from deep within you—your soul. A new path is sought. You establish a new path, having learned the lesson of knowing the impact of poor communication.

Once you have learned, you will look to the stars and be thankful that the opportunity was given to you to see, regardless of whether you thought at the time the universe had supported you or not. It always will. It knows the right moment to give you the right gift. Even something which appears bad can be a gift in disguise. The universe knows, so have faith!

"Courage is knowing what not to fear."
—Plato

The next stage is to live that thought and only speak of it through the conscious act of knowing it has arrived. Do not speak of it as an expectation, control what it is, or speak in relation to the timing of it. Be ever mindful of the thing you desire; speak of it in prayer—to conscious others, if you must—with the knowledge of its delivery. This creates the power of belief in thought. In the beginning stages of learning to consciously create, stay with tricking the mind, and be vigilant to negative thought. Stay positive.

Negative thought will express as negative words and behaviors, and will slow the process of healing, as the power of doubt is just as creative as the power of no doubt. Since doubt is what we have been conditioned to all our lives, to change this takes mindful attention, vigilance, and faith—and the courage to hold all three in your awareness!

Remember that we are undoing years of reacting unconsciously from past experiences and judgments, hoping for an outcome and consuming intolerable amounts of energy. We are reacting to life unconsciously through thoughts, words, and actions that are based around scarcity and survival, manipulation, control and expectations. We need to be conscious of undoing this.

Now you are creating a new reality based on conscious creation through your heightened awareness and present moment creative thinking. You know the outcome is certain because the present is not invested in either past or future time. It is certain!

Conscious creation is manifested in silence—a powerful present awareness in Self. Your power comes from the deep inner Self, the place of silence, stillness, and high vibrational energy that we must attune ourselves to if we are to consciously create.

> *I lived in the joy of my creation—sustainable peace and joy. I was not like some silly clown that couldn't wipe a smile from my face, but rather, I lived in grace and in my knowledge. I stopped the talking that created the judgments—both my own and those of others. I adsorbed myself in the wonderful people I met through healing, books, and passions acquired and developed over the previous two years with quiet appreciation and gratitude. I stopped taking things for granted and became grateful for the things that were already in my life. In particular, I started to enjoy the love of my family and to be truly grateful for all the abundance that already existed in my life. In fact, for the first time, I had a true appreciation for the things I had in my life.*
>
> *I focused on positives, and when I felt my path deviating into regression from fear of not receiving or feelings of lack, I meditated in silence for only a couple of minutes at a time. Thereafter, I expressed more gratitude, focused on positives in my life, and expressed my desire through prayer and visualization. I felt my way out of the past and soothed my way into the present. It was not always easy, yet I found as I regressed into past behaviors of control and expectation or anxiety and fear, I realized what was happening, felt the feelings within, disconnected the negative thoughts associated to those feelings, and virtually dropped them—just like that. At a group therapy meeting, a wise old man named Gerry, a member of the group for over thirty years who experienced enormous grief in his life, taught me the simplest of secrets to letting go of negative thoughts. He looked at me, smiled, and from a position of holding both fists clenched and facing upward he simply turned his fists over to face the ground and opened his hands.*

It is important to note here that between the conscious and the unconscious, it is the unconscious that has the power. Therefore, it is very important for each of us to know two things as we start the cycle of consciously creating—what we desire in life and whether we are really staying on track. We have to be very mindful and watchful of our behaviors as we consciously create.

Let your behaviors be a sign to show you where you are relation to conscious creation. Your behavior is your guide to how you are feeling. Your feelings are your guide to what you are thinking.

Are you ready for what you desire? For example, if you use control or you use cocaine—it doesn't matter what addiction—then this is a sure sign you're not feeling good or confident about your desire. Look for the thought behind those behaviors. As you practice this, you will be quicker at picking up the symptoms, and as you regress, you will become alert and aware quicker and learn to drop the thoughts that create these reactions in you. Your mind and body must work together, not in ways you have been conditioned. Use your mind and body to observe your behaviors, thoughts, and words in order to show you the truth of your current reality. This will soon become instinctive.

This is the work of the soul. You will not be disappointed when the thing you desire doesn't manifest as you think it will. By using your power of awareness and instinct, you will instantly know with your present-moment awareness that the power lies within you to change your reality. Trusting in your Self is a gut feeling.

> *Miracles instantly started to occur in my life once I knew I had the power—inner power, not ego power—to heal myself. I knew that it was the only path to salvation for my wife, who still had not attended one counseling session, as it was for my children, who had experienced the pain of their mum and dad separating, and for me. It was the only way for me to find lasting peace and joy within.*

The Five Steps of Conscious Creation

1. Choose your most perfect desired outcome, and allow this thought (or prayer) to be the dominant thought and desire. Stay with it. (Don't be afraid of the word "prayer." Pray regularly. Repeated desire produces the strongest effects.)
2. "Swim in the sky." Set your frame or mood to a higher frequency. Think of all the wonderful things that desire will bring. Think of what you might do or how many possibilities exist for you on their arrival. Feel the physical sensations of thoughts that please you—swim with them.

3. Be the thing you desire to happen. Think it, feel it, and don't wait to see it before you believe in it. If you want more of anything, give it away first; there is no such thing as scarcity other than in the mind. Remember, however, that this is about you, not about another person or a thing. You must be it, feel it, and allow the universe to do the rest, regardless of the reaction in another. Good thoughts and intentions, and the question, "What would love do now?" are good guides.

4. Do the things you would do if your desire had already been given to you. Act it out through feeling it in every part of your body. By feeling it, you can actually trick the mind into believing you have it. In the quiet of your home and the silence of your mind, go over the process of doing the things you would as if you had received your desire already. Do not become attached to, or obsessed with the thing, however; get on with your life. Use gratitude.

5. Know you have received what you desire—or a grander version of it. Maintain complete faith. Express gratitude repeatedly until a positive mindset is firm. Trick your mind. How would you act to another or others? You have it, so what would you do? Act it out through feelings of gratitude and demonstrations of appreciation.

Important notes to remember for conscious creation:

- If you speak of what you desire, speak only to other conscious souls as if the event has occurred. Speak of it without expectation. Speak of it with grace and quiet confidence. Loose talk will bring judgments from people who are less conscious than you into your frame of events. If others need to ask or question your motives, stop talking. Hold your grace, and change the subject. If people listen without judgment and with a caring attitude, then they are conscious souls. No judgment—either yours or that of others—will suffice when consciously creating, and the only opinion and path you choose that matters is yours!

- Maintain faith in your belief. Faith is the most important tool you have, despite being the hardest to apply, for without your control, you will feel lost. Without your seeing, you will have trouble believing. You must have faith and maintain faith, knowing the thing you desire is on its way. Rejoice that the thing you desire is here! Without expectation, the thing you desire will be given you. It may not be in the order or preciously how you thought, but with faith in the power of the universe, your higher power, and all things, you are a part of in its entirety; it will be given to you in the form and manner that is perfect for you at this point of your evolution. It can only be as good as, or better than, what you desired.

- Put no time limit to what you desire. Remove the hourglass, for disappointment is the only conclusion to any expectation—especially time. Can you see now why we struggle with faith? You think faith is receiving it when you say you desire something. Yet if the greater power of all knows the exact and most appropriate timing for its arrival for your highest good, then the sooner you de-focus from time and focus on knowing without time, the more imminent its arrival. It is widely accepted that creating consciously in spirit is instantaneous; the physical constraints to creation is the purpose of our knowing this. In spirit consciousness, the "what is" is to create instantly. In physical form, we are searching for creating "what is" instantly. Conscious creation is our physical remembering and "connected-ness" to our spirit consciousness! We know how good "what is" is when we create in physical form and realize our power of creating! This is one aspect of one's spiritual evolution.

In my own life, I came to understand that conscious creation was the way to prosperity at a whole new level—a level made real through consciousness and knowledge, not by attacking, manipulating, constant unease, anxiety, or basing relationships on how complete they made me feel or how mutually beneficial (financially or otherwise) they were.

As a result, I finally discarded all forms of expectation of any result in relation to my desires. This was my most difficult challenge. My entire life was based on expectation. Being in the present moment and being fully aware was a release from the agony of always expecting a result. I started to experience freedom within. Without expectation, there was no longer pressure—just the joy of doing. What happened thereafter became faith in knowing that the best was on its way—and without fail, it was every time! In other words, the how and the when are for the universe to work out.

The only thing we should ever allow ourselves to expect is a miracle, as miracles are directly linked to inner consciousness and inner Self. When expectation of inner consciousness or love exists, then only love can strengthen within you!

Just have faith. Trust in your silence, for it is from within silence that love cultivates, illuminates, and creates.

CHAPTER EIGHTEEN

Silence

"The hush of heaven holds my heart today. Father, how still today! How quietly
do all things fall in place! This is the day that has been chosen as the time in
which I come to understand the lesson that there is no need that I do anything.
In you is every choice already made. In you has every conflict been resolved. In
you is everything I hope to find already given me. Your peace is mine. My heart is
quiet, and my mind at rest. Your love is heaven, and your love is mine."
—*A Course in Miracles,* lesson 286

Why have we become so disorientated and transfixed by pain and drama?

The feeling of separation was part of our early experiences through conditions imposed on us. Through design, these conditions determined the choices we would make in relation to the belief of who we are and who we wished to become. Neither was real.

It is in this lack of Self-knowledge that guilt manifests as our reality—thinking and doing with guilt becomes the vehicle for creation. In this mindset that carries guilt what is it that we create? Obviously not what we desire. The compelling energies of guilt—thinking and doing with expectation, resistance, and control—conceal the very core knowing of who you truly are.

Inside us is a place where knowledge is simply known and wisdom acted out in our physical world. We are not still long enough to listen to or hear our inner wisdom speak to us through our instincts. The difficulty many of us face is that the words we speak do not sustain or invite peace and goodwill. Words are powerful in their creation of our worldly experience and easily create the experience of pain or peace by their very use.

Peace comes from spirit, and spirit is your intrinsic nature of who you are. It knows all there is to know. We give no time to the silence to listen to the inner Self—our spirit. Instead, we choose to express words over faith in our inner beliefs. It is easier to have a judgment than a belief in someone or something, because that is how we have been taught. Too often, the words we use are negative. Often they derive from thoughts of our past experiences. We express them to others in a manner that creates more judgments and criticisms as they react unconsciously to our own. The process of creation works against the very thing we know to be the truth in all things—that there is only love and unity. To attack another is only to attack our Self.

Too often, we choose not to listen to Self, and instead delve into the physical world of words, and the drama created by them. Where is our silence? In your silence, you will be given the answers to all of life.

You can only experience the spirit of you from a place of silence. It is here that you will understand its existence and benefit from its joy. Our words and thoughts echo loudly—too loudly to truly hear and see the abundance that exists all around us. We are caught up in all things physical. It is all we understand. Our physicality is our belief that we are born, we die, and there is literally nothing after, unless we have been good. We struggle, resist, give in, fight hard, protect, defend, and attack, and in so doing, we believe we will be accepted and made worthy. We believe this is life—the norm—and often are readily accepted by unconscious souls, as like attracts like. It is in these relationships and the dramas that play out within them that the opposite of your current reality becomes known—the false reality we believe in and the drama created by it is not a place of unity, but only a place of separation. Aligning with this separateness ultimately is the catalyst that gives us our belief in unity.

As the world is separated, you choose a side, and that side is aligned to a group of others with equal mindsets. These others strive to survive and take all they can to achieve a sense of self worth and acceptance—all in the name of survival. They are compliant and afraid to speak their mind, choosing to forego their own needs for the needs of others. They are outwardly happy and inwardly filled with anxiety and concern. There are many differing personalities that make the world go around. Yet they all share a common reality—they are all separated from Self. It is the way we are taught by our parents, teachers, and authority figures. It is conditioned in school, at home, on television, in society, and by government and religion; separation is our teaching.

Separation is what we know so well yet fail to see. In that separation, there are feelings of scarcity, lack, and disconnection. No wonder there is no peace, for how can this peaceful state be found when the feeling of scarcity exists? It is a scarcity that exists without and therefore it is felt within. It becomes our form of communication.

We have become so attached to words that we use them unsparingly. We are content with them, as they offer us security and commonality with others. They describe who we are, and we repeat them often. Regardless of their use, we feel no better. We subject ourselves to the whim of the result we achieve from expressing them in the manner our past experiences would have them spoken.

We are complete; yet we are incomplete. Our reluctance to just let go holds us in a place of ignorance. We choose the path we know well, regardless of the constant pain we feel. We continually refuse to seek the path of knowledge.

Sit quietly, if you can, and listen to the sounds around you. Do you feel restless? Can you enjoy your own company for more than a minute? Can you stop the constant chatter in your head or the thoughts that you need to do something—anything—and the constant urge to keep doing? It is time to ask for answers, because you are hurting yourself and those you love. Your pain becomes an expression of your emotions through denial or attack. The world you see is not real and has no basis for permanence. Until you find permanence, everything around you will be shaken and tested. Permanence can only occur in the Self, and this Self can only hear its calling in the silence within you.

Why is there a constant need to tell our stories? Have you ever wondered why you can't keep quiet? Is it because you needed to prove you were something against the backdrop of feeling like nothing. You are insecure by the nature of your past or simply feel empty in the absence of Self-love. The constant need for validation comes from the lack you feel within. Our childhood woes, our life experiences and our true feelings are all too easily ignored; the truth of our anxiety is hidden for fear of non-acceptance and rejection. We feel we must keep up a brave face.

When we do start to speak in a positive way? We are not so naive that we think people will let us be without judgment and criticism and shower us with positive thoughts and blessings in return if we do speak of positive things in our lives—or are we? In reality, to speak and share positive messages often deters others from hearing and receiving well. It is too easily accepted on the surface; however, in the quiet of others' homes, another reality is too common: the reality of non-acceptance. Others are often too easily influenced by envy—or worse. Their judgments manifest a new reality. Our journeys inward are set well before our experiences begin. Our life maps foreshadow the same ultimate conclusion for all. This becomes our reality—what we see we believe, what we think today becomes our tomorrow.

> *When my world as I knew it collapsed, most of the people I held in high esteem—yes, those hundred or more upon whom I had lavished wine and celebration—turned their backs on me, were opinionated, or simply vanished. It was their time, perhaps, to take sides, feel validated, or give opinions based on their own life experiences. For a short time, their lives had meaning, and in this process, their lives would feel happier. I realized a part of me was destroyed, as it had been at age eleven when my best friend was no longer permitted to play with me, sleep over, or be seen in my company because his family believed I was the son of a bad man. This part of me had never really recovered until my fifties. Society had turned its back on the family with money and status once there was none left. A part of me was shattered by resentment.*
>
> *However, when the hurt was gone, my greatest gifts were presented to me. My life lessons had been realized, and my life journey set me on a new path.*

With every crisis, there are many gifts on offer. It is important that we see opportunity here, for it is here that our greatest experiences will occur and our greatest purposes will be learned. Mine was to forgive, and the first person I forgave was me.

I forgave myself for all the wrong ever done to me. The world I saw had a completely different meaning—a completely different reality. It was less about acquiring riches and more about acquiring love of self and prosperity of the soul. I was in a place where I could truly love all others. My children could be given the tools that I had never been given, and their lives would be enriched by those gifts, thereby enriching others. If ever I could give my children a gift, then the tool to enrich their lives and others with love would be the greatest.

Our lives are made of words, and our words shape and express our experiences. This is all done in the name of the turbulent, volatile ego—the adapted ego self we manifest, which demands everything and leaves us with nothing. Look for the signs and know all can be diverted. Your life can turn around immediately, but you will need courage to do so, as the ego is a formidable opponent.

You know the signs now. Don't ignore them, for you can retain all that you have and live in complete peace and joy, but you need to listen to the spirit in you, for the spirit in you knows all. This is not ego gratification, but fact. How can you trust yourself and the words written here just enough to start the process of conscious creation?

To date, you have reacted to everything that passed you by. You judge, criticize, and condemn life, live with fear, anxiety, or constant unease, and still choose to ignore your reality. Together, we manifest the unity unconsciousness of a reality none of us can bear to tolerate much longer. Our governments manipulate us, as do many religions. Fear has become the basis of our society. Fear begets fear, and fear manifests more negative influences in our lives.

Where is the peace? Do you find peace in attack, a false belief that you will be saved by your incessant thinking, planning, defending, controlling, or denial? If you listen to enough people, they will tell you that, yes, resisting and fear is where you will find peace. Attack protects our way of life, and just like you and me, our society operates in the same way. Scarcity creates worry, anxiety, and concern. It is this worry and concern that has made us so steadfast in our determination to protect our way of life, regardless of the millions upon millions who are suffering. We attack anyone who jeopardizes our way of life or challenges what we have made of ourselves.

Where is the love? It's as if we're saying, "Let's keep ignoring it. Let's destroy the planet because we can." All that is beautiful, but fragile is being systematically destroyed by the feeling of never-enoughness, of scarcity within us as individuals and as a society as a whole. We are manifesting its demise. Its demise will cease the minute your consciousness shifts from your outer world to your inner world. Surely no one who is shown the pain they feel and the alternative of peace within would continue on the path of pain. That is the path you are on. You see the signs, but are you going to listen to the inner you? The inner you will guide you away from the place you feel no rest or love.

Give yourself the time to know that you are love and to remember it, for it is who you are.

In order to link to spirit within, you must decide to release the ego. Make a conscious decision that your ego may not be doing you any favors. Ask yourself, "How do I feel most of the time? Can I rest? Do I need to keep doing, or am I restless when not doing? Do I feel unfulfilled? How do I communicate with my loved ones? Are they happy or just trying to make me happy? Are they connecting with me and I with them? Do I need to attack if things don't go my way? Am

I easily threatened, or do I panic when a plan doesn't go the way I thought or someone states an opinion I don't agree with?"

There are many telltale signs we easily ignore. Stop ignoring them, for that path is destructive to you. Yes, you will receive your lesson, and yes, you will learn—but why not avoid the pain, the crisis you must surely meet, and the dark night of the soul? Help heal the world, keep all that you have, and live without fear in complete peace and joy.

1. The first stage of healing is *intentional*. It is done by recognizing and facing our truth.

   Our lives are full of expectations and demands we place upon ourselves and everyone around us. These demands cloud our vision of the power we hold within—the power that can simplify our lives and offer us complete peace. We grow older and somewhat wiser and look back with frustration and anger for missing out. Outer possessions, financial gain, and security were met at a price—a hefty toll on our health and those we love.

   Your life has been chaotic. You have either given up on life and failed to find the peace that accompanies this outcome, or you've applied yourself wholeheartedly without rest or reprieve to relentless thought for the purpose of achieving and acquiring. You have planned and deployed all manner of strategies and learned much, and your planning continues to this day. Tired of life battles and incessant thought, you employ the benefit of hindsight and patience. Yet all is experienced without awareness of the unrest within you. After seeing your truth in the unease of it all, you search for peace and acknowledgement of yourself.

   You now seek a new path, believing from the wisdom you have gained that the journey can be easier and more fulfilling. You now seek peace within. It is why you are here.

   The ego must be discarded, but it will be formidable in defense. Yet within easy reach, a life that is far more beneficial awaits you. You sought reward in everything you did and now it is time to do without material reward. A new reward is awaiting you that is far more beneficial than you have ever imagined possible. It is time to observe with full awareness and to do so with anticipation and without expectation.

   Be aware, for now you must trick the mind into releasing you from your past, which has kept you confined to unease and discomfort most of your life. It is time to feel your body, the conduit to your inner Self—your soul. Here is the place of all knowledge, and here resides great wisdom. Now we must trick the mind to allow us the time to hear our inner messages. We trick it by being totally aware in the present. When we deviate from this path, we will revert to unconscious acts of defense and attack based on our misconstrued evaluations and perceptions. This will resonate in the body as discomfort and pain, which we can feel and then act upon quickly with silence and present focus through awareness.

A Powerful Path to Self-Healing

When you experience body pain, go to the place of silence and be totally aware of the pain you feel. It may be numbness, perhaps a knot in the stomach, a weakening of a body part, or a sickening feeling. Be totally mindful of it. Keep it in your awareness, and focus on your breath and its rhythm to release the pain.

Now be aware of the thought behind it. Watch the mind, and the negative thought will appear and be recognized. Be aware of it, and accept it. Now that you have accepted it through your awareness of it, choose a positive thought to replace it or simply drop the negative thought altogether and allow no thought by being aware of the breath.

Any negative thought that creates pain within you feeds life to that unease and is expressed through your body as an emotional pain. Your reality is heavily invested in pain, and from this perspective, no creative thought can flourish—only more negative thought.

Let's create a reality. For example, let's say you have knots in your stomach because you have an idea that a loved one has violated a core value. The idea manifests itself into a negative thought, the thought feeds the idea into your perspective as your reality, and the body picks up the pain and amplifies the negative flow of energy within you.

When this happens, your mind and body are working in unison, feeding negative energy in a circular pattern, keeping it alive, and manifesting more of it. As it grows, so does the appetite for more negative energy. Negative thought creates even more negative thought, and the cycle continues, projecting outwards: We express unloving acts and the drama of life continues.

Your world now becomes the illusion you manifest. This is now the world you see—an unloved and unloving world. You are literally creating an unconscious reality based around a perceived fear.

Now all you see is the reality you have created from a perception based on an idea.

The ego is in control of your every thought and is using the body to create pain. We do not look within and continue to focus on the outer connection, creating a pattern of pain for all. Life cannot be seen in abundance; we are literally blinded by our obsession.

Without a *heightened sense of awareness,* it is impossible to go to a place of forgiveness and healing, and our thoughts and actions thereafter will be reflected in self-created images from the perspective of anger or rage, pain, jealousy, inadequacy, lack of control, feelings of unworthiness, and so on.

2. The second stage of healing is a *heightened sense of awareness.*

Now are we at a point of conscious creation or unconscious reaction? Let us not be creatures of habit, but creatures of creation. No reality exists unless you give meaning to it. Most of the time, the world you see is the world you created, and that world has no end to pain and suffering.

Where is the love?

My wife abused herself in ways I never thought possible after leaving me. Care was all I felt for her. In hindsight my ego couldn't accept her leaving. I was out of control just as I had been as a child growing up. I was revisiting my past and now my past was a part of my reality once again. Blinded by my ego, I felt I needed to protect her, and the more I heard of her pains acted out on stage, the more hurt and angry I became. From this perspective, I felt anger, jealousy, and then rage. My own judgments became my reality. Everyone was in the firing line, and attack was easy. My reality was now based on illusion, and incessant thinking was founded on negativity, grossly exacerbated by my version of events.

The point here is that when all was said and done some eighteen months later, I had more Self-awareness and Self-love. In this state, I would have allowed her to express her pain in her way without interference. I would have allowed the natural course of all things to play out in the physical world without interference. My wife was a grown woman who needed to heal herself in her way without my emotional reaction, which was determined by my judgments, not hers. Her purpose was merely to experience a new reality, her own reality—the basic right of all. Yet does being a partner, provider, good person, or whatever label we give to ourselves or another allow our expectation thereafter to be placed on another? No.

More to the point, when sufficient time had passed and healing within became my most wonderful reality and experience, I could say with complete honesty when I looked back that 80 percent of the pain I experienced during this time had been born in my thought, created from a whisper, spoken of constantly, and exaggerated by my reactions and actions.

Whatever you resist will persist, and whatever you speak of will become your experience.

What you say today will become your reality tomorrow!

Heightened awareness must be maintained if we desire peace of mind and complete bliss in our lives.

Heightened awareness can be developed by anyone.

During a group interactive seminar, a colleague said that she felt her life was pretty good. In fact, a number of people really felt like everything was okay. Others, of course, recognized a certain discontentment or unease that they lived with and were happy to speak of it. Interestingly, I continued to speak with the one colleague who shifted in her chair several times, yet continued to say that things in her life seemed just fine.

When my colleague, Cindi, was asked if there was anything troubling her, she said, "No, not really. I did have a bit of an incident with one of my friends, but it is over now."

We asked if she would share it with us all.

Cindi continued by telling us how a friend, Mary-Jo, had brushed her aside some six months earlier for no apparent reason. Mary-Jo just didn't want to know Cindi anymore. Cindi continued by saying to the group how it wasn't her fault and that she really tried to make it up to Mary-Jo for three months and couldn't break through. Mary-Jo simply didn't want to know her anymore. Cindi again reaffirmed that she considers her friends like family and that it did hurt her, but she had tried for three months to do everything possible to resolve the differences, which she couldn't quite understand in the first place.

When another colleague asked Cindi if she still felt uneasy about it, she hummed and arred, and then said, "No . . . yes . . . not really . . . I suppose so."

Cindi was asked why she persisted for three months, especially considering the fact that she felt she had done absolutely nothing wrong.

Cindi replied, "Because I consider all my friends like family."

When the session ended, I asked Cindi if we could have a coffee together. She accepted, and we spoke further. I asked her about the three months of trying to solve something that obviously took a lot of good energy away from her and suggested that perhaps her past may have had something to do with it.

She said, "Oh, no. My past wasn't the issue—this was just because I considered this girl like family."

Knowing Cindi was from a divorced background, I asked a little about her mum and dad's relationship with each other. She went on to say that her dad didn't really like her mum; he didn't talk to her. I asked how that had made her feel as a child growing up.

She said, "Terrible."

I suggested that her sense of having to solve the problem with someone who clearly wasn't a friend—let alone family—was perhaps due to her past or childhood screaming to resolve the issue of a mum and dad she loved. Perhaps this was not the first time she had done this. She spoke on, and indeed, it wasn't.

By the end of our discussion, Cindi had thought a lot about herself and her behavior and appeared quite pleased to have the burden of blame and resentment lifted from her subconscious. In her awareness, she had a chance to deal with the cause of her issue and to forgive all participants in this—her dad, mum, and friend. Most importantly, of course, she forgave herself. She feels she is a good person who did nothing wrong; she was not at fault, and she can release any guilt.

If we look at this closer and remind ourselves that this girl, for all intents and purposes, appeared content and happy within that meeting.

She knew no better; yet she harbored deep feelings of resentment, which probably stemmed back to childhood. She was conditioned by the body pain associated with those numerous hidden feelings and emotions, such as anger, anxiety, resentment, blame, or feeling unloved or cared for. This was so much projection for just one reality that she, like most of us, no longer felt the pain and emotions within the body. It becomes a blur; the pain is like the skin of an onion, layer upon layer, deadening the senses.

Instead of dealing with her pain earlier in life with awareness, those emotions were left unattended to surface somewhere down the track with someone else. Perhaps someone pushed a wrong button that reminded her of the pain she felt. A simple thing said by a loved one or someone close could activate the trigger. The pain was released; the ego was in control.

Perhaps the past will manifest itself into fatigue at work, tiredness, or lack of vitality. But do these feelings and behaviors ever go away until we are made aware of the very cause? The cause is found in our past. It is time to come to terms with our truth. We must find the cause. It is here that healing begins.

One week later, my colleague's mum came up to me in the street and said, "What have you all done to her? She's on fire." You see, that was a big weight to carry around—and many of us do it. We carry huge weights and then release our emotions in all the wrong places and to all the wrong people—the ones we truly love. She is working now with counselors and meditation to help her resolve past issues.

After all, who in your perception hurt you—a loved one?

There is a place we can go that is familiar and close; yet it seems to be the most difficult place for us to find. The place is called inner silence. It is here—and only here—that anything and everything you want to know can be answered. It is the place where everything you ever desired can be given to you.

A young man in his late twenties came to me and said, "You know, I can't understand my lack of control over sex. I love my wife, I think, but I just can't stop the feelings I have for other women. I'm a sex addict. I always think about it. If things go wrong at home, I'm off looking for it. And I feel so guilty about it afterwards." Having no formal qualifications myself, I thought he should see someone about it; however, he persisted in speaking with me. I considered all the counseling and personal work

I had attended and the number of years of life experiences I had, and I thought it best to listen and speak openly to him.

After listening for some time—an hour or so—I asked him to close his eyes and follow his breath inward and outward. I said, "This is a very simple form of meditation—easy for anyone to do, and very effective." He closed his eyes. There was a sense of tiredness in him as he contemplated his admission. For ten minutes, he rested quietly. I rested my mind and body as well in order to tune in with him.

I asked what life was like growing up in his family, and he told me that his mum and dad were really fantastic—they loved each other, loved him, and took him and his sister on holidays regularly. On his fourteenth birthday, his dad gave him a motocross bike, and they went riding together. Whenever on holidays, his dad and mum were always generous, giving their children whatever they asked for. They were not overly strict and gave their children a midnight curfew. His parents supported both him and his sister in everything they did. They were hardworking. His mum was a perfectionist who wanted the best for the family.

I have heard many times that there are three things you can control in your life—food, drugs, and sex. Knowing this younger man for as long as I did, I had seen that he never seemed to be at peace. I wondered why he needed to control and medicate his feelings with sex. Where were the feelings he was having coming from? What was the cause?

I had known him for over ten years, so it was easy enough for the two of us to talk. He did stress quite a bit. His head rarely rested from thinking of all sorts of things. He mainly thought about relationships and work, relationships being the dominant anxiety area. There was no genuine restfulness apparent, yet as I said, he was outwardly happy but inwardly anxious and concerned.

We continued the conversation. He told me that his dad and mum were supportive. Even on one occasion, after he got a sixteen-year old girl pregnant, his dad did not scream and yell, but was supportive and consoling, saying words of comfort like, "Don't worry, son, we will get through this." He recalled that news of the pregnancy was the talk of the town. He vividly recalled how well his mum and dad supported both him and the girlfriend during this time.

It occurred to me then to ask about the love between his mum and dad, and he said, "Perfect. They really support and love each other—always have." It sounds perfect, doesn't it? It was, apparently, and still is. Everything was perfect, he said, even the pressure on him. As he grew older, his mum wanted him to be 'perfect': to do a better job, be better in school, and whatever else. The fact is that we are not perfect.

This friend of mine had quite a number of disappointing relationships, struggled in his marriage, and considered himself a sex addict. Not only that, but he stressed about it often whenever he sought outward pleasure, and then carried the guilt of it around for days. Making matters worse, he regressed to thinking of past relationships and tried to self-diagnose whether there was anything he could have done to salvage them.

I asked, "Do you feel guilty that you feel you cannot replicate that perfect environment you had when growing up? Do you feel you cannot live up to the same sense of perfection, belonging, success, support, giving, and loving you received as a child? Is it the constant need to be validated for your feelings of being less than perfect?"

We sat for an extended period, and I asked him to soul search—not by thinking, but more from feeling his way. He breathed in deeply, and I asked if he could follow his breath for a few minutes in and out of his body, minimize thinking, and simply search for the feeling in the question.

His reply, after ten minutes of silence and contemplation, was, "Yes. I do. I feel I can't be like them; I'll disappoint them. I loved what they gave me and how they were always there for each other and loved us completely. I suppose I always dreamed of a relationship like that—like Mum and Dad. I felt the pressure of not living up to their standard. They didn't come out and say it, but Mum was always pushing us—for our own good, of course." He laughed. The response came without hesitation.

A week later, we caught up with each other again, and he said he really thought about what we discussed. He felt a huge weight lifted from his chest. He felt like he really wanted to control those feelings of being out of control and not go looking elsewhere for what he had at home with him. He went on to tell me what a beautiful week he and his wife had had and that he felt much better about himself. He could sit peacefully at home with his wife without those nagging feelings he would have just before darting out the door to fulfill some part of what it was that was lacking within himself.

In the end, it appeared all he was looking for was awareness. He wasn't the bad person he at times thought of himself. His relationship was different to that of his own parents' relationship. He just needed to know he didn't need to be perfect and always look for validation from somewhere else. He started to accept his imperfection—the imperfection of physical creation. As is said in rehabilitation, we are all perfectly imperfect. He knew he had all the love and validation in him and his life right in the present.

The feeling of guilt—the most severe emotion if left unchecked or unnoticed—manifests in all sorts of negative ways in all areas of your life. Consider this: without getting to the cause, how could you possibly release those emotions and behaviors that break down any form of love that exists within and around you?

Unless you take the time for you and find the place within—the silent sanctuary that exists within you, the most liberating of all places—then you will never realize what awaits you. Your life will become outwardly focused, and the real treasures of your life will go amiss. You will struggle for everything in life, because what becomes your reality is made from an unloving self—the self that is always searching for something. That self needs to struggle and fight for its survival, and its survival becomes dependent on those outer things; that need has become who you are. That self becomes separate from the very essence of who you are. Your true Self resides in love and joy and bliss.

If you carry guilt, resentment, or blame, then by the very nature of what these are, you have not forgiven a part of your life or someone for something. Over the course of the next several weeks, this young man forgave himself for the torment he put himself and others around him through. He chose not to live with that guilt anymore.

The young man felt liberated and much happier within—all from one act of finding the cause of the problem that was burdening him and keeping him within the prison of past thoughts and mind identification. It was a prison where his only escape was control—control over sex, in this case. Someone else may have a different addiction.

We spoke further several times, and he did hit some low points when the past crept up and consumed him. He had feelings of blame towards another. Excuses of boredom crept in. He felt he was not having fun or missing out. He felt sensations of being held back by another, and the list went on, until he realized these were merely images in his head. He adopted simple meditation techniques, changed negative thoughts with positive ones, and followed the breath technique alone for up to five minutes at a time. On each occasion, he described his mood shift as dramatic. He described how, with the knowledge of where his thoughts stemmed from originally, he was better able to deal with his current feelings, thoughts, and behaviors whenever they took a turn.

He found the primary cause of his sex addiction. It was found in facing his truth.

On and on it goes. When does it stop? I am a sex addict, and I like to have fun; this is my fun. I know no better, as I have no idea why I feel unhappy. It is who I am, so I accept it without looking. The world is unhappy just like me; it is normal—just watch the news if you want proof. What I see is my reality; it must be right. My wife is always unhappy. She doesn't appreciate me. Why can't she understand me? I have had enough of this; I'm unhappy. But I love her—I really do. If only we could stop fighting. Why does she not cook for me? I work all day; what did she do? I care for him; he gives me no attention. He doesn't speak to the children; he is tired after work—or whatever it is that he does.

Too often, when you do sit down and take notice, it is too late. The damage is done.

Why is this? Because we weren't aware of the cause of the pain we felt. We can't unless we go to a place where we can drop our guard and feel peace. Often, during a crisis, we go to that place—not by choice, but because our defenses are flattened and our egos are dismantled, which gives us a chance to evaluate and look within.

Don't wait for a crisis before you see. The love you have in your life already exists in you and all around you. It is time to seek it out. It takes courage to fight the ego. It will do everything in its power, using the mind and body, to keep you under its control. It has protected you for long enough; now it is destructive to you. It is time to let it go.

3. *Vigilance* is the third stage of healing.

Fear cannot last forever, as your experiences, which are besieged in fear, will ultimately lead you away from the very thing you believed was the only reality. This is the purpose of experience: to teach you and allow you to remember that only permanency can come from within. Everything else sought outside of oneself is impermanent, and it is in this impermanence that your experience will lead you back to yourself.

The best way to connect to conscious living is to disconnect from incessant thought based on attachment and neediness. To not think in this way is to allow all to be and experience the best of life. It is this thinking that traps the body and the mind in a duality of uncertainty. To be certain and firm in eliminating thoughts that connect us to past experiences (and thereby our judgments) will shift our consciousness to a higher level of acceptance of all that is and show us our purpose to perfect unity—the unity of you, us, and everything. Unity, forgiveness, love, acceptance, peace, prosperity, and joy are all states of being felt in connection with the inner Self. Silence is your connecting medium.

We become free to access inner knowledge as we discard old beliefs. Inner silence opens the door to this knowledge. Inner knowledge is accessed by letting go of the world in which we apply reason to everything. The more reason we apply, the less inner knowledge we access. Reason is defending a position of who we think we are. We all possess this inner knowledge; it lives in the memory of every cell in our bodies. It is our connectedness to everything that is. Remembering it is undoing what we have believed to be our identity and the means by which we see our world and the people within it.

It is in the silence and journey inward that connection to your outer and inner world can coexist in perfect harmony. You must be conscious of your inner Self and alert to your outer world at the same time. This is the true intention and purpose of life—the path you seek and your soul's desire. It is the perfect union between the physical and your natural state of being.

It is the path of enlightenment!

You need to be firm in your belief. Firmness is as vital as intent. Firmness assures you will guard against the bad habits of attack, blame, judgment, criticism, resentment, self-pity, expectation, and so on— behaviors that have kept you in a state of anxiety. Break these habits, because they have no meaning to your purpose. Certainty and firmness will ensure your release, and it will take certainty and firmness to keep you on guard against the prevailing ills that wait to control you once again. They will come through thought and stir up the body pain to breathe life into itself. Be vigilant at forgiveness! Forgive and accept. Be alert to this.

The experiences of life are either fruitfully accepted or sadly rejected. Your decision to accept will create miracles and a beautiful new reality. Your rejection will keep you in the state of fear, and your actions and reactions will stem from this fear. Fear endeavors to destroy everything it connects to; yet it cannot survive in consciousness, the light of your being—love.

No guilt should be suffered as you journey through life, regardless of the circumstances. Awareness and acceptance of what is are all that are required to break barriers of human consciousness and set you on the path of conscious creation. The simplest way to reclaim your rightful place is to delve into the depth of silence and hear the answers that you are now seeking.

To do this, you must be ruthless in eliminating thoughts held over from the past that are limiting your experiences. You are free to choose your destiny and the path of your journey—the numerous possibilities that are available to you in every moment of time—and your experiences (regardless of what they are) are your purpose for being here. To know your Self—as was your intention—is not to fight and resist, but rather to accept and forgive.

All acceptance is forgiveness, and forgiveness is felt in the depth of silence. The inner Self is not restricted by thoughts of lack, and whenever we experience a heightened awareness through silence, we are connecting to the place where fear does not exist. The strength of who and what you are will surprise you, but to get there, a certainty must be maintained. You must be certain that your path is what you are seeking, and you must stay vigilant against the backdrop of all life fears. Fears are nothing more than an illusion. They are self-created and impermanent.

This journey starts within.

Words cannot describe the knowledge you have already. If each cell in your body contains enough information to fill the *Encyclopedia Britannica* and more, what is there to say? It can only be felt. Your knowledge is felt within the body and made aware by the mind, for the body is the conduit to the soul. It is the feeling manifestation of physical form accessed through the mind. The mind belongs to the soul. The mind operates not just from the brain, but also every cell within you. Every cell participates. How do we access the place of all knowledge? By feeling it.

We feel this knowledge in the quiet of Self—the place where our minds and bodies rest. Nothing you have is permanent but the inner magnitude of love that radiates within. Nothing else can be real, for all else is an illusion created by the ego—the adapted other self that will keep you in the tormented state of constant thinking. This constant thinking is a never-ending thought process of survival, acceptance, validation, want, and the constant search for love. It is here that you fight hard for your very existence. In the pain of that resistance, the acknowledgement of the journey to the inner you will surely come.

"Your vision will become clear only when you can look into your own heart. Who looks outside, dreams; who looks inside, awakes."
—Carl Jung

The Inner Journey to Silence

Feel the meaning of this statement for a moment. Then stop, rest your body, and allow your thought to be consumed by calmly focusing on your breath. Do this for just two minutes. Have you any idea how much energy you consume each day on thoughts and words to prop up your very existence?

Use the following four steps to guide you effortlessly into connection with Self.

1. Before you sit in silence for those valuable moments, go swimming in the sky. Change your state instantly. Go to the place you love so much, and just be—daydream. Remove negative thought with positive visualization. Thereafter, sit quietly to commence the journey inward.

2. Now say to yourself, "I'm going to rest now for two minutes" —and just sit and rest. Close your eyes and rest. We now seek the silence of the mind: pure, blissful silence! If you hear a sound, let your mind wander to it; do not judge it, but allow it freedom from judgment. Just go there quietly. If your mind is consumed by sounds, focus once again on your breath. Once you are focused on the breath, replace that focus with the awareness of the breath, thus making it a gentle focus: simple awareness and nothing more.

3. Do not try to explain your state or resist it in any way. Allow all to be. All thoughts, agitations, and unease, or any sounds—just simply go to them with openness and allow all to just be. In this state of acceptance and awareness, the thought and unease will dissipate. When your thoughts are activated, don't feel bad. Feel like you have achieved a moment of awareness. You're one step closer to wisdom and peace within.

4. Always return to your breath and be aware of your breath. Your breath will become gentle, and with practice, it will be almost as quiet as the mind. You will start to feel the peace of it as it takes you inward. The repetition of breath technique is an active form of meditation, as is all repetition.

   Active meditation can be felt in gardening, knitting, or hitting a ball against a wall. The next time you do even those things of a repetitive nature value them for what they are. Learn to enjoy them completely.

   You can practice active meditation even by walking. I use this practice to strengthen the power of conscious creation. Instead of breath awareness, when walking, I use the mantra of prayer associated to my desires. Powerful verbal and spiritual affirmations are repeated over and over; each time, they become a little closer to your reality. Do not underestimate the power of prayer because of a misguided belief in the way prayer has been used to create fear (i.e. repent for your sin).

Remember, there is no vengeful God or angered Supreme Being. There is instead love—and only love—and when all is said and done, that is exactly what we will be left with, the thing we have searched for all our lives. Don't leave the pain of your past until it is too late, creating crises that will affect you and your loved ones. Learn to appreciate all you have right here and now. Seek love out! Start with gratitude. Find gratitude whenever you can—say it, respect it, focus on it, and repeat it. Let it become habitual. Learn to appreciate everything in your life. Be thankful for it.

Breathing Meditation: Powerful Inner Transformation

Here are six steps of a powerful breathing meditation.

1. Let's practice the technique of the journey inward. First, simply start breathing; let the breath be intentional and pronounced. Breathe air through your nose into your deep diaphragm, and then slowly breathe out through your mouth. By slowly, I mean three times slower than you breathe in. As you breathe in, you should see your stomach rise. Now do this more pronounced version of breathing at least five to six more times, if you can, with no intervals between breaths.

2. After this, it is time to slow your breathing and the intervals between breaths. The deep, intentional breaths will have put enough oxygen into

your body for you to be able to slow your breath sufficiently. However, do not be alarmed by the incessant thoughts that will creep in. Remember, this is about acceptance of everything that occurs—of everything that is heard, felt, and thought.

3. Allow your breath gradually to get quieter and shallower. As it becomes quieter, follow it with your mind. Your mind will start to relax and go within. Remember, as a sound or thought occurs, do not be troubled. Let it be. In this awareness, simply return to the breath; soon you will barely hear it.

Practice makes perfect; however, this is one of the simplest and most effective techniques for finding the mental space within the body. You will find moments of great rest.

4. Now I want you to think of sunlight and allow it to flood over your body—beautiful, warm sunlight. Feel its warmth. Your mind has the power to feel it simply by thinking it. Better still, just imagine it. Allow the white light to wash over you, and bring it into your being. Feel its warmth, relaxation, and peacefulness.

5. Now imagine the light completely covering you—swirling over, around, and through you. Once you have this image clearly in your mind, begin to breathe it in, and let the light swirl freely within you through your breath, gently massaging you from within. Just feel it; don't try to understand it—simply imagine it. Allow it to happen.

6. Be silent, let go, and rest.

If you feel agitation or restlessness, find the source within the part of your body that is experiencing it. Be aware of the exact place of unrest, and observe it. Allow the light to wash over it, and as you breathe outward, you will see and feel that anxiousness or dark area being released from you. It will dissipate by the very awareness and focus you are now giving it—an awareness you have rarely given it before.

Remember, this is only for five to ten minutes. Within these minutes, you will find a few valuable seconds of rest and acquire valuable knowledge—the power and knowledge within you. Do not be afraid of new sensations you may experience. You may experience moments of deep restfulness—almost as if you are losing control. In fact, you are letting go of control.

You may experience a feeling of separation from the body. This is very nerve-racking at first, because your entire life has been consumed by the mind with body identification. It has become who we are. Our thoughts, which have been expressed through the body, run our lives. You may acquire insights of the sadness you feel and become agitated, quickly running to your usual defense of dismissal to protect your self-made identity.

Whatever the feelings, accept them wholeheartedly. Let nothing concern you. Just go with your feelings; go with every sensation, and know that a few valuable seconds will plant the seed towards heightened awareness.

When you feel any anxiety in doing too much or too little, boredom, or an expectation or demand creating disruption in your day, then go to this place, for you will find a few valuable moments of complete contentment.

Do not talk about it; this is your time. It can't be explained, and when you talk about it with those who do not understand it, you are bringing physical judgment to it from others who have not experienced it. It is here that your own feelings are judged and criticized; you then revert to old ways—habits which have kept you in a place of unconsciousness and of not knowing where true peace lies.

Your silence within and without is important for you now. Speak of positive, conscious actions only with others of likeminded awareness, which will lift your consciousness as you empower each other. Group consciousness is a powerful creator. Involve yourself with like energy, and your consciousness and awareness will grow. When you are strong enough to find silence your ally, then you will become the teacher, and others will be guided by your strength within.

We are embarking on a journey of undoing. There are many years of poor conditioning that have yet to be undone, and they are undone by the exact opposite of what we always do. Now we no longer do, but simply do not do. We feel our way for feeling is what we are, and the physical is the conduit to the soul—the all-knowing self. Self is the place we long to remember. The body is designed for this process.

Do you prefer the prison of your mind? Do you want to be a slave to your imagined senses and restlessness to unknown forces within and without? We don't stop. Instead, we prefer to run the gauntlet of experience until the experience consumes our every thought—complete mind-body identification—and our separation feels complete. It's the separation of our true Self from God (or whatever you believe to be your higher power) —the perfect unity consciousness—that causes the anxiety. Only love of Self can cure the pain and reunite you with your Self—the only place that is your salvation and freedom. You are the master of your destiny, and through your awareness, the very things that have clouded your vision to this point in your life—your mind and body identification—can now be utilized to release you through intent, awareness and *nurturing* vigilance— nurturing with Self love. It is called the feeling manifestation of your soul's desires.

In which way is your destiny going to be determined? It is your choice. Our lives are determined by our choices. As Deepak Chopra writes, "You and I are essentially infinite choice-makers. In every moment of our existence, we are in that field of all possibilities where we have access to an infinity of choices."

It is in complete silence that we hear the voice of God!

Do you feel the anger and anxiety welling up within? Why should you be told there is another way? Why, after all you have been through, should you need to be told to start again? Believe it or not, it does not take long to change compared to the length of time it has taken to imprison you. In fact, it is a heartbeat by comparison.

Go to that silent place, and allow awareness and your breath to ease those thoughts of resisting. Go there often, and the process will speed up for you. The practice of heightened awareness strengthens each time you do, and each time, your consciousness will grow and strengthen within. Your remembering will become a little clearer. Remembering is the bountiful knowledge of the soul, and this knowledge is soaked in wisdom.

In time, you will feel complete joy. You will feel joy whether you have something or someone or have nothing. The higher your consciousness, the less demand you will have of yourself to acquire outside things to feel good. Then the act of doing becomes totally enjoyable, and the expectation you place on yourself to acquire becomes irrelevant, for peace and happiness derive their source from within, not without.

"The mind, once expanded to the dimensions of larger ideas, never returns to its original size."
—Oliver Wendell Holmes

Death is the ultimate silence. Yet there is no death. Some refer to the day of death as "remembrance day," meaning, the day we remember who we are and why we came here. We have learned to fear death as if it is final, which is another ego mind-identified control mechanism to keep us in a state of separation and anxiety. We need to learn to use this misconception as a strength, not a weakness.

The strength is seen in living. We must be grateful for everything and everyone in our lives. Every journey we take can be seen as an effort or adventure. Each person can be seen as an opportunity to gain something or an opportunity to give something. It is in the non-permanence of things that the moment of doing and having should be appreciated, lived, and enjoyed.

If it was said that life is but a game—a grand game, designed specifically for you—and that all of its experiences are nothing but an illusion, would it take on a different relevance to you? Would you take it seriously? Would you be more grateful and appreciative?

If permanence is found within and the within is the home of all that is, then the silence within is the language of the soul. It is the language of all wisdom and all knowledge. What is wisdom but the knowledge to know what to do with the knowledge when you know it? Yet the language of our lives is based on drama and emotion. The unease is a consequence of the separation from our true Self. The true Self is the same Self of all life in all form, the matrix of all that is, or the glue of the universe.

We own it; yet we prefer to ignore it in place of pain and fear, because we simply don't remember. You are a marvelous creator. This life was designed for you to find your higher purpose and discover who you are—the true you, the inner you.

It is not death that we should fear, but not living life—we are missing out on it. We are choosing anxiety and fear as a way of life.

Conclusion

We fear because ego has no base except a body—an impermanent organism. We falsely believe we are only a body. Most believe God created our bodies. Who created the body? God! Who can we blame? Of course it is logical to assume false beliefs from false teachings. We end up blaming our Self, our higher power—the same power that is one and the same power within all existence. We falsely believe our bodies are who we are. We are not bodies; they are not who we are, yet we think we are just bodies with brains, as if our minds are constricted to a certain area to think with—as if that's all there is to us. We experience the feeling of separation and loss as if we have no say or control over our reality. The truth is our reality is the only thing we have control over.

We all too often believe we are subjected to the whim of life and find ourselves playing victim to it. The truth is we are the creators of our reality. We are powerful and imaginative beings who endlessly create through our false beliefs. In resisting life, our minds work excessively hard to maintain our false beliefs, maintaining the perception of being a self that is not real. Ego created the adapted other you for the purpose of defending against the fear you experienced and now believe so strongly in. The mind never stops scheming, thinking, manipulating, attacking, resenting, begrudging, and hurting, and it does it all under the guise of a false, perplexed perception of self.

The ego is a monster, and it will consume you. You will turn simple events into stage productions. The mind will not rest, and this we choose as the way to live our lives. Why? We choose separation from true Self, higher power, God, the spirit, each other, the world, and everything else.

It is not worth it in physical terms, as the pain we experience in our lives is often unbearable—or worse, we no longer feel the pain, for its consistent presence has made it feel normal. Imagine for a moment how wonderful it is going to feel when you connect within to the stillness and silence of all that is—all knowledge, wisdom, and love. It is at the core of your being. It is your soul.

Is it funny that we go through life angry, betrayed, and full of self-pity and resentment, and yet we never stop to ask why? We just assume to know why. And our answer to it is more hurt and pain inflicted on someone or on ourselves. Retribution and gain soften the impact we feel. Someone has to lose, but we do not care, providing it is not us. We are invincible. We are strong and determined, and we put up a good fight, laugh, cry, and celebrate our victories. We get angry or wallow in self-pity at our defeats. There is rarely a kind, heartfelt appreciation to the victor—just envy or worse.

Still, we go on without noticing the unhappy self in all the battles. We have no awareness. You are a great warrior; there is no doubt. Just being your Self is an amazing achievement of creation, but we don't realize that, for we are lost in our own illusion, and we doubt our existence is anything more than a fleeting moment of gain and loss—winner take all. This is insanity. What else could it be? Aren't we going to die and be no more? Those thoughts are the insanity!

You are great beyond greatness. You are the creator of all you are and all you do, because you are the same Self as all the universal energy possesses. You are one with it, and in the power of silence, you will connect to it. You are not separate; you are joined. You are one with everything and everyone. You are greatness made manifest, so live life a new way. Connect to your true Self and experience abundance, prosperity, wealth, and love like never before. It is your birthright and inheritance, so claim it.

When nothing else seems to work for you, your silence will be your greatest energy. Access it, and at every opportunity, repeat it until the energy connection becomes readily available. In every moment of your experiences there lies the opportunity to access the knowing place. Every experience gives you the opportunity to be aware of your enslavement. The power of your silence will release you.

Our experiences make us who we are. We feel detached when we are young and carefree, and then, with great expectation, we become entrapped by our expectations; the lust for adventure is replaced by the burden of doing. We do things to succeed—to survive—and the ones closest are the ones to blame. After all, we are doing it for them, aren't we? Not quite.

We just lost our zest for life through past conditioning and learning, instead choosing the life of slavery of mind and body. The ego is the great creator of dismay and disillusionment.

So choose freedom now!

There is no freedom without the soul. Without the soul connection, there is no genuine, deep love of Self. We are free spirits by our very nature. We do not need outside things to fill the spirit, as spirit lives within us. It is available to you in this moment and any other moment; it is simply a matter of choice.

Connect to the inner Self through the power of silence—the place where the heart and soul unify and connect with your outer physical realm. Feel the wonders of life, and see the beauty of this world. To master life is to build the bridge between your inner and outer world. The power of silence is the vehicle for peace and joy—your release from the prison of your mind and the enslavement of your body.

Your life experiences will be of men forever seeking you out for their own gain. These experiences are normal to the thinking man. To have no mind to their plight and to rise above their attacks and judgments is the greatest of all our freedoms, for no longer are you controlled or controlling. Life can only be exciting, full, and rich; everything done will be in joy, and every relationship will be peaceful.

Peace and joy are close—getting the mind to move from outside itself—a separate self—to inside Self as part of the whole. Are you ready to reclaim your life and make it heaven on earth? That's the only question. It is the destiny of the soul!

Make the choice to live. Reclaim your birthright—the inner you that longs for your return and the perfect harmony with everyone and all there is.

Yet we are resolved to hang on to our old ways from fear. The fear is not born in us, but taught to us, and we can't stop thinking. The fear of not being good enough, not achieving, not having, not belonging, loving, and being loved manifest and destroy all that we love with our minds to comfort the ego for its own unreasonable reasoning. How can we truly feel?

We must look within and ask for guidance to heal. Create this desire by your thoughts and prayer. Remove the fear only with love, let love grow within, and you will find true inner peace—a journey for liberation and a life lesson achieved.

The only way true peace can enter is via the inner Self. The inner Self has the power to heal, and no other means is capable of this. Any other means are based on separation, and separation is the cause of the problems. It is not understood how your soul achieves this end, because it is perceived as alien to your physical form and alien to all you have been taught to believe.

Your spirit or soul—the inner you—is not something we can identify in words or talk about and expect to connect with. It is felt within, without words and definition. It is the power of all things, and your connection is in the stillness and silence of your mind—the move away from mind-body to mind-soul. Your awareness and access to mind-soul is through feeling.

Stop fighting life, and life will give you everything you desire in return. You must rid self-pity and resentment in order to connect to your inner world. Once this is achieved, true forgiveness in all others and self will free you. The inner silence will be found, and joy will be felt in all aspects of your life. The process to joy and peace will grow each day. Each day, the challenges will be there with you, as the ego self will fight for control. Each day, it will lose its grip a little more, and you will strengthen in knowledge through the courage of your awareness.

Do not wait for the crisis in your life, a life-or-death situation or the dark night of the soul, before you act. Access the knowledge now, as you have the power to do so. We all do. Do not allow self-assessment to determine your path. Instead, allow trust and acceptance to be at the core of your experiences. See an alternative where once there was none. Look for the many possibilities in every moment or any relationship that exists for you—the possibility that any attack can be seen from a loving perspective.

Any reality can be changed in a moment's notice to a different reality—a reality felt and heard as the soul directs.

Your entire life has been spent longing for silent connection. You've searched for connection to Self within, the connection to all energy and all knowledge, and unity with all things. Our fear made our illusions real, and our illusions made our pain real; our pain made our search for silent knowledge real. It was our purpose to realize this truth. This is the importance of our lives; without pain and separation, we would have no other desire than the all-loving Self that we are. Yet this cannot be static, as all life cannot be static. Life is about evolution and growth; it is equal to all that exists in nature. It is the natural order of things to evolve, grow, and expand. Evolution of all is known as the breath of God.

Once we connect, our lives are severely altered forever; the healing is complete, and others will be healed in your presence. It is the miracle of transformation and heightened consciousness.

Categories of People

There are three main types of unhealed people **(and we're all unhealed to some degree and equally capable of total healing).

1. While some people are caring and helpful, they are limited in their ability and cannot survive on their own.

2. Others are self-centered and conceited. They are jealous by their nature and willing to kill for positions of power. You can recognize them, as they always talk about themselves and highlight their attributes to progress and to prove themselves.

3. Still other people are indifferent to life. They wait for opportunities that never seem to come, yet stand in grandiosity with what might be. One thing they all have in common is that they cannot survive or be as they think without others to satisfy their neediness, do their bidding, or complete their dreams. While we may look at those around us and feel incomplete, defining others as complete and unaffected is wrong perception. It is important to realize that the majority of the world population falls into one of these characterizations.

Without the three aforementioned types of attachment and attributes defining who we are, how could our lessons be learned? To learn our lessons, we must consider what is important: connection with Self, learning to live in peace and joy of Self. This, then, will Self-create more of the same, which will all be expressed in love. Love flows from Self, and Self, then, can love. The need of another is not Self-love, but self-neediness. Nothing in love is anything other than love. It is not neediness, attachment, attack, self-pity, or any other definition other than its own definition: pure love. Anything else is ego, not love.

Our illusionary self is created from our experiences—created from ego—categorizing us into one of these three groups; yet none of us, as divine souls, fall into any of these categories. The soul needs nothing; it has it all, and all is it. It possesses the knowledge and wisdom of all that you will ever need. You are divine in purpose and stature; you have the power of the universe at your disposal. You are a creator—magnificence in all forms, including the physical. Your purpose is to evolve spiritually. Your path is to lighten the path of others—to lift consciousness throughout the world—and you have the power to do so. Remembering is all that is required, and your human form was designed for this process. It is the process of healing and reclaiming true Self.

How you choose to live your life will be based on your choices. Trust and have faith in the process of life, and allow it to unfold. Know that it is your soul's purpose to bring to you all you require in order to evolve. Every experience you encounter is an experience you choose in your life. Realize the truth in this statement and your world will take on new meaning and new direction, for the purpose of your path exists in your inner knowledge. Life is leading you there; help yourself and go within. You now have the power of silence as your guide.

In the silence of Self, you can hear the voice of God.

There sits the secret that nobody knows?
We live to relive all of our woes.
Freeing us from the past and just letting go,
There is the secret that we already know.
But are blind to see,
For our ego says, "No."
We distance ourselves away from the truth,
Lord Almighty forgiving our dues.
How easy it is to continue to grow, with ignorance, hatred, and all for
the show.
But in the center of our life sits the secret
We already know!

About the Author

Gregory Nicholas Malouf, a successful Australian businessman and entrepreneur, suffered constant abuse as a child. He consequently became a workaholic in order to run away from his past and allow himself to live the "perfect life," or so he thought. He was earning triple figures each week, throwing lavish parties, and could do anything or go anywhere in the world he wanted when his world collapsed. For the first time, at age fifty, he realized that his priorities were misguided—he was living a lie. He suffered from anxiety and obsessive control disorder—two of many addictions he had suffered in his life—why? Because he had not been able to confront the truth of his past. Through a genuine intent to find life abundance, he has faced his past and found the truth that limited his life. Today Malouf shares his lessons on how to truly liberate your mind and body, live in the present with gratitude, consciously create the life you desire and finally find the abundance you deserve. Whether you were under nurtured or over nurtured, you are living with anxiety, fear, or dissatisfaction, Malouf has written *Silent* and founded the Epsilon Healing Academy for those who believe what he needed to believe: that there must be a better way. And there is!

Glossary of Terms

Anxiety	A permanent state of worry and concern. A mental disorder usually caused by the build up of fear. A toxic energy spilling out into the body that is usually caused by layers of fear.
Bliss	Radiant, loving energy centered within the heart chakra and radiating outward. Complete fullness and Self-fulfillment felt as a vibrating energy within the body.
Consciousness	A loving knowingness of the meaning and purpose of life. An intentional path of peace, joy, and bliss. A conscious or knowing awareness of life and our connectedness with it and all people and things. A light, high vibrational, loving energy that connects and holds life within it.
Dark night of the soul	The crises in our lives that can impact our lives at a moment's notice. The reality we believed in is seen for what it is: a distortion. Our lives come crashing down around us and our defenses are shattered. We are left in grief.

Divine energy	Light energy that resonates at a high speed. It attracts only other energy of like kind. It is one with all energy, as it does not restrict. It is free-flowing and highly creative energy—the pure, loving energy of all life.
Ego	Self-made, adapted self. The part of us that we created so as not to feel the trauma, hurt, and pain of our past. A fearful self made to protect our wounded inner child.
Fear	Fear is born by not understanding a situation at hand (the ego being challenged).
Joy	Complete connectedness to life, and through it, that which we are enjoying. A constant state of happiness, and a sense of connection to inner and outer form alike.
Law of the universe	The loving value that applies to all existence. Values of life in total. Its highest value is connectedness to all people and all things in existence as one.
Matrix	The body of energy within which creation exists. The life-giving energy that allows the transference of energy within existence. The glue of the universe in which energy flows.
Negative energy	Dark, dense energy that requires other dark, dense energy to survive. A forceful exertion of one's self. It is a usable power that is restrictive and limited by its destructive power.
Pain	A life given. To be human is to experience pain or loss—for example, loss of a family member or loss of a job. Outcomes of imperfection.

Peace	Calming effect of loving energy within the body and a mental state of connectedness with all life, people, and things.
Positive energy	Light energy that resonates at high speed. It attracts only other energy of like kind. It is one with the divine and conscious energy of existence, as it does not restrict, and it is free-flowing, high, creative energy.
Self	The inner, loving, all-knowing Self. The Self that is our high "I am," which is connected to the greater consciousness of all life.
self	Our adapted other self. The small, ego self made to protect and nurture us when were most vulnerable. The self we created to control that which we were hurt by; the very self that now controls us—controls our every thought, word, and action. The self that resists and controls to satisfy its false needs and wants.
Separation	The separation from our true spiritual Self. A move away from moral law to man-made law. A fear-based reality that is foreign to our inner Self.
Shadow	Our ego self that falsely mimics who we are. It is our other adapted self we created to give our self a sense of worth. It is our ego self.
Shame	This is the shame we act out within the reality of a fearful self or an unloved self. It is often caused by toxic shame we carry into adulthood from our childhood lessons.

Soul	The housing of our physical being that is connected to spirit within all life. Our core essence. It is one with and part of our true Self.
Suffering	A choice we each make to prolong pain through non-acceptance of it. A fear-based reality.
Toxic shame	Toxic and carried shame from our past, especially our childhoods. Shame of others that we carry through life. This shame causes our guilt and fears.
Unconsciousness	A fearful reality acted out unknowingly. The act of reacting to life rather than acting thoughtfully within it and being controlled by our ego, believing we are at the behest of life, not the creators of it. A fearful state of being.
Unity consciousness	The loving connectedness of two or more people aligned energetically. Unity consciousness is a powerful, loving, creative tool. Individual consciousness masses together to make form or matter manifest; it manifests peace and joy.
Unity unconsciousness	An unknowing mass of energy culminating by two or more individuals knowingly manifesting fear into reality, such as in the form of war or famine.
Universal consciousness	The loving connectedness of all life. It exists within the universal law of intelligence. It is the moral law of all creation; the oneness within every part of existence is its function.
Wounded child	The small child who suffered hurt and trauma yet was too vulnerable to do anything about it. Feelings became repressed within.

Silent Resources

Epsilon Healing Academy Programs and Services to Help You Build a Community

To facilitate your progress in harnessing the power of silence, my team and I created the following materials, services, and programs to provide you with further support.

Access Free Downloads, Blog, and Newsletter

Go to Gregory Malouf's blog at www.EpsilonHealingAcademy.com to subscribe to our monthly online newsletter, which will keep you updated on new insights from *Silent*. The blog is also the hub of ongoing discussions and has links to other resources.

Connect via the Social Networks

I welcome connection. Follow me on Twitter: @gregorymalouf, Facebook: Gregory Malouf, and LinkedIn: Gregory Malouf. You can also join the Epsilon Healing Academy on Facebook and LinkedIn. Please contribute there and become part of the growing community.

Epsilon Healing Academy Coaching and Seminars

More detailed assistance for you on your *Silent* path is available through videos, video conferencing, and webinars. For more information on these services, please visit www.EpsilonHealingAcademy.com.

CPSIA information can be obtained at www.ICGtesting.com
Printed in the USA
LVOW100331100912

298105LV00001B/5/P